Economic policy and technological performance

Centre for Economic Policy Research

The Centre for Economic Policy Research is a registered charity with educational purposes. It was established in 1983 to promote independent analysis and public discussion of open economies and the relations between them. Institutional (core) finance for the Centre has been provided through major grants from the Economic and Social Research Council, the Leverhulme Trust, the Esmée Fairbairn Trust and the Bank of England. None of these organizations gives prior review to the Centre's publications nor do they necessarily endorse the views expressed therein.

The Centre is pluralist and non-partisan, bringing economic research to bear on the analysis of medium- and long-run policy questions. The research work which it disseminates may include views on policy, but the Board of Governors of the Centre does not give prior review to such publications, and the Centre itself takes no institutional policy positions. The opinions expressed in this volume are those of the authors and not those of the Centre for Economic Policy Research.

1 February 1987

Economic policy and technological performance

Edited by

PARTHA DASGUPTA

and

PAUL STONEMAN

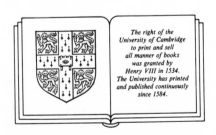

The right of the
University of Cambridge
to print and sell
all manner of books
was granted by
Henry VIII in 1534.
The University has printed
and published continuously
since 1584.

CAMBRIDGE UNIVERSITY PRESS

Cambridge

New York   New Rochelle   Melbourne   Sydney

Published by the Press Syndicate of the University of Cambridge
The Pitt Building, Trumpington Street, Cambridge CB2 1RP
32 East 57th Street, New York, NY 10022, USA
10 Stamford Road, Oakleigh, Melbourne 3166, Australia

First published 1987

Printed in Great Britain at
the University Press, Cambridge

British Library cataloguing in publication data

Economic policy and technological performance.
   1. Technological innovations —— Economic aspects
   2. Technology and state
I. Dasgupta, Partha   II. Stoneman, Paul
338'.06   HC79.T4

Library of Congress cataloguing in publication data

Economic policy and technological performance.
  Includes index.
   1. Technology and state. I. Dasgupta, Partha.
II. Stoneman, Paul.
T49.5.E28 1987   338.9'26   87-9387

ISBN 0 521 34555 3

Contents

Tables

Figures

Preface

This volume contains the proceedings of the conference 'Economics and Technology Policy' organised by the Centre for Economic Policy Research and held in London on 1–2 September 1986.

Financial support for the conference was provided by the Department of Trade and Industry, British Telecom and the Centre for Economic Policy Research International Foundation to whom we express our gratitude. We would also like to thank Monica Allen for all her efforts to ensure the smooth running of the conference, Wendy Thompson for help in developing the conference proposal and in financial administration, Stephen Yeo for his assistance in getting this volume to press and especially John Black for all his efforts as Production Editor. In addition, on behalf of all the authors of the papers in this volume, we wish to thank the participants in the conference not only for their comments on these papers but also for their contribution to a most constructive and enjoyable event.

PAUL STONEMAN
PARTHA DASGUPTA

Participants

Christiano Antonelli   *Organization for Economic Cooperation and Development*
John Barber   *Department of Trade and Industry*
John Black   *University of Exeter*
Jeremy Bray MP   *House of Commons*
Robin Brighton   *Segal Quince Wicksteed, Consulting and Management Services, Cambridge*
J. B. Cowie   *British Telecom*
Cathy Cunningham   *Cabinet Office*
Partha Dasgupta   *St John's College, Cambridge and CEPR*
Paul David   *Stanford University*
Giovanni Dosi   *University of Sussex*
Henry Ergas   *Organization for Economic Cooperation and Development*
Paul Geroski   *University of Southampton*
Zvi Griliches   *Harvard University*
Philip Hills   *Department of Trade and Industry*
Tom Hoehn   *Malmgren, Golt, Kingston & Co.*
Derek Howarth   *Department of Trade and Industry*
Bruce Lyons   *University of East Anglia*
Douglas McWilliams   *IBM UK Ltd*
David Mowery   *Carnegie–Mellon University*
Ariel Pakes   *Harvard University*
Keith Pavitt   *University of Sussex*
Christian Pothoff-Sewing   *Unilever PLC*
Ron Smith   *Birkbeck College, London*
Luc Soete   *University of Sussex*
Joseph Stiglitz   *Princeton University*
Paul Stoneman   *University of Warwick and CEPR*
Peter Swann   *University of Bath*

Susie Symes   *HM Treasury*
Wendy Thompson   *CEPR*
John Vickers   *Nuffield College, Oxford and CEPR*
Michael Waterson   *University of Newcastle*
Jeffrey Wheatley   *British Telecom*
Geoffrey White   *HM Treasury*

CAMBRIDGE
UNIVERSITY PRESS

The right of the University of Cambridge to print and sell all manner of books was granted by Henry VIII in Royal Letters Patent

have pleasure in sending for review a copy of:

DASGUPTA.ECONOMIC POLICY TECHNOLOGICL
Price: £25.00 H/b (0 521 34555 3)
          (Price in Dollars $34.50)
Publication Date: 15TH OCTOBER 1987

It is requested that no review should appear before this date.
May we ask you to let us have a copy of any review published
or, if you send a copy of your journal, to indicate the pages on
which a review appears?

The Edinburgh Building, Shaftesbury Road, Cambridge CB2 2RU
Telephone (0223) 312393

Introduction

PARTHA DASGUPTA and
PAUL STONEMAN

I   Motivation

A great many research problems in economics, as in other disciplines, we would imagine, are internally generated by the subject. Seminal contributions are those which formulate new questions, or pose old questions in a novel and tractable manner. Such contributions often have the habit of attracting large research followings in rapid succession, refining, extending and embellishing the original analysis. It is at this stage that the problems analysed are internally generated; that is, prompted exclusively by the earlier contributions. This is the Baroque stage in a problem area.

Such 'cumulative causation' in the temporal characteristics of research output is not difficult to explain. There are strong dynamic scale economies in any one line of research. The second paper on a well-formulated problem area is a great deal easier to write than the first, the third easier than the second, and so on. There are exceptions, of course; there always are. And in any case, 'cost reduction' cannot go on indefinitely; at some stage decreasing returns set in. But there are extensive spill-overs in learning in the field of academic research. This sets in motion for a time the phenomenon of cumulative causation originating from the initial investment in the production of an 'idea'.

We say this with some feeling. It has been recognized for a long while that 'knowledge' (or 'information'), the output of research and development (R&D) activity, possesses unusual properties – among which the feature we began with is an instance. These properties make it most unlikely that the market mechanism can be relied upon to produce knowledge in appropriate amounts, and to use it efficiently. Furthermore, careful work in economic history has established the importance of technological change for the rise in the productivity of labour hours. Then again, industrial case-studies have indicated the importance of investment in R&D on technological improvements.[1] And yet, the economics of R&D policy, more generally technology policy, is still in its infancy. And this, despite the astonishing pace of intellectual activity which has prevailed in the field of analytical public economics over the past decade and a half.

A major stumbling block in the development of the analytics of technology policy matters has been the fact that our understanding of the pre-requisite *positive* aspect of the problem area was until recently slow to develop. Recent work in the field of industrial organization has shown that in decentralized environments resource allocation mechanisms involving technological competition are quite different from those involving the familiar price competition among atomistic agents.[2] A major purpose behind our organizing a CEPR conference on the economics of technology policy was to attempt a systematic account of these differences and to initiate a discussion of policy matters. In this Introduction we will not summarize individual contributions; the essays are non-technical and quite comprehensible. Given the frequency with which we are informed that no two economists ever agree and that the subject is in a crisis, it is quite remarkable how congruent are the views of the authors (as were those of the discussants) on the problem areas that need to be broached with care.[3] This is reflected most vividly in the frequent overlaps among the contributions. There are some recurring themes, concerning mostly the nature of this elusive commodity, knowledge, and the way in which we ought to view the development of a decentralized economy's investment in the production and use of this commodity. In the remainder of this Introduction we will summarize these common threads.

II   Knowledge as a commodity

Knowledge, all too frequently, is both a consumption and a capital good. A mathematical theorem is often valued for its beauty, as well as for its potential for the generation of further theorems. (Of course, often a theorem assumes beauty precisely because of its fecundity.) Often knowledge is a pure capital good; for example, process inventions. It is less frequently a pure consumption good. Even a new harmony is an input in the production of musical ideas. The value of knowledge as a capital good – that is, as an input in production – is a derived value, often highly conjectural, as in the case of very basic research. But at an analytical level this distinction, between capital and consumption goods, is not of great moment.[4] In what follows we enumerate a few of the key features of knowledge which make the economics of technology policy so problematic a field of discourse.

(i) *Knowledge as a public good.* Unlike private commodities, if one person gives another a piece of information it does not reduce the amount of information the first person possesses. Thus, given a fixed quantity of knowledge it is the cost of *transmission* which should determine how widely it ought to be disseminated. But often such transmission costs are negligible.[5] This implies that the knowledge ought to be freely available. But if this were the legal position, then in the absence of any further government intervention there would be *under-production* of knowledge, as the economics of public goods has emphasised. Three routes are possible for the purpose of overcoming this problem. The first is to grant producers of new knowledge intellectual property rights to their discoveries and allow them to charge (differential) prices for their use by others. This was Lindahl's solution to the problem of the efficient production and allocation of public goods.[6] The second is for the government to engage directly in the production of knowledge, allow free use of it, and finance the expenditure by the imposition of lump-sum taxes. The third is to encourage private production of knowledge by the imposition of (differential) subsidies for their production and the levying of lump-sum taxes to finance these subsidies. This last is the Pigovian solution to the problem.[7] These issues are raised in the contributions of Dasgupta, Barber and White, Lyons, and Ergas.

(ii) *Knowledge as a fixed cost in production.* A piece of knowledge does not need to be produced more than once.[8] The point is that the same piece of information can be used over and over by as many people as wish to, at any scale of operation (Arrow 1962). Thus the production of a piece of information (e.g. the discovery of a cheaper method of producing a marketable commodity) is rather like a fixed cost in the production of goods and services. Now fixed costs are by definition a source of scale economies in production, raising an attendant set of problems in the field of public policy. Issues relating to this feature are discussed in the contributions by Dasgupta, David, and Stiglitz.

(iii) *Durability of knowledge through its use.* Knowledge, like trust, and unlike most commodities, decays if it is unused and, if anything, grows with use. Many medieval crafts are now lost to us because they have not been culturally transmitted down the generations. This much is clear enough. Also transparent is the fact that the more it is used the more durable it is; that is, the less likely it is that it will be forgotten. But in fact knowledge has further peculiar properties. It is difficult not to learn more in the process of *using* a piece of knowledge. Learning-by-doing, learning-by-using, increased efficiency in the 'technology' of learning through the actual process of learning – learning to learn – are concepts that are familiar enough. The stock of knowledge often increases through the very *use* of knowledge. Now, this can have consequences that are profoundly different from those arising in conventional production models. The presence of such learning possibilities implies not only an intertemporal *externality*, it implies – if powerful enough – dynamic scale economies in production activities. In recent years the implications of such scale economies have been explored at length. (See e.g. Arthur 1985, David 1985, Farrell and Saloner 1985, Katz and Shapiro 1985, Arthur, Ermoliev and Kaniovski 1986, and Dasgupta and Stiglitz 1985.) A strong implication of its presence is the irreversible nature of economic activity, the possibilities of small changes in such activity (or in the economy's underlying parameters) resulting in large changes over the long haul in the economy's characteristics, as it veers away more and more from its original trajectory. The idea of 'cumulative causation' is precisely this. In the presence of such intertemporal scale economies, myopic decision rules, or policy *reforms*, are unlikely to be even approximately adequate. A sequence of 'local' improvements cannot be guaranteed to locate globally optimal policies. This is familiar from work in social cost-benefit analysis of projects in the presence of static economies of scale in production. The problem assumes far more serious proportions when such scale-economies are intertemporal. It is possible for industries to get locked into inefficient technologies. In such situations only a big push can move them off the errant paths and towards more satisfactory trajectories. One then needs some idea of ways of achieving this. The contributions of David, Barber and White, Lyons, Stiglitz, and Stoneman in this volume address this class of issues in different contexts.

(iv)   *Moral hazard and adverse selection in the production of knowledge.*   Here we are concerned with the organization of research within the research unit. Not only is the production of knowledge shot through with uncertainty, there are serious moral hazard and adverse selection problems operating in such organizations. It is much more difficult to assess the efforts and intentions of scientists than their performance. Furthermore, the intrinsic ability of scientists and technologists is not observable, only their past record. Thus the allocation of researchers to their tasks and the zeal with which researchers engage in these tasks is likely to be inefficient, not only in a first-best sense – that is obvious – but also in an informationally constrained sense. (See Greenwald and Stiglitz 1986). These issues are touched upon in the essay by Dasgupta, but they have not been fully developed.

(v)   *Knowledge absorption and trade.*   Problems arising from these four basic features are compounded in a national setting where firms are capable of making pre-emptive moves with research and development as their weapon and in the international setting when national governments make unilateral moves through the use of trade and industrial policies. The classic argument for the protection of a domestic infant industry was based on one such problem. Recent work in international trade theory (e.g. Brander and Spencer 1983) has addressed a number of such possibilities and the welfare losses that are involved in the absence of co-operation. The contribution of Lyons in this volume discusses these issues.

III Summary

Three features therefore stand out; that knowledge has the attributes of a public good, that there are strong scale economies involved in its production and use, and that the uncertainties involved in its use and production are acute. These features should not prevent us from discussing technology policy issues. The welfare economics of R&D investment is a perfectly viable subject. But it will not be an easy one to master.

NOTES

1 See e.g. Griliches, ed. (1984), and the contribution by Griliches and Pakes in this volume.
2 For a wide variety of essays elucidating this, see Stiglitz and Mathewson, eds (1986).
3 We note here that participants were academic economists, economists from government, industry and the OECD, and one Member of Parliament.
4 But see the essay by Dasgupta in this volume where it is argued that different social organizations may *view* knowledge in different ways.
5 Transmission costs are different from the costs of educating people to make *use* of the information. In the text we are concerned with transmission costs, not education costs.
6 There are, to be sure, incentive problems in demand revelation, and we are ignoring them for the moment.
7 For a more formal exposition of this, see e.g. Dasgupta and Heal (1979), Chapter 3.
8 By this we do not mean the need for independent confirmation of a new discovery, which is a different matter altogether. The need for confirmation by others, or by oneself, is to evaluate better the characteristics of the newly produced discovery, e.g. whether it has been accurately stated.

REFERENCES

Arrow, K. J. (1962), 'Economic Welfare and the Allocation of Resources for Inventions', in R. R. Nelson, ed., *The Rate and Direction of Inventive Activity*, Princeton University Press.

Arthur, B. (1985), 'Competing Technologies and Lock-in by Historical Small Events: The Dynamics of Allocation under Increasing Returns', mimeo. Stanford University.

Arthur, B., Yu. M. Ermoliev and Yu. M. Kaniovski (1986), 'Path-dependent processes and the emergence of macro-structure', *European Journal of Operational Research*.

Brander, J. and B. Spencer (1983), 'International R&D Rivalry and Industrial Strategy', *Review of Economic Studies*, **50**.

Dasgupta, P. and G. Heal (1979), *Economic Theory and Exhaustible Resources*, Cambridge University Press and James Nisbet (London).

Dasgupta, P. and J. E. Stiglitz (1985), 'Learning-by-doing, Market Structure and Industrial and Trade Policies', mimeo. University of Cambridge.

David, P. (1985), 'Cleo and the Economics of QWERTY', *American Economic Review*, May (Papers and Proceedings).

Farrell, J. and G. Saloner (1985), 'Standardization, Compatibility, and Innovation', *Rand Journal of Economics*, **16**.

Greenwald, B., and J. Stiglitz (1986), 'Externalities in Economies with Imperfect Information and Incomplete Markets', *Quarterly Journal of Economics*, **101**.

Griliches, Z., ed. (1984), *R&D Patents and Productivity*, University of Chicago Press.

Katz, M. and K. Shapiro (1985), 'Network Externalities, Competition and Compatibility', *American Economic Review*, **75**.

Stiglitz, J. E. and G. F. Mathewson, eds (1986), *New Developments in the Analysis of Market Structure*, Macmillan (London).

1 The economic theory of technology policy: an introduction

PARTHA DASGUPTA

I Introduction

An important channel through which firms engage in non-price competition is research and development (R&D). R&D expenditure designed
to locate new or improved products and to lower manufacturing costs of
existing products influences the structure of the industry. At the same
time, industrial structure is a determinant of the incentives that firms
possess for engaging in such forms of non-price competition as R&D
competition. This mutual relationship was a central theme in Schumpeter (1950), although his discussion was not in a form that is amenable
to tests. It is somewhat paradoxical then that until recently the investigations Schumpeter's writings stimulated were for the most part empirical. Here, there have been two broad trends. One has been the
case-study approach; the other, an analysis of interindustry data by way
of regressions undertaken between variables such as the degree of
concentration, the intensity of R&D activity, the number of patents
issued, growth in demand for products, and so forth. Elsewhere (see
Dasgupta 1986) I have attempted to summarize a number of empirical
findings from the latter route and have presented simple theoretical
constructs which can account for them.

These constructs, and indeed most of the theoretical investigations in
recent years on the economics of technological change, have aimed at
explanation, not *design*; they have addressed an aspect of what is often
called 'positive economics'. Theoretical economists working in the field
of technological change have not in recent years demonstrated much
passion for issues in public policy.

This is surprising. In the literature which preceded the current burst of
activity in this field, *three* forces were seen as determining the nature and
extent of R&D efforts in an industry: the degree of appropriability
of R&D benefits by firms (Arrow 1962), the extent of the market

(Schmookler 1966), and innovation opportunities (Rosenberg 1976). The first of these, *incomplete appropriability*, occasioned by the fact that *information* – the output of R&D activity – has some of the attributes of a pure public good, provides *prima facie* evidence of market failure, and therefore a case for government attention. This was one of the thrusts of Arrow's classic 1962 article. There was another, that the production of information (or more broadly, knowledge) is shot through with uncertainty much of which, for reasons to be discussed below, cannot be insured against. The absence of adequate risk markets should also alert us to the need for government attention.

Recent work in the field has suggested in fact that matters are yet more complicated. In Dasgupta and Stiglitz (1980a) it was noted that the degree of appropriability of R&D benefits depends not only on technological opportunities – of maintaining secrecy, for example – and the legal code – patent laws, for example – it depends as well on the industrial structure, and this last should not be treated as exogenous, but in turn should be explained. In short, the degree of appropriability depends on the industrial structure and industrial structure depends, at least in the medium and long term, on the degree of appropriability – a classic case of mutual dependence. This is one reason, there are others, why discussions on public policy in the field of technology become complicated.

II   Scale economies in the production of information

Research is directed at the acquisition of information. In particular, each step in a research programme is designed to yield information to the investigator. Naturally, research involves the expenditure of resources, so not all information is worth seeking. Nor in general does the acquisition of information *eliminate* uncertainty. But this does not provide one with a ground for not acquiring it. For even though it would not eliminate uncertainty the acquisition of information may alter the planned activities of the people acquiring it. Therein lies its value.

In the language of statistical decision theory the acquisition of information is the observation of a signal which allows one to update the probabilities one associates with various possible events. A useless – or non-informative – piece of information is one which does not alter these prior probabilities. A perfect piece of information is one which enables one to know with 'certainty' which is the true event of nature. Most information is of an intermediate kind.

When one conducts an experiment one does not know in advance what the outcome will be. But usually one can catalogue the various *possible* outcomes and, what is most important, one can assess in advance the implications that would follow from each such possible outcome. Thus, in the extreme, one knows in advance what the optimal subsequent course of actions is for each possible outcome. One calculates the maximum expected net benefits flowing thus from each possible outcome of the experiment. Presumably, one has a prior subjective estimate of the likelihood of each of these possible outcomes. Taking into account the cost of the experiment one estimates the expected net benefits of the experiment itself. Presumably, there are many possible experiments to choose among. One now chooses that which offers the maximum expected net benefits.

There are of course deep problems with this formulation of the R&D problem. Experiments (mental or laboratory ones) throw up on occasion previously *unthought-of* possibilities, that is, states of nature which one cannot in advance describe. No one that I know of knows how to incorporate such possibilities into decision theory. At a crude level one can view them as a 'black box' – a residual event, after all mutually exclusive events one can enumerate have been written down. It is the *revision* of probabilities if the world does enter the black box which I do not know how to formulate. In what follows therefore I will ignore this issue. There are more basic problems to discuss.

The point I wish to highlight in this section, due originally to Roy Radner and Joseph Stiglitz, is that under a wide class of plausible situations regarding one's attitude to risk there are increasing returns to scale in the value of information at very low information levels. By this one means that it is not worth investing even a tiny amount to learn a tiny bit. If it is worth seeking information of a certain kind it is worth seeking it in largish chunks. I will not labour the point here, but the implications are surely that as a general rule the number of research projects society ought to initiate is bounded, due not only to the usual reasons of indivisibilities in production, but also to the nature of information as a product.

III   Science and technology as social organizations

This conference is to discuss the economics of *technology* policy. But I hope very much that we will not neglect *science* policy. Questions concerning these two fields are connected and, as I will argue below, connected in a way usually not appreciated. It is not uncommon to be offered the distinction that science deals with the general while technology deals with the particular, that science is concerned with principles while technology concentrates on applications, that science resides in the abstract plane of ideas while technology is grounded on the development of products and manufacturing processes. Such distinctions can of course be made, although with far greater difficulty than would appear at first blush (see Dasgupta and David 1986). The point, however, is that such distinctions, even when they can be made, concern the *characteristics* of the output of research, they concern the *type* of information produced by research endeavour.

Information is a commodity, but it is not a single homogeneous commodity. Such distinctions as those above are based on commodity characteristics. They do not pose any novel problem for the policy maker. To be sure the prospective benefits of certain types of information may be much harder to estimate than others. Thus it is well appreciated that the benefits of basic research – the output of which is an input in further research – are likely to be more conjectural than those of highly specific applied research. But this difference is a matter of degree, and nothing of analytical moment depends on it. Today basic research is conducted not only at universities but also in what one calls 'industry'. And applied research has never been exclusive to commercial firms and individuals seeking their fortune. In a recent essay Professor Paul David and I have argued that there is a far more potent distinction for policy makers, occasioned by the fact that there are today two broad *social organizations* – we may call them science and technology – that are moved by distinct *attitudes* towards the output of research. (See Dasgupta and David 1986.) We argued that science, as a social organization, views knowledge as a *public consumption good*, while technology regards it as a *private capital good*. Their collective attitudes being different, their norms and codes of conduct are different.[1] An important feature of the 'scientific ethos' is that scientists are obliged to disclose all new findings and submit them for critical inspection by other members of the community. In submitting their findings to their peer group scientists, *qua* scientists, surrender claim to exclusive control of that information. In fact, the social norm is uncompromising: *complete* disclosure is the rule.

In technology, as one would expect, the community rules are quite different. Disclosure is not the order of the day, reticence, and on occasion downright secrecy, is; for members of the community of technologists are motivated by the privately capturable rents than can be earned from their findings. One may then draw a sharp distinction between science and technology in regard to the disposition of their respective research findings and express it in the form of a social imperative: if one joins the science community one's discoveries must be disclosed completely, whereas if one joins the technology community such findings must not be fully revealed to the rest of the membership.[2]

A social organization is different from the members it comprises. The difficulty with disclosure in science is that in general it dilutes the incentive on the part of the scientists to produce knowledge in a decentralized environment. Society at large may seem to solve this problem by allocating funds for science through public bodies. But what is the guarantee that scientists won't slack? The institution of science has attempted to meet this problem by nurturing the *rule of priority*. And somewhere between full disclosure (in science) and secrecy (in technology) lies another private incentive mechanism: the institution of patents, which technology often relies upon.

The priority rule, which is used by the scientific community to reward its members, serves two purposes at once. First, it establishes a contest for scientific discoveries. Since effort cannot in general be monitored, nor induce intention, reward cannot be based upon either. A scientist is thus rewarded not for his effort, nor his good intention, but for his achievement. An alternative would be a fixed fee, but as one collects such a fee whether or not one has produced anything of interest, it dulls the incentives to work hard. Moreover, since it is difficult in general to determine how far behind the winner the losers of a scientific race are when discoveries are made it is not possible to award prizes on rank. Thus science does not usually pay 'runners-up', unlike tennis tournaments. The optimum type of payment scheme, one which is compatible with individual incentives, is thus one where, roughly speaking, the 'winner takes all'. Priority mimics this.

The second purpose the rule of priority serves is in eliciting public disclosure of new findings. Priority creates a privately-owned asset – a form of intellectual property – from the very act of relinquishing exclusive possession of the new knowledge. It is a remarkable device. In science priority often *is* the prize. Priority is the basis upon which scientific societies award various tokens of public recognition and is also the ground for claims to informal recognition of one's accomplishments by one's scientific colleagues. The rule of priority is thus a particular form of reward, or payment, to scientists.

I want to compare this form of reward with that in technology. The rewards of the technologist, *qua* technologist, are linked to the often-private appropriated rents from the production of knowledge. The beneficiary of such additions to knowledge – which may or may not have met the test of being additions to knowledge – is presumably willing to pay for them. This creates the possibility of a reward structure that is not linked with priority of discovery.

Secrecy provides a means of capturing rents from new findings. But secrecy is not completely reliable. Apart from anything else there may be little to prevent rivals from making the same discovery at a later date and sharing the rent. The institution of patent protection attempts to remedy this. Patent systems in principle allow individuals and firms to disclose their findings without diluting the rents that they can earn. The system in effect offers a private reward for disclosure and makes the award on the basis of priority of disclosure. The reward itself is tied to the private rents that can be earned from the new knowledge, which in turn the patent is intended to help secure. By connecting disclosure with the right to exclusive use of discoveries the patent system undertakes to solve the problem of financing the pursuit of scientific, that is, publicly disclosed, knowledge.

The patent system is both interesting and problematic because it represents a conjunction of the distinctive and antithetical mores of science and technology in regard to the treatment of new information. Looking backward it seeks to reward additions to knowledge that are disclosed, and does so on the basis of priority. But to finance the award it looks ahead to a contrived limitation of access to the new knowledge. As an invention it incorporates a fundamental feature of the reward structure of the scientific community which seeks to create intellectual property from a public good. However, by leaving the determination of the economic value of that property to the workings of the *market*, the assignment of patent rights necessarily inhibits the utilization of that public good.

Professor Paul David and I have elsewhere elaborated upon this way of looking at the science–technology distinction and have shown that it explains a number of seemingly puzzling features concerning the institutions of knowledge production (see Dasgupta and David 1986). Here I have summarized certain aspects of our findings so as to emphasize one point: both science and technology have instituted a reward structure for their members that, roughly speaking, precipitates a race among rivals. *As a very first approximation* then, the winner in both science and technology, takes all. For this reason the economics of technology policy bears a strong resemblance to that of science policy. The benefits of a scientific discovery may lie far away in the future and, more to the point, be highly conjectural. But then so often are the benefits of a technological innovation. It is a matter only of degree, their difference, not of substance.

IV   The issues

There are at least five interrelated questions in the economics of science and technology policy:

(1)   What research problems ought to be on the agenda?

(2)   How many and what kinds of research projects (or research strategies) ought to be pursued in tackling them?

(3)   How ought resources to be allocated among the chosen research projects?

(4)   Who ought to be conducting the research?

(5)   How ought research personnel, i.e. technologists, to be compensated for their effort?

I have posed the normative questions here because we are to discuss technology policy at this conference. One may similarly pose their non-normative versions; that is, questions concerning the manner in which science and technology, as social organizations, resolve these issues. In any event, the non-normative versions need to be explored first if for no other reason than that public action must of necessity be undertaken in a private, decentralized, environment. In other words, one must locate the inefficiencies and, more generally suboptimalities, of the 'marketplace'.

In recent theoretical literature on the microeconomics of technological change (1) and (3) – and their non-normative counterparts – have been much discussed (e.g. Loury 1979 and Dasgupta and Stiglitz 1980a, b). (2) has been addressed in a partial way by Loury (1979) and Dasgupta and Stiglitz (1980b), under the rather unsatisfactory assumption that the risks associated with the available set of research strategies are independent of one another.[3]

In a recent article Professor Eric Maskin and I have explored the general case where choice has to be made from a number of available research strategies that are less or more correlated with one another. (See Dasgupta and Maskin 1986.) In Section VII below I will discuss some of the issues that arise in this context. Question (5) has been discussed in recent years, for example by Lazear and Rosen (1981) and Nalebuff and Stiglitz (1983). Finally, question (4) has, for the most part, been ignored in the literature.

In what follows I will discuss each of these questions in a brief manner. I want to say, however, that the brevity will be due, not to lack of space – Paul Stoneman has not imposed any such constraint on me – but to the fact that I understand only a small part of these issues.

Before I do this though it is as well to ask again why we might expect the 'market' to answer these five sets of questions in an incorrect manner. Earlier we noted two reasons which had been highlighted by Arrow, the non-appropriability of the benefits of research, and the absence of an adequate set of risk markets. The first has been much discussed in the literature and gives rise to familiar remedies, the public subsidy of research in science and the institution of patents in technology, among other measures. In what follows I wish to concentrate attention on the implications of the second of these reasons – the absence of an adequate set of risk markets – and a third reason which also Arrow mentioned but did not do much with. This third reason concerns the fact that information, once produced need not be produced again, because it can be used over and over. Information input in production is like a *fixed cost* and can be used for any scale of productive operations. Thus consider the manner in which society values the outputs of parallel research teams. The point is that of the discoveries (or inventions) made by rival research units only the 'best' is worthwhile to society. For example, among available techniques of manufacturing a commodity society only wants to use the best-practice technique. To take another example, there is no value added when a discovery is made a second, a third, or a fourth time.[4] To put it sharply, the winning research unit is the sole contributor to social surplus, except in-so-far as the presence of the eventually losing research units provided a spur to the winning unit into greater effort and thus a better outcome (see below).

Now compare the social valuation of the outputs of rival research units with the way research units themselves value them under the 'winner takes all' compensation schemes discussed in the previous section. The point to note is that society does not care *who* is successful in solving a given scientific or technological problem, it cares that the problem is solved. But for the individual scientist or technologist the identity of the problem-solver matters greatly: *each* wants to be the successful one! Thus suppose there are two research units in competition and two possible outcomes of each unit's research: success (S) or failure (F). Writing as (S,F) the event where the first research unit succeeds and the second fails, and so on for the remaining combinations, and ignoring R&D costs, society is clearly indifferent between (S,S), (S,F), and (F,S). But under the 'priority' and 'patent' systems of reward, neither competitor will be indifferent between them. For example, the first competitor will prefer (S,F) to (F,S). This non-congruence between private and social rankings of final outcomes is a source of distortion and a reason for public concern. (For further elaborations of this point see Dasgupta and Maskin 1986.) And it is this particular non-congruence which I wish to keep in the foreground in the discussion which follows.

There are at least three sets of agencies involved in the production of knowledge: the individual researcher, the 'firm' and 'society' at large. For example, there is the lone inventor, the researcher working on his own for fame (public disclosure of discovery) and fortune (rents from the discovery). There is also the case of the individual firm (or corporation) employing research workers in its laboratories, pitting its technologists against those of its rivals in the search for a new product or a new process. Obviously in this case we have to distinguish the benefits to the firm on successful completion of the project (e.g. monopoly profits backed by a patent) from the benefits to the successful research unit (e.g. bonuses, promotions, esteem and so forth). Furthermore, one must distinguish the firm's benefits from the benefits enjoyed by 'society'.

All this is obvious and I have drawn attention to it solely because in what follows I shall, for expositional ease, often not distinguish between the research unit and the 'firm' for which the units work. (An exception will be Section V.) For my purposes here nothing will be lost by this identification. I shall therefore often restrict myself to two sets of agencies: research units and government agencies.

I should finally reiterate that the five questions we have raised above are, as is typical in economics, interrelated. But considering them simultaneously would be a hopeless task. I therefore take them up separately.

V   Who should do the research?

This is a problem in 'adverse selection', involving as it does information asymmetries among agencies regarding the innate abilities of potential research workers. Some people are better at one field of enquiry than others. Other people are better at other disciplines. A person's knowledge of his own abilities typically will differ from his potential employers' knowledge of his abilities. But he will not necessarily know more. Self-delusion can easily prevail; one of the characteristics of a good teacher is the ability to spot talent.

Much of university training consists of tests designed to screen potential researchers. The most accurate 'tests', however, are those which involve candidates actually conducting research. If such research output is not public knowledge potential employers will not know the outcome of these tests and will therefore not be able to screen candidates. Suppose for example that science were to cease to exist and we were left only with a technological community. Since in such an environment non-disclosure is the order of the day, not only would each enterprise in technology have to rely on its private knowledge pool, thus producing an enormous amount of duplicative research; it would be forced to employ research workers from a population with a higher dispersion of talent and a lower mean talent.

Science, as a social organization, continually provides the public service of screening research workers, enabling technological enterprises to have vastly better information about the personnel they are about to employ. Nevertheless, it is a service which is widely unappreciated. The argument that if there is some useful R&D to be done it *will* be done in technology and that it will be done by cheaper means and without recourse to the public purse, betrays a staggering lack of understanding of the economics of science and technology. Research *accomplishment* is the best measure of a person's innate research *ability*. If at some early stage in a person's career this is not disclosed there is potentially a serious misallocation of resources: the person in question may end up in the wrong technological enterprise, at the wrong job.

VI   The public choice of projects

We are here regarding the output of a research project as information and we are regarding information as a commodity. So we need to use the theory of social cost-benefit analysis for the choice of research projects. The social (as well as private) benefits of research are uncertain, possibly highly so, but then so are future benefits of the Channel Tunnel. I wouldn't wish to regard the two types of uncertainty as identical, but to concentrate on their differences would be to miss an awful lot. Thus in choosing a research project one is choosing a (possibly subjective) probability distribution of net benefits over time. This implies of course that questions (1) to (3) in my list of five are highly related. Nevertheless, it will be useful to separate them.

In social cost-benefit analysis of investment projects it has been found useful to distinguish the product-mix of projects from the 'choice of techniques' problem. For example, a social planner might be interested to know whether society ought to invest in the production of rayon or dacron and would simultaneously then be interested in discovering the 'optimal' techniques for manufacturing rayon and dacron. Clearly you can't answer the first question without simultaneously answering the second.

Likewise, for R&D investment. The 'products' are probability distributions of *different kinds* of benefits. And so we are faced with a portfolio problem in investment. But we have here a portfolio problem which is different from the usual real investment portfolio problems faced by society. For a *given* product the benefits are, as we noted in Section III, not additive: only the best outcome counts. To illustrate the difference consider the installation of two manufacturing plants designed to produce the same commodity. As usual, there is some uncertainty in the return from each plant. If the realized rates of return on the two plants are 5% and 10% the aggregate return is some average of the two figures. By way of contrast consider two research projects designed to investigate the same technical problem. As we noted earlier it is only the better outcome which counts: society will simply ignore the worse one.

To formalize all this, suppose there are N potential techniques (or research projects) for solving a particular technological problem. Thus I am here concentrating attention on the 'choice of techniques' issue. Let x_i ($i=1, \ldots, N$) be the fund allotted to the ith technique. Assume for simplicity that the outcome of project i can be represented by a real number. But the outcome is uncertain. So let $h_i(x_i, \tilde{e}_i)$ be the output of the ith project, where $\tilde{e}_i$ is a random variable and h_i is a random real number. To put it another way, if x_i is the investment in the ith research project (the ith technique), the outcome, h_i, is a probabilistic one. Since only the best outcome counts, society will value the realization of the portfolio investment by the function max $\{h_i(x_i, \tilde{e}_i)\}$.[5] So now suppose that $\bar{X}$ is the total amount available for the specific technological problem under review. Then the portfolio problem is to find x_i (≥ 0) for $i=1, \ldots, N$, which maximises the *expected value* of max $\{h_i(x_i, \tilde{e}_i)\}$, subject to the budget constraint $\sum_i^N x_i = \bar{X}$.

Now the first thing to note about this problem is that if h $(x_i, \tilde{e}_i)$ is a *convex function* of x_i – and this includes the case where h_i is *linear* in x_i – then the optimum portfolio consists of a complete specialization in one research project, even if the project uncertainties are independent of one another. (See e.g. Nalebuff and Varian 1983.) We conclude that for diversification – that is parallel research – to be desirable h_i has to be sufficiently concave in x_i, at least for moderate and large values of x_i. In other words diversification in R&D pays only if diminishing returns set in sufficiently rapidly. (See Loury 1979 and Dasgupta and Stiglitz 1980b.)

But there is an important caveat to this conclusion. The phenomenon of moral hazard – or hidden action – is likely to be far more important in R&D than in ordinary investment. In other words, the idea that $\tilde{e}_i$ is exogenous is wrong. Thus suppose that diminishing returns do not set in, even for large investment levels. I want to argue that there can still be a case for parallel research. For research output depends not only on the capital equipment provided to the research worker and the worker's innate ability. It depends also on the zeal with which the researcher works; and finally it depends on genuine chance elements. Of these, neither the chance factor nor zeal can be monitored by the employer. Thus, by observing the researcher's performance the employer cannot judge whether it was a combination of hard work and moderate luck or less than hard work and much luck which led to it. This is why scientists and technologists must not be paid for their zeal or good intentions. In addition, the rationale for not paying a researcher a fixed fee, even when he is averse to risk and the employer (e.g. the government) is not, is that he will otherwise have an incentive to slack. I conclude that a research unit's remuneration should be based on its performance.

But matters can be improved upon from the employer's point of view by introducing a *race* among rival research units. If then, two rival research units were to be established, both working along *similar* lines, payment to each could be tailored to the performance of *both*, that is, the employer could introduce relative compensation schemes. In short, establishing rival research units is a way of introducing competition and it can be so designed as to encourage both units to work harder than each would in the absence of competition. Priority and the patent system are both special instances of reward systems based on relative performance.[6] Given that only the best outcome among the rivals is of value to society it might seem a waste to establish more than one research unit: there is more than one unit to support. But if the original moral hazard problem is acute this cost is more than recovered by the expected gain in research performance. (See Mookherji 1983).

VII   The private choice of projects

All this is on the side of the coin concerning public choice of projects. I want now to ask after the behaviour of *private market* forces when the winner of the patent (or priority) race collects the social surplus from the discovery. (If it does not, there is an obvious distortion in the market, and this can be corrected for by a subsidy or tax on the market value of the invention). Naturally, I will assume that diminishing returns set in for large enough investment in any one research project. It will also be realistic to suppose that at low enough investment levels there are increasing returns. For simplicity I take it that each firm can choose a single research project. Each firm chooses its investment level given the investment levels of rivals.

Begin by assuming that all feasible projects are probabilistically independent of one another. Then it is simple to see that *if there is free entry* into the patent race *and if* R&D does not involve any sunk costs there will be a tendency towards too many firms in market equilibrium. This is because in the absence of sunk costs, free entry will dissipate expected private returns from research. (See Dasgupta and Stiglitz 1980a.)[7] Rent dissipation through free entry is today a familiar notion.

An R&D tax would restrict entry and reduce the waste which results from excessive competition.

But waste can take many forms. Rent dissipation involves an excessive *number* of competing projects. We can ask whether, even if the number of competitors were right the rivals, under the pressure of market forces, would choose the right projects and the right investment levels in these projects. In a recent work Eric Maskin and I have shown that they would not. There is a pervasive pressure on private firms to choose excessively risky projects (see Dasgupta and Maskin 1986), and thus on average one would expect the market to display too large a spread in the realized quality of research. The reason can be traced back to the non-congruence of social and private goals occasioned by the 'winner takes all' form of compensation. We discussed this in Section II. Patent and priority races encourage excessive risk-taking precisely because each rival wants to be the winner, whereas society does not care who wins. Excessive risk-taking is privately beneficial because it raises the chance of victory: the chance of making a high-quality discovery. To be sure, it increases the chance of defeat as well, but this is the downside of the spectrum, the quality of the invention is low, and so there is less to lose in being the loser.

Of course, for this argument to be valid public and private attitudes to risk must be approximately the same. There is, on the other hand, a claim, hallowed by tradition, that private firms are more risk-averse than the government. If this is so there will be a force working in the direction opposite to the one I have outlined above. The claim is very plausible if the 'private firm' is a small investor. It isn't all that plausible if we have giant corporations in mind.

In fact Maskin and I have shown that, when both society and the individual research units are risk-neutral, the patent (or priority) system encourages another form of bias in the choice of research projects: excessive R&D expenditure, leading, on average, to too high a rate of technological advance. The underlying reason for this result is the same as above, that each competitor wants to be the winner of the race, whereas society is indifferent who wins.

Corrective R&D taxes are an obvious set of tools to remove the biases resulting from the patent system which I have outlined so far. A bias which is more difficult to correct concerns the degree of correlation among research projects in market portfolios. So far I have assumed that the available projects are independent of one another. In fact, of course, this is an extreme hypothesis, research projects being less or more correlated depending on how unrelated are the underlying ideas on the basis of which the projects are designed.

So suppose there is a large number of available research projects, 'similar' projects in the set being by definition those which are highly correlated positively. To have a well-posed problem I suppose that project characteristics are otherwise identical, such as their means, variances and so forth. Suppose, for simplicity, that there are two firms which compete by choosing R&D projects and that all decision-makers are risk-neutral. What will be the market equilibrium correlation in relation to the socially efficient correlation?

Suppose to begin with that all projects cost the same. It is then both privately and socially profitable for the firms to choose projects that are of as low a correlation as possible; since this will minimize the chance of their producing close results. (See Bhattacharya and Mookherji 1984.) To induce 'interior' solutions, that is, to permit a genuine tradeoff between costs and benefits, we must either postulate risk aversion or that costs vary with projects in such a way that a firm's research cost is reduced if its project is more correlated with that of its rival. In a recent paper Dasgupta and Maskin (1987) have explored the latter hypothesis and have shown that the market encourages *excessive* correlation among R&D projects. The moral is unmistakable: both scientists and technologists choose overly similar research strategies; society ought to encourage greater diversification.

VIII Conclusions

In this essay I have tried to outline what appear to me to be some of the basic issues in the economics of technology policy. The position from which I have begun is that research is aimed at the production of information. In developing public policy prescriptions one must therefore study the nature of the product in question. This was indeed the route initiated by Arrow in his classic paper. The salient points would seem to be these:

(1)   Under a wide set of circumstances there are economies of scale in the value of information at low information levels. This, in conjunction with more conventional scale economies of production, implies that the market for information is non-competitive.

(2)   Of the several competing ideas directed at a product or process design only the best is of use to society. This implies that research portfolios need to be analysed in a way which differs markedly from conventional financial or real investment portfolios.

(3)   Closely related are the facts that information possesses affinities

to pure public goods and it is like a fixed cost in production. A piece of information can thus be shared with no erosion to it and can be used over and over again at any scale of operation.

(4)   Science and technology are distinct social organizations, differing by way of the goals which guide them. The differences in their goals explain why science insists on information disclosure and why technology encourages secrecy. It was noted that because of these differences science plays a vital role in screening research personnel for technology.

(5)   The winner-takes-all form of compensation to research units, occasioned by the priority rule in science and patent laws in technology, encourages excessive R&D investment and excessive risk-taking on the part of R&D units competing for the prize.

(6)   Set against (5) are forces pushing in the reverse direction of insufficient R&D investment and insufficient risk-taking, occasioned by incomplete appropriation of benefits on the part of research units, greater risk aversion on the part of private individuals than is displayed by 'society', and so on.

(7)   Free entry into research would seem to imply an excess of entrants. And finally

(8)   There is reason to believe that rival research units select overly similar research projects, resulting in an excessive occurrence of 'multiple' discoveries. Market portfolios are thus inefficient.

The economics of technology policy is in its infancy. It is not often one hears the argument that public attention should be directed at the choice of R&D projects by private firms; this is surprising. It is widely appreciated today that R&D investment has a strong influence on an economy's performance. It is also appreciated that information, the output of R&D, possesses exceptional characteristics. Furthermore, we have now seen that R&D technologies possess features which make the activity of information production particularly problematic. And yet the massive recent literature on public economics has barely touched upon these matters. The microeconomic theory of technology policy, like population policy and the public finance of military expenditure, is somewhat of a step-child in our profession.

NOTES

1 David and I did not of course mean that science is not interested in applications, nor did we mean that it is interested exclusively in knowledge for

the sake of knowledge. Scientists regularly investigate phenomena with a view to applications. But science insists on the publicness of knowledge – and universal publicness – and is ultimately concerned with knowledge and its applications as consumption goods.

2 I am avoiding qualification, caveats and so forth for the sake of brevity. For an elaboration of this theme see Dasgupta and David (1986).

3 Dasgupta and Stiglitz (1980b) also discussed the other extreme, and equally unsatisfactory, case of perfect correlation among projects.

4 By this I do not mean independent *confirmation* of a theory, which is a different matter altogether.

5 Contrast this with a financial, or real, investment portfolio, where the aggregate value of the N projects would have been $\Sigma h_i(x_i, \bar{e}_i)$.

6 It should be emphasized that such forms of contests (or tournaments) are of value only if the rival research projects' exogenous chance factors are correlated. (I am still assuming that there are insufficient diminishing returns to R&D expenditure in each research project so that there are no gains from diversification.) If the risks are independent there will be no gain from rivalry, because by observing relative performance one cannot infer anything about relative effort levels.

7 The argument – that rents are dissipated under the conditions postulated – is similar to the theory of contestable markets. See Baumol *et al.* (1982). By an absence of sunk costs I mean only that research expenditure need not be committed until the date of entry.

REFERENCES

Arrow, K. J. (1962), 'Economic Welfare and the Allocation of Resources for Inventions', in R. R. Nelson (ed.), *The Rate and Direction of Inventive Activity*, Princeton University Press.

Baumol, W. *et al.* (1982), *Contestable Markets and the Theory of Industrial Organizations*, Harcourt Brace Jovanovich (New York).

Bhattacharya, S. and D. Mookherji (1984), 'Portfolio Choice in Research and Development', mimeo. Stanford University.

Dasgupta, P. (1986), 'The Theory of Technological Competition', In J. Stiglitz and F. Mathewson (eds), *New Developments in the Analysis of Market Structure*, Macmillan (London).

Dasgupta P. and P. David (1986), 'Information Disclosure and the Economics of Science and Technology', in G. Feiwel (ed.), *Essays in Honour of K. Arrow*, Macmillan (London), forthcoming.

Dasgupta P. and E. Maskin (1987), 'The Simple Economics of Research Portfolios', *Economic Journal*.

Dasgupta P. and J. Stiglitz (1980a), 'Industrial Structure and the Nature of Innovative Activity', *Economic Journal*, **90**, 266–93.

(1980b), 'Uncertainty, Industrial Structure and the Speed of R&D', *Bell Journal of Economics*, 395–410.

Lazear, E. and S. Rosen (1981), 'Rank Order Tournaments as Optimum Labor Contracts', *Journal of Political Economy*, **89**, 841–54.

Loury, G. (1979), 'Market Structure and Innovation', *Quarterly Journal of Economics*, **93**.

Mookherji, D. (1983), 'Optimal Incentive Schemes with Many Agents', *Review of Economic Studies*.

Nalebuff, B. and J. Stiglitz (1983), 'Prizes and Incentives: Towards a general theory of compensation and competition', *Bell Journal of Economics*, Spring, **14**, 21–43.

Nalebuff, B. and H. Varian (1983), 'Some Aspects of Risk Sharing in Non-Classical Environments', in L. Soderstrom (ed.), *Arne Ryde Symposium on Social Insurance*, Elsevier Science Publishers (Amsterdam).

Rosenberg, N. (1976), *Perspectives in Technology*, Cambridge University Press.

Schmookler, J. (1966), *Invention and Economic Growth*, Harvard University Press (Cambridge, Mass.).

Schumpeter, J. (1950), *Capitalism, Socialism and Democracy*, 3rd Edition, Harper and Row (New York).

2 Current policy practice and problems from a UK perspective

JOHN BARBER and GEOFF WHITE*

I Introduction

1 This paper is in four sections. The first tries to place technology policy in the context of economic policy generally. The second discusses a number of questions about the scope of technology policy and the sort of issues with which, in principle at least, it should concern itself. The third puts forward an economic rationale for technology policy when economic policy is based on the presumption that the allocation of resources is best left to market forces. The final section provides a summary of current Department of Trade and Industry (DTI) policies towards science and technology.

II The role of technology policy in economic policy

2 Technology policy should be seen as part of economic policy. Economic policy can be regarded as that set of policies whose principal objective can be variously expressed as fostering wealth creation, increasing the long-run growth of productive potential or national disposable income, or maximising the sustainable long-term level of consumption, according to taste. Technology policy can be regarded as consisting of those economic policies specifically concerned with ensuring that firms, consumers, and government have access to appropriate and up-to-date technology at the lowest possible cost; with fostering invention and innovation; with encouraging the diffusion of innovations, new technologies, and technological best practice; and with ensuring that industry takes advantage of the economic opportunities offered by worldwide developments in science and technology. Technology policy

* Department of Trade and Industry and HM Treasury respectively. The paper represents the views of the individual authors and not necessarily those of the organizations by whom they are employed.

may be viewed as a particular subset of the instruments available to economic policy as a whole, together with the particular intermediate objectives to which those instruments are directed. Technology policy shares the common objective of wealth creation with other branches of economic policy and its instruments can be regarded as just some among the many available for achieving that common objective.

3   Technology policy is therefore ultimately concerned with wealth creation and not with the pursuit of technological achievement for its own sake. The technological objectives set out above are pursued because they are seen as playing a vital role in the process of wealth creation. The success of technology must be judged not just on how far these intermediate objectives are achieved but also the extent to which this achievement is translated into output and productivity growth, and improved living standards. This in turn means that the success of technology policy is conditioned by a whole range of economic factors, many of which lie outside the purview of technology policy proper. These wider economic factors are however the concern of other branches of economic policy and consequently the outcome of technology policy is affected by the success or otherwise of a whole range of other economic policies.

4   To give an example, innovation can be thought of as the successful exploitation of technical change. The economic benefits of innovation are only realised when a new product is successfully brought to market or a new process is successfully brought into use. The extent of successful innovation will therefore depend not only on the quantity and quality of technological inputs, but also on competence in production, in marketing, and in all aspects of management. It will for example also depend on the financial strength of the firm concerned, on the scale on which it can launch the innovation, on the size and growth of the potential market for the innovation and the strategic position of the firm in that market, on the strength of any competition, as well as on the availability of labour and bought-in components and capital equipment.

5   If the UK Government wishes to improve the innovation performance of UK firms it has to decide whether it would be more appropriate to encourage firms to undertake more R&D or whether it should direct its attention to one or more of the numerous other economic factors which determine whether firms innovate successfully. The decision will depend on an analysis of which factors currently constrain the innovation performance of UK firms, on the availability of policy instruments which can influence those factors, on the effectiveness with which these instruments can be used, and on available financial and administrative resources. This will not only require analysis of the complex workings of a modern industrial economy, but must also take account of a wide range

of economic, political, legal, social, institutional, organizational, and psychological factors which govern the choice of available policy instruments and the ways in which they can be used.

6   In recent years the relative importance attached to technology policy has increased both in the UK and elsewhere. The reasons for this appear to us to be as follows. Firstly, the prime objective of macroeconomic policies is now seen to be the creation of a stable financial framework in which macroeconomic forces can operate effectively. This has led to an emphasis on supply side policies of which technology policy may be seen as one. Secondly, this change has been associated, partly perhaps as a result of the stagflation of the 1970s, with a shift away from policies which promote economic growth by stimulating demand towards policies which improve the efficiency with which resources are used. Again technology policy is seen to have a role to play in this. Thirdly, with the increasing sophistication and variety of goods and services and the rise of the NICs, there has been increasing stress on the role of non-price factors in ensuring the international competitiveness of advanced industrial countries. Successful exploitation of the increasingly rapid pace of scientific and technological change is seen as playing an increasing role in non-price competitiveness and indeed, in price competitiveness as well.

7   Fourthly, within the area of industrial policy there has been increasing disillusionment with a number of forms of direct intervention in industry including industrial restructuring, attempts to create national flagships in particular industries or sectors, rescuing lame ducks and the like. Government's ability to provide finance, use preferential procurement, or even prevent competition is seen as increasingly irrelevant in the face of rapidly changing market conditions, or where the firms being assisted lack the necessary managerial or other capabilities. Policies are therefore directed more to working with the grain of market forces, and to providing firms with assistance to improve their innovative and competitive capabilities without weakening their commercial responsibility for their own actions and the incentive for them to stand on their own feet. Intervention is directed much more at the objective of correcting failures in the market mechanism rather than towards grand strategies.

8   Lastly but not least the rise of new science-based industries, such as those associated with information technology, which offer enormous economic potential, has further increased the importance attached to science and technology as a source of future wealth and prosperity. Such industries are heavily dependent on R&D as the main source of their technology, and even the use of their products often requires significant technological know-how. Consequently measures to increase the proportion of national resources going to R&D in these industries and to

increase the dissemination and improve the use of their products are seen as an important new element in technology policy.

III   The scope of technology policy

9   This section of the paper examines the scope of technology policy in more detail and with particular reference to the UK's situation.

Sources and use of technology

10   To begin with, as stated above, technology policy should be concerned with the use and exploitation of technology as well as with its source. In addition, technology policy should concern itself with all the sources of technology, and not just R&D on which firms draw and with the various ways in which these sources of technology can be exploited. As Keith Pavitt has argued in a series of papers, firms differ systematically in their principal sources of technology. He identifies four main types. First, *supplier dominated firms* which are typically small and found in traditional manufacturing and non-manufacturing sectors. Most of their technology comes embodied in their purchases of capital equipment and components, and in-house technological skills are weak. Second and third, he identifies two types of what he calls production-intensive firms. *Scale-intensive firms* are typically producers of bulk materials through continuous processes, or of consumer durables through mass assembly. The main sources of their technology are in-house production engineering activities plus technology embodied in purchased capital equipment. *Specialized suppliers* live in symbiosis with the scale-intensive firms to whom they supply capital equipment. Their sources of technology are their in-house design and development capability plus the experience of users. Fourthly there are *science-based industries,* e.g. electronics, whose source of technology are in-house R&D plus the output of the public science sector. These are also the industries which are most likely to benefit from collaborative R&D.

11   Pavitt warns that this taxonomy is still only tentative and requires further elaboration and validation. However, it provides a useful reminder that technology policy must concern itself with a variety of industries which differ not only in the sources of their technology and the means by which the latter is appropriated, but also in terms of the typical size of firm and the relationship between those firms and their suppliers and customers. Firms can obtain the new knowledge and techniques which they incorporate in their products and processes by in-house R&D; by reading the trade press, and scientific and technical journals;

by licensing technology from elsewhere; by buying new types of machinery or components; through in-house production engineering skills and learning by doing; by drawing on the experience of their customers; by learning from other firms using similar equipment or processes; by recruiting highly skilled staff; by use of consultancy; by commissioning R&D from outside; by collaboration with other firms, etc. Technology policy must concern itself with these activities and others which there is not room to list here.

12   Technology is only commercially valuable to a firm when it has been embodied in the design of a new product or incorporated in the firm's production system. Technology in its commercially (and therefore economically) useful form tends to be firm-specific at least to some extent. While this is obvious in the case of technology which a firm has developed through its own efforts it is also generally true of technology acquired from elsewhere. For example where a firm licenses technology from abroad it may need to undertake a certain amount of R&D to understand what it has acquired and to adapt it for use in its own activities. By this means it converts the acquired technology into a form specific to itself. While one can conceive of polar cases, where the amount of effort required to adapt acquired technology to the purposes of the firm is minimal, in general firms will have to expend at least some resources in appropriating technology acquired from elsewhere. The effort and cost involved in appropriation will render the acquired technology firm-specific. In one sense costly appropriation will represent a waste of resources as it is bound to involve firms in 'reinventing the wheel', in finding out for themselves what other firms already know. However, it may also be an important source of innovation, as the firm may wish to adapt the technology in a way as yet peculiar to itself, or may simply stumble on some new discovery by serendipity.

13   There are a number of implications for technology policy in the way in which firms acquire technology from elsewhere and make it specific to themselves. Firstly, activities such as R&D and production technology should be the focus of policy not just because they are sources of innovation but also because they are involved in appropriating technology from elsewhere. Secondly, the whole process highlights the importance of diffusion of product and process innovations and of transfer of technology. Thirdly, it focuses attention on the means by which technological knowledge is transferred between firms or from universities or research establishments to firms. A particular mode of technology transfer will transfer technological information specific to one establishment (technology transfer within multi-establishment firms

is not costless) to another, with a greater or lesser degree of efficiency which is inversely correlated with the effort which has to be devoted to appropriating the information by the receiving establishment. Fourthly it reminds the policy maker that innovation without prior diffusion or technology transfer and pure diffusion without any subsequent innovation are polar cases. The processes of developing and transferring new technology are inextricably linked.

14   The problem facing the firm is to acquire and appropriate, in a form specific to itself, those technological capabilities which best enable it to exploit the market opportunities which it faces and to do this in the most cost-effective way. This means it must be aware of what technology is available and at what cost. Firms' awareness of technological opportunities therefore becomes an important concern of technology policy.

Production versus use of technology

15   Consideration of the fact that sources of technology differ across sectors, and of the separate but linked process of innovation and diffusion suggests two more lessons for technology policy. Firstly it should not just concern itself only or even primarily with the producers of technology, those firms and industries which produce capital equipment and components which are the source of new technology for other firms and industries, but also with the users of technology. Typically it is the producers of major new technologies which attract the attention of policy makers, partly because of the technological glamour and prestige which surround them, but also because they often constitute coherent and forceful political lobbies. However, it is far from clear that the bulk of the economic rents from an important new technology will be earned by the equipment producers, and it may be more economically rewarding for a country to make effective use of a new technology than to be a producer. This may be particularly so where equipment producers are being subsidised by their governments in a number of countries, and the technology has a wide range of uses.

16   One answer is for policy makers to encourage both the production and use of new technologies. However, limited financial resources may impose the need to make some kind of choice. Moreover there are some policies for aiding producers, e.g. preferential procurement, which may prevent users from obtaining access to superior (foreign) sources of technology.

17   In practice the choice between supporting the production and use of a technology may not be quite so stark. In order for a country to make

effective use of a technology it may be necessary to possess some knowledge of how it is produced. There may also be some advantages for domestic users in having a domestic source of supply. Also even if a country does not find it economic to produce the full range of equipment and components associated with a major new technology, it may be able to exploit effectively particular niches within that range. Moreover, the existence within an economy of knowledge of the production and use of a variety of technologies creates an environment which is conducive to innovation, particularly innovations involving the convergence of several technologies. Innovation is likely to flourish where a network of contacts exist between people with knowledge of a wide range of technologies and a range of entrepreneurial talents and experience. This is the kind of environment in which technological serendipity is most likely to result in important new products and processes.

18   The second lesson which can be drawn is that technology policy should concern itself with all sizes of firms – small, medium and large – across the full range of industries. It must concern itself both with firms which are in the worldwide forefront of technology in their sector and with firms which are technological laggards even by domestic standards. In the case of the UK it is far from clear whether there is more to be gained from encouraging state-of-the-art breakthroughs, say, in aerospace technology, than from raising the standards of small engineering workshops to the best German or Japanese practice. In a situation of tight constraints on public expenditure such choices may sometimes have to be made. It goes without saying that the needs of a small and technically backward firm in a mature industry are very different from those of a large and sophisticated producer of high technology products. However, in a situation in which most of UK industry does not consist of either large or high technology firms the needs of the former cannot be ignored.

The technological spectrum

19   The linear model of innovation which shows a steady progression from pure scientific and engineering research through applied research and so on to final commercial exploitation is largely discredited, but it does serve to illustrate another important choice which faces the maker of technology policy. That choice is whether to concentrate support towards the research end of this spectrum or on the closer-to-the-market phases of innovation.

20   The arguments in favour of concentrating support on the research phase are as follows. Firstly, since basic applied research is more likely to

give rise to externalities or spin-off than close-to-the-market development, firms are more likely to spend less than the optimal amount from a national point of view. Secondly, because research involves a much lower commitment of resources than development (and development much less than production and marketing) the financially constrained policy maker will find that he gets more leverage for limited funds in this area.

21   Thirdly, it is perhaps easier for a policy maker to choose between economically promising technologies at the research stage than to choose which of several potential new products should undergo final development and go into production and be put on the market. It is not too difficult for governments to hire economic and technological experts, to consult both academia and industry on a confidential basis, and to monitor developments abroad, in order to arrive at a view about what technologies might have a promising economic future. They may well get it wrong in many instances but it is not obvious that a well designed government exercise to identify promising technologies will suffer from a marked disadvantage *vis à vis* similar efforts by firms. Against this, it is much more difficult for governments to hire or develop in-house commercial expertise whereby they can successfully second guess decisions made by commercial firms about product and process development, production, and marketing. The strictures against attempts to pick winners even by consensus have much greater force at these later stages of the innovation process. Moreover the problems posed by lobby groups and vested interests will be much greater the closer government intervention is to the market place.

22   Fourthly, there is the role which government plays in supporting academic science. There seems little doubt that the private sector is unlikely to fund the socially optimal level of scientific research and that a major role is justified for government in this area. We discuss below the distinction between science and technology policies, but technology policy must take cognizance of whether academic science provides the necessary underpinnings for the nation's technological needs, and must concern itself with the pull through of promising scientific discoveries into the commercial domain.

23   But there are also arguments in favour of Government support for close-to-the-market innovation activities. Firstly, the later stages of the innovation process are much more influenced by the pull of market forces and their effects on wealth creation are much more direct. There is always a risk with Government programmes to support applied research that they become captured by the technological establishment and become too technology driven, with too little attention being paid to

the ability of the country concerned to exploit the research results. Successful innovation involves a complex interaction of both technology push and 'demand pull' and governments must try and ensure that their technology policies give appropriate weight to both.

24   Secondly, there are many small and medium size firms whose only innovation activities consist of close-to-the-market design and development activities. These are the kind of firms who are most likely to suffer from market failure in the provision of capital, especially risk capital, and have the greatest need for Government support. These firms are nearly always engaged in incremental innovation, and they are very unlikely to be involved in significant breakthroughs in major technologies, but the aggregate impact of their innovation activities on wealth creation is too important to be neglected.

25   Thirdly, in the case of the UK the evidence suggests that the main weakness in innovation performance has been not so much in the invention of new products and processes as in their commercial exploitation. There are a number of possible reasons for this, including deep seated factors such as myopia or inadequate investment in human capital, not all of which can readily be influenced by technology policy alone. However, given that the ultimate success of technology policy depends on commercial exploitation, the UK's failing in this respect is a problem which technology policy cannot ignore.

26   A well-thought out technology policy will concern itself with market failure wherever the latter may occur in the innovation process, the exact balance varying according to national circumstances and the likely effectiveness of government interventions. However, since the ultimate objective of technology policy is wealth creation and technology does not result in wealth creation if it is not exploited, technology policy should concern itself with economically exploitable technologies[1] and with the exploitation process itself. If firms within a country are poor at exploiting available technology a technology policy which concentrates on making more technology available is likely to yield disappointing results in the end.

The role of firms

27   The primary role in the economic exploitation of new technology rests with commercial firms. As was pointed out in paragraph 4 above, the success of firms in exploiting technology depends on the full range of their commercial capabilities and not just on those technological factors, such as the level of R&D, which are the primary concern of technology policy. Technology policy must pay regard to the strengths

and weaknesses of national firms as well as to the goals and strategies they adopt and the factors which lie behind them. In the case of the UK this is particularly true where the development and production of major new technologies are concerned.

28   Another important concern of technology policy is the rate at which new, especially technologically-based firms, are formed, and in the UK at least, with the propensity for them to grow and compete with existing large firms. This again involves a whole range of factors, many of which are not technological as such, including the entrepreneurial ambitions and talents of scientists and technologists, the attitudes of venture capitalists and other providers of capital, the nature and growth of demand for innovative products and processes including the attitudes of public purchasers, the level and structure of taxation, etc. The rise of new large high technology firms from small beginnings adds an extra element of flexibility, particularly in the electronics industry, to the response of the US economy to technology opportunities, which appears to be lacking in Europe where the same firms, somewhat transformed, seem to dominate decade after decade.

The international dimension

29   It is essential for technology policy to have an international dimension. In the case of the UK it is sometimes pointed out that 95% of the world's R&D is carried out abroad and, while much of this R&D is probably devoted to appropriating existing technology rather than discovering new technology, there is obviously a large and developing stock of technology overseas which UK firms could take advantage of. There are many sectors in which UK firms are less advanced in their technology than many of their competitors in other advanced industrial countries. (There are of course a number of sectors where UK firms are in the forefront of new technology.) However, obtaining access to and appropriating overseas technology may be often difficult and sometimes costly. Intellectual property rights, language, distance, and secrecy all present barriers to international technology transfer. Without a certain existing level of technological competence UK firms may simply not be in a position to absorb state-of-the-art technology relevant to their sectors. Lack of skilled technologists, managers, or operatives may present a barrier to adopting leading edge technology from overseas.

30   There is some evidence that an important barrier preventing many UK firms from absorbing more advanced foreign technology is that they are not aware of its existence, and do not undertake the systematic

search activities which would make them so aware. It is always possible to set up government-sponsored data bases, or use embassies as scientific and technological listening posts, in order to improve the knowledge of UK firms about foreign technology. But if the firms themselves are not prepared to use such facilities then little will have been achieved.

Technological collaboration

31   An increasingly important element of UK technology policy is to encourage collaboration between UK firms, and between UK firms and their foreign counterparts. Collaboration between domestic firms in the same industry (a) enables them to pool technological knowledge; (b) permits them to share the costs of generic research where technological and commercial benefits may be long-term and very uncertain, and thus between them to cover a wider range of technological possibilities than any of them could have afforded alone; (c) enables them to share the costs of the heavy up front R&D which may be necessary to enter certain markets; (d) if properly managed can enable them to accelerate the development of technology. Collaboration between domestic firms whose relationship is that of supplier and customer can also yield significant benefits. The supplier benefits because such collaboration can enable development of a new product to be informed by the detailed requirements of a customer and by the actual performance of a prototype in use. The supplier can also benefit from the demonstration of the qualities of a new product to other potential users. The customer benefits because of early access to the latest technology and by the opportunity to have an innovative product tailored to its precise requirements.

32   Collaboration between domestic firms may be particularly appropriate where they face much larger foreign competitors or where they are technical laggards by international standards. From the point of view of the technology policy maker encouraging firms to collaborate is a way of helping them help themselves by pooling technology, sharing R&D costs and avoiding duplication, and internalising externalities. Collaboration between firms can be extended to include universities and government research establishments, thus improving technology transfer between academia and industry, increasing the proportion of academic research which bears some identifiable relationship to wealth creation, and improving the dissemination of the results of in-house government-supported R&D.

33   Collaboration between UK firms and their European counterparts offers particular advantages. In a number of sectors, particularly in the area of information technology, European firms are indeed smaller

than their US and Japanese competitors and in some instances less technologically advanced as well. European collaboration as well as offering the same advantages as domestic collaboration offers some additional advantages. In some sectors eg main telephone switches, procurement policies based on national preference have fragmented the European market and have resulted in European firms enjoying much smaller domestic markets than their US or Japanese counterparts. European technological collaboration enables the often high R&D costs of developing new products in these sectors to be spread across a European-wide market, thus enabling European firms to compete more effectively in world markets. Fragmentation of the European market can result in, or be the result of, a variety of different standards for the same product in different European countries. European collaboration can provide the means to overcome this problem and achieve common product standards throughout the European market. In time collaboration between firms from different European countries could result in the emergence of pan-European firms having a scale of operation and size of 'domestic' market which enables them to match the leading US and Japanese firms.

34   Of course collaboration with European partners is not always the best option for UK firms seeking international links. Given the importance of the US market for many new technologies and the capabilities of US and Japanese firms in many sectors, it may sometimes be more appropriate for UK firms to collaborate with suitable firms from those countries. Conversely, an advantage of European collaboration is that it is more likely to involve a partnership between equals, thus increasing the potential for mutual benefit. Above all it provides the opportunity to break down barriers within the European market and reduce the fragmentation which has placed European firms at a disadvantage in world markets. Where opportunities for unifying the European market in this way arise it will be particularly important for UK firms to participate effectively, otherwise they could face a permanent deterioration in their competitive position.

35   Collaboration between firms can be costly, particularly when it takes place across national boundaries. It involves extensive negotiations to set up the collaborative arrangements and difficulties such as the allocation of intellectual property rights. Differences in corporate and national cultures, entrenched attitudes against cooperating with competitors or simply against cooperating with other firms at all, and differences in objectives, must all be overcome. Once a collaborative project has been set up considerable effort and expense may be needed to coordinate the efforts of the various partners particularly if they are from more than one country. Thus despite the advantages of interfirm

collaboration it is not likely to occur on anything like the optimal scale without encouragement and assistance either by national Governments or the European Commission. As firms become more accustomed to collaborating and to coping with the costs and difficulties involved the need for such assistance may diminish.

36   The existence of international collaborative programmes and opportunities for international collaboration which may make heavy calls on limited budgets faces technology policy with the problem of comparing the benefits of such collaboration with the benefits from supporting purely domestic activities. In particular there is a choice between encouraging the development of a particular technology on a purely domestic basis or assisting national firms to develop and acquire the technology by means of international collaboration. In many cases the outcome of the choice will depend on factors specific to the particular technology or industry in question, and it is difficult to lay down general principles. However international collaboration will often be favoured where the firms are large producers of a major technology with high up front R&D costs and where demand is characterized by national preference. By contrast, policies which are directed at small firms and at the use or diffusion of technology will tend to be undertaken on a national basis. In some circumstances firms may require a measure of prior domestic support to build up their technological capabilities so that they can profit from the opportunities for international collaboration.

The relationship between technology policy, science policy and public procurement

37   There are several areas of Government policy, which while they do not have wealth creation as their prime objective and are not formally part of technology policy, nevertheless have a profound effect on the *intermediate* objectives of the latter. We now wish to consider whether two of these areas of policy – science policy, which embraces the public funding of the advancement of knowledge, and public procurement, particularly in the area of defence but also in the areas of health and environmental protection – should be more closely integrated with technology policy.

38   There are those who would argue that both science policy and public procurement should be subordinate to technology policy to a significant extent. The argument tends to be two-fold. The first is based on opportunity costs. The resources of qualified scientific personnel and sophisticated research equipment that are devoted, say, to astro-physics or defence procurement, may have alternative,

more productive use in the commercial exploitation of technology. Wealth creation and economic welfare would therefore be enhanced by the transfer of such resources out of astro-physics and defence procurement.

39   This argument is closely related to the second, namely the tendency for science policy and public R&D procurement to become compartmentalized activities, with institutional rigidities. The consequence can be that each category of public R&D funding becomes so separate that it disregards both the beneficial and adverse effects it may have on other parts of the research community. An example is the preoccupation of basic science with peer evaluation to such an extent that wider purposes such as industrial and economic benefit may not be adequately reflected. Another is the risk that defence R&D procurement may have too little regard to the opportunities for civil exploitation of the technologies which it fosters.

40   There is no doubt that rigidities of the above kind do occur and that they can cause distortions which result in divergencies between opportunity costs and the prices actually paid for the resources in question. The question is what to do about them. There are two polar solutions. The first is that each category of public funding of R&D should be implemented as efficiently as possible against the specific objectives for which it is intended. This approach accepts that there are different purposes for science policy, public procurement of R&D and technology policy and that the efficient pursuit of each is most likely to give rise to optimal allocation and use of technological resources.

41   The second approach is to suggest that all public funding of R&D should be assessed against some over-riding and central criteria such as 'wealth creation'. This is associated with recommendations for a 'top down' approach to the organization and management of all public funding of R&D, usually in a centralized and coordinated way. This is in contrast to the alternative approach which emphasises a pluralistic, 'bottom up' model of determining R&D priorities.

42   UK Governments have tended to prefer the pluralistic approach on the grounds that it allows choices and priorities to be determined by those who are closer to the scientific, technological, and market opportunities, or the needs of the public service in question. It also facilitates a diversity of approach to scientific problems and encourages the competitive exploration of alternative technologies. A risk with the 'top down' approach is that it could become captured to some extent by industrial interests so that science and public procurement of R&D became regarded as a means of augmenting private productive capital. By concerning itself with the simultaneous achievement of too many

objectives the 'top down' approach may suffer from excessively bureaucratic management and the lack of clear criteria for success.

43   Of course the distinction between science policy, public procurement, and technology policy is not a rigid one, though it does give rise to different incentive structures (for example as between the scientific and the technological communities). Nevertheless in circumstances where the public sector resources devoted to undertaking or financing R&D directly relevant to wealth creation are inevitably constrained, and UK firms' own spending on civil R&D is at best running flat and is falling behind that of their overseas competitors, it is becoming increasingly difficult to ignore the effect which the massive defence R&D budget could (and inadvertently does for good or bad) have on wealth creation. In the case of public funding of science, concern that resource constraints may mean that UK science will not undertake the activities which UK industry requires of it, and disquiet about the failure of UK firms to exploit many of the more important discoveries emerging from British universities, suggest a need for better coordination between public funding of science and of the technological strategies of UK industry.

44   There is thus a need for careful consideration of the nature of the institutional barriers between technology policy, science policy, and public procurement of R&D and where these barriers should be set. It is important that each category of public funding of R&D should be assessed in order to ascertain as far as possible what its effects are on its own programme objectives and its wider economic consequences for wealth creation. Only then will it be possible to identify the marginal trade offs which can inform the designing of institutional arrangements.

45   There is one particular segment of the spectrum from basic science to commercialized innovation where the distinctions between science, technology and public procurement of R&D policies may be particularly harmful and where there is need of greater central coordination and direction. That is the segment which is occupied by what are sometimes referred to as emerging or strategic technologies. These terms are not always precisely defined, but it is generally recognized that the technologies referred to have at least the following two broad characteristics:

(a)   They are emerging in the sense that they offer possibilities of collaboration between the scientific and technological communities because their development calls on a wide range of scientific and technological disciplines and, although they are far removed from final commercial application in specific products and processes, their potential is discernible.

(b)   They are likely to have a wide range of applications in industry and elsewhere in ways which are likely to cause production and consumption patterns to be significantly transformed.

The need for central coordination is probably strongest at the point where the development of one of these technologies is about to become set on a particular trajectory because of the dominance of one particular user or group of users. Once the development of a technology becomes locked onto a particular trajectory it may take a form which is unsuitable for exploitation in other markets or by other types of user. Development in other directions or transfer to other users may be made more difficult. At this stage it is particularly important to consider all the options for exploiting the technology and to ensure that none are inadvertently precluded because demand was largely from one particular type of user.

IV   The economic rationale for technology policy

46   A successful technology policy must rest on an analysis of the factors which may be constraining the technological performance of firms, and an an analysis of how the influence of these factors may be ameliorated. Appropriate policy instruments must then be designed and applied. The implementation of such policy instruments is only justified if their benefits outweigh their costs, though, because of the uncertainties involved, this cannot be guaranteed *ex ante*. Given that their outcome cannot be guaranteed, the net economic effects of technological policy measures should be subject to *ex post* evaluation.

47   The analytical complexity of these tasks and the amount of information which must be brought to bear upon them are considerable. As the policy maker's analytical capability is bound to be limited, and he can possess only a fraction of the information available to market participants as a whole, any decision to intervene will be rough and ready. Not only is there a risk of miscalculating the effect of policy measures on their chosen target, or even of choosing the wrong target altogether, but distortions may be created elsewhere in the economy. And in so far as intervention involves public expenditure there are costs both in terms of the resources foregone by the private sector and the economic distortions caused to incentives by the taxes used to raise the revenue. Since governments are not subject to the same commercial incentives and disciplines as the private decision taker there is also a greater risk that they will deploy resources inefficiently.

48   For these and other reasons the economic, including the technology, policy of the present UK Government is based on the presumption that the allocation of resources is normally best left to the workings

of the free market. Where there are defects in the market mechanism the first aim of policy should be to eliminate these. Nevertheless it is recognised that there are cases where defects in the market mechanism cannot be sufficiently remedied or where they can only be remedied after a long period of time. Where such defects can be identified it is accepted that there is an *a priori* case for intervention to offset their effects.

49   There is some evidence that market failure may have inhibited the exploitation of new technology in the UK, and that we have lost ground relative to the other major OECD countries since the late 1960s. For example in 1985 industry's own funding of R&D was a lower proportion of GDP in the UK than in the USA, Japan, West Germany and France. Moreover while the proportion so devoted by these four other countries was growing, in the case of the UK it was at best flat. The UK share of foreign patents taken out in the USA has declined from 20% in the 1960s to around 8% in 1983/84. This is a greater decline than that of any other country. International surveys indicate that UK managers are less aware than their foreign counterparts of the opportunities (and threats) offered by new technology and that UK firms accord less priority to identifying the effects which new technology might have. Import penetration in UK high technology sectors (defined by the OECD as those industries with a high R&D intensity) has risen more rapidly than in the comparable sectors of other major OECD countries or than in the case of UK medium and low technology sectors. Our export performance in high technology sectors is however somewhat better. There is no lack of case study evidence suggesting that technological standards of much of UK industry are lower than their counterparts, say, in the USA or West Germany. Recent studies by the National Institute for Economic and Social Research suggest that the UK has a poorly trained and educated workforce compared with its main competitors, and other studies have suggested that this is also true of British management. While the main role in revitalizing British industry must be played by industry itself, it is recognized that there is a role for government where its interventions can be expected to rectify market failure and enable firms to remedy technological and other deficiencies in their performance, without offsetting adverse effects elsewhere in the economy.

50   There is, as far as we know, no single accepted way of classifying those instances of market failure which justifies Government intervention and which takes account of the allocation of resources in a dynamic as well as a static context. However, for the purposes of technology policy the following taxonomy covers most of the relevant sets of circumstances:

(a)   *Risk.*   Firms, their managements, and their providers of capital may be averse to risk (and to uncertainty). This may cause them to devote insufficient resources to the development, appropriation, and exploitation of new technology;

(b) *Information.* Markets can only allocate resources efficiently if participants are well informed about the opportunities open to them and the likely consequences of their decisions. There is evidence that UK firms, particularly small firms, lack this necessary information, particularly in respect of new technologies, and that the market mechanisms which might provide this information are inadequately developed;

(c) *Competition and Market Structure.* In some cases high up front R&D costs may constitute a barrier to market entry. Where this results in inadequate competition, intervention to help firms overcome this barrier may be justified;

(d) *Externalities*, i.e. where the actions of individual firms give rise to benefits which accrue to others, e.g. their customers, and which they cannot appropriate themselves, or costs which they are not obliged to bear;

(e) *Dynamic aspects of Innovation and Economic Change.* There are circumstances in which the decisions of firms and of their suppliers of capital do not take account of the longer-term dynamic benefits which may result from a particular course of action. Perhaps the best-known case of this is that underlying the so-called 'infant industry' argument. Another is where domestic firms are unwilling or unable to devote sufficient resources to R&D at a time when technology is changing rapidly, in order to lay the technological foundation needed to compete for the substantial economic and commercial opportunities which may arise later on. In some instances the potential applications of the technology are very widespread so that the future economic opportunities open to the UK would be significantly restricted if we lacked an adequate capability in that technology. If market forces fail to bring this about then it *may* be appropriate for the government to intervene. Although it is neither possible nor necessary for the UK to maintain a major presence in every important technology we cannot afford to be absent from all of them.

The above list of market failures is not exhaustive, nor would it satisfy a fastidious theorist. Its purpose is to provide some practical guidance to help those involved in policy implementation to identify those circumstances in which government intervention may lead to net benefits to the national economy.

51   Of course identifying an instance of market failure is not sufficient to justify intervention in pursuit of the objectives of technology policy.

An appraisal of the benefits and costs (including the costs associated with the policy instrument itself) of the particular intervention should be attempted in order to ascertain whether it might result in a net benefit to the economy as a whole. If intervention is to be economically beneficial then, *inter alia*, the following conditions will need to be satisfied:

(a)   The activity supported would be additional in the sense that it would not have occurred in the same form or at all, without government assistance;

(b)   That the supported activity results in economic benefits which are greater in the case where support is given than otherwise;

(c)   That the extra benefits which result from support exceed the opportunity cost of providing it together with the costs of displacement or distortions elsewhere in the economy.

The effects of any particular act of intervention will be subject to a considerable degree of uncertainty, and any decision to intervene will be a matter of judgement as to where the balance of probabilities might lie. A decision to intervene in a particular case should only be taken if there is a reasonable chance that the benefits will exceed the costs by a margin which offers the nation the prospect of an adequate return on the intervention programme as a whole.

52   Where Government assistance is given to industry it should normally be on a temporary basis and confined to enterprises and activities which can reasonably be expected to become viable in the long run without continuing support, or where the intervention would otherwise result in long-term benefits to the economy. There are some instances, e.g. the more basic forms of research, where permanent intervention may be justified, and others where a case for temporary intervention is repeatedly recreated by changing circumstances. However, intervention should seek wherever possible to improve the working of the market mechanism and should avoid situations in which the intervention itself becomes the predominant reason why the market failure persists.

53   The importance of this framework for technology policy lies not just in the guidance it provides for successful intervention but the discipline which it imposes on the policy maker to analyse as far as is practicably possible the reasons for a particular action and what its implications might be. This analysis needs to include the necessity for the intervention, to identify the market failure which is preventing an efficient allocation of resources, how the intervention will overcome this market failure, and with what results.

54   Where UK officials engaged in technology policy propose that Government support be given in a particular instance, for example a

grant towards an R&D project undertaken by a firm, they are now required to identify the type of market failure which justifies that particular intervention. They are also required to try and identify what change in the firm's behaviour will be brought about by the provision of support. Officials are asked to try and identify the benefits which would accrue, with and without support, both to the firm and to the rest of the economy (in order to identify any externalities). They are also asked as far as possible to identify any loss of producer surplus resulting from the displacement of other activities either within the assisted firm or elsewhere in the economy.

55 Of course appraisals of this kind are clearly very difficult to undertake. They would tax the expertise of the most eminent economic experts in the field of technology policy, and it must be remembered that the officials involved in implementing technology policy are rarely, if ever, professional economists. More significantly, perhaps, they involve difficult decisions about commercial matters which neither government officials nor professional economists are well placed to make. Except in the largest cases where the resources involved justify calling in economists, accountants, and secondees from commercial firms, the appraisals are carried out by Government officials following a simplified set of procedures. The results of the appraisals tend therefore to be rough and ready, with the assessments often of a qualitative rather than a quantitative nature.

56 It is important to match the level of sophistication and thoroughness of appraisal with the amount of Government support involved. This is not just because administrative resources within DTI and elsewhere are limited, but because appraisal places burdens on the recipient firms, e.g. demands for information, justification etc. Too heavy a burden of appraisal will deter firms from applying for support and negate the whole objective of the exercise.

57 An important element of UK technology policy is that expenditures are subject to *ex post* evaluation. The purpose of this is to examine the costs and benefits of support after the event with a view to discovering:

(a)   How far the original appraisal was borne out by events;
(b)   Whether or not the benefits of the support have in fact exceeded the cost, i.e. whether the support provided value for money;
(c)   How the value for money of similar types of support given in the future might be improved.

Like appraisal, evaluation involves a substantial element of judgement and can at best lead to only broad-brush or tentative conclusions. It has the advantage of hindsight but suffers from the disadvantage that many of the facts to hand at the time of appraisal may no longer be ascertainable. In the case of support for technology it may be many years before all the economic effects work themselves out, by which time the particular scheme under which the support was awarded may have been discontinued, thus reducing the value of the lessons from the evaluation. In most cases interim evaluations are undertaken during the active life of the scheme. The results of such interim evaluations are even more tentative but are often of more practical value.

V   Current Department of Trade and Industry policies towards Science and Technology (S&T)

58   This final section of the paper provides a brief description of DTI policies towards science and technology.[2] Virtually all of the measures included under DTI S&T policy fall within the purview of technology policy as defined in this paper.

59   In 1979/80 support for science and technology amounted to £142m, or around 6% of total expenditure by the Department. By 1985/86 support for S&T had risen to £409m, or about 27% of total DTI expenditure. By 1989/90, it is expected that nearly 47% of the Department's budget will be devoted to S&T policies. This shift is taking place, however, within a DTI budget which peaked at £3.2bn in 1981/82, falling to just under £1.5bn in 1985/86, and is forecast to fall to just under £1bn by 1989/90.

60   The Department's policies for promoting science and technology can be divided into the following four categories:
(a)   Funding of the four DTI Industrial Research Establishments (IREs)[3] and the National Weights and Measures Laboratory;
(b)   Selective financial assistance for R&D projects undertaken by individual firms;
(c)   Measures designed to promote technological collaboration between firms and between firms and the higher education sector;
(d)   Programmes designed to promote application of best practice techniques, greater awareness of the new and emerging technologies and the supply of essential technological skills. These programmes are referred to collectively as 'non-project support'.

61   Out of DTI current expenditure on Science and Technology of just over £400m about £45m is accounted for by the net cost (excluding major building works) of the four Industrial Research Establishments. Another £90m is accounted for by support for aircraft and aero-engine

R&D and for civil space. Support for general industrial R&D accounts for around £220m, while support given for other schemes designed to promote certain areas of high technology account for a further £30m. Of the £250m which is accounted for by assistance to industry (other than aerospace) about 70% was accounted for in 1984/85 by support for projects carried out by individual firms, compared with 10% for support for collaborative projects and 20% for non-project support. In 1988/89 it is expected that single company project support will take up just 36% of support for general industrial R&D and new technology compared with 23% for collaborative support and 41% for non-project support.[4]

62   Underlying this change in the future pattern of DTI S&T support is a fundamental review of technology policy carried out in late 1984/early 1985. The review assessed the Department's experience with past schemes of assistance. In the area of support for individual company projects the evidence showed a tendency to support incremental developments rather than radical innovations. Non-project support, on the other hand, was found to have induced changes in company attitudes to innovation and to have accelerated the wider adoption of best management techniques.[5]

63   The review recommended that resources should in future be focused on those activities which offered greatest leverage from limited funds, and have the most widespread economic impact. On the basis of the available evidence, and on advice from industrialists taking part in the review, it was accepted that this meant increased emphasis on non-project support. It was concluded that financial support for projects undertaken by single companies should be more selective, concentrating on projects which were more innovative and/or more risky in relation to the size of the applicant company, and which offered a potentially greater economic return; this more stringent approach would be somewhat relaxed for small firms. The review recommended a modest increase in the support given to collaborative R&D projects.

64   Thus while support for single company projects will continue to be available, non-project support and support for collaborative projects, both domestic and international, are to receive increased emphasis. The focus of Departmental support will also increasingly tend towards the development and application of key enabling technologies, such as microelectronics, the benefits of which are likely to be spread over large parts of the economy.

65   The shift away from project support further reflects the recognition that a successful innovation performance requires not only expenditure on R&D (which project support seeks to encourage) but mechanisms and incentives for the diffusion and exploitation of

innovations. Non-project support, such as awareness programmes and advisory and consultancy services, encourages the application of new products and processes rather than increasing their supply. Given the UK's oft-cited weaknesses in exploiting its scientific and technological advances this policy response seems highly appropriate. The expansion of collaborative project support may also be expected to encourage diffusion and application, involving as it does the sharing of know-how between firms and/or academic institutions. Other non-project support measures, such as those designed to improve education and training, facilitate increases in real supply of skilled manpower and help to ensure that increased expenditure on R&D is not dissipated in higher factor prices.

66   The main DTI schemes and initiatives (excluding those concerned with aerospace) under the four categories set out in paragraph 59 are briefly described in turn below. A number of the support schemes for industry are now marketed under the umbrella title of 'Support for Business'.

Industrial Research Establishments

67   The four Industrial Research Establishments carry out a variety of functions. The National Physical Laboratory (NPL) is responsible, with some assistance from the National Engineering Laboratory (NEL), for measurement standards in the UK. These functions include comparisons with national standards laboratories worldwide to ensure the traceability of the measurements standards used in the UK to a common international standard, accreditation of laboratories providing measurement services to industry as well as the direct provision of calibration services to industry, and the development of measurement technology. The Laboratories also have statutory functions, e.g. the Laboratory of the Government Chemist acts as a referee analyst under various Acts of Parliament, and provide analytical and advisory services both to DTI and to other Government Departments. They also carry out R&D into promising areas of technology. A good deal of their R&D work is carried out in the context of consortia and clubs involving both industrial firms and universities and polytechnics, thus facilitating the effective transfer to commercial enterprises of the particular technology involved. The IREs provide industry with advice on technological matters and with testing facilities, and undertake R&D and design work for research and trade associations and individual firms. They also organize conferences, seminars and courses and issue publications. Where appropriate and feasible services to industry are charged for.

Support for projects undertaken by single companies

68   The main programmes which come into this category are as follows:

(a)   *Support for Innovation (SFI):* This is a comprehensive facility available to all sectors, offering selective financial support to firms undertaking R&D projects. The main form of assistance is grant aid of up to 25% of eligible costs for development projects and up to 50% for research projects. Projects have to be innovative (a significant advance for the industry or sector concerned), additional (would not go ahead on the same scale or timescale without support) and offer good potential economic returns. Offers of assistance under SFI averaged around £140m per annum up to the end of 1984 but since the Review mentioned above have been running at a much lower level.

(b)   *The Microelectronics Industry Support Programme (MISP):* This scheme (started in 1983) provides for total grant assistance of £120m over seven years for R&D and/or capital projects which contribute significantly to the improvement of the competitiveness, strength and independence of the UK microelectronics industry. An earlier MISP scheme which provided total assistance of £55m closed in 1983.

(c)   *The Fibre Optics and Optoelectronics Scheme (FOS):* This scheme is similar to MISP but directed at the UK fibre optics and optoelectronics industries. It was launched in 1981 with a total budget of £25m which has since been increased to about £55m.

(d)   *Software Products·Scheme (SPS):* This scheme provides support in the form of grants of up to 25% of eligible project costs for the development and marketing of software products (packages). The current level of expenditure under this scheme is of the order of £6–7m per annum.

Support for Collaborative Projects

69   The main programmes in this category are as follows:

(a)   *The Alvey Programme:* This programme brings together the DTI, Ministry of Defence (MoD), Science and Engineering Research Council (SERC), higher education institutions (HEIs) and firms to undertake pre-competitive research into advanced information technology. The programme focuses on four main areas – Intelligent Knowledge Based Systems (IKBS), Man/Machine Interface (MMI), Software Engineering, and Very Large Scale Integration (VLSI). The programme started in 1983

and is due to run for five years with a total spend of £350m
(£150m from the Government, £150m from industry, and £50m
from SERC).

(b)   *Support for R&D undertaken by Research Associations (RAs)*:
RAs were originally set up as a means of carrying out R&D on a
cooperative basis for particular industries or technologies. Projects undertaken by RAs may be eligible for grants of up to 50%
of eligible costs if they involve longer-term research or generate
significant externalities. In other cases e.g. development projects which are closer to commercial exploitation, the maximum
grant is 25%.

(c)   *Joint Optoelectronics Research Scheme (JOERS)*: JOERS is
designed to support pre-competitive research into optoelectronics involving collaboration between industry and academic
institutions. The scheme was launched in 1982 with a total
budget of £25m (provided by DTI and SERC) but additional
funding of £11m was made available in March 1986.

(d)   *EUREKA*: Eureka is a pro-European programme which is
designed to encourage market-led civil R&D projects undertaken on a collaborative basis by firms from more than one
European country. The scheme was launched in 1985. UK firms
participating in such projects are eligible for support on a similar
basis to SFI. So far DTI expenditure in support of Eureka has
been small but is expected to increase considerably over the next
few years.

The DTI also provides support for collaborative projects centred at
research establishments run by other Government Departments including projects designed to facilitate civil spin-off from military R&D. It
also supports a variety of other small collaborative programmes covering
technologies such as advanced robotics.[6]

Non-project Support

70   The DTI runs or is involved in a wide variety of schemes in this
category. Some of the more important ones are described below under
four different headings:

(a)   *Education and Training Initiatives*: These include:
—   *The Engineering and Technology Programme*: A £43m
three-year programme (of which £12.5m has been contributed
by DTI) announced in March 1985 to create 5,000 additional
student places in higher education in engineering and technological subjects by the end of the decade;

— *Micros in Schools Programme:* A £15m scheme which has helped 27,000 primary schools and 5,600 secondary schools purchase a microcomputer and related equipment;

— *Software in Schools Scheme:* A £3.5m scheme to promote the use of educational software in schools;

— *The Computer-Numerically Controlled Machine Tools Scheme:* A £7m scheme that has enabled further education colleges to purchase advanced UK made-machinery for use by engineering students;

— *The Information Technology Centre Scheme:* At a cost of £13m to DTI, this joint DTI/MSC scheme has established 170-plus centres (ITeCs) providing training for unemployed young people in IT skills.

(b) *Technology Transfer:* The Teaching Company Scheme (TCS), which is jointly funded by DTI and SERC, establishes programmes in which academics work within firms on specific projects designed to improve the firm's efficiency and competitiveness. Technology transfer is also improved by a variety of other DTI schemes, particularly those designed to promote collaborative research.

(c) *Awareness and Application of New Technology:* The DTI runs a number of schemes designed to increase the awareness and understanding of new technologies and to encourage their application by UK industry. Technologies covered include microelectronics, advanced manufacturing technology (AMT), and computer-aided design, manufacture and testing.

(d) *Advisory and Consultancy Services:* The Department runs a variety of information, advisory and consultancy services which aim to help companies, particularly small companies, improve their productivity and manufacturing efficiency, quality assurance, product design, marketing, and application of new technology.

In addition the DTI also provides assistance for industrial design via the financial support it gives to the Design Council.

71   Of course, as was made clear earlier in the paper, the DTI is not the only UK Government Department whose policies have a significant impact on the objectives of technology policy. The impact of science policy and defence and other areas of Government procurement have already been discussed. Macroeconomic policy, taxation policy, and policies towards education and training also have an important impact on the technological performance of UK industry. In addition UK firms and academic institutions can apply for support under the various schemes

financed by the European Community such as ESPRIT (Information Technology), RACE (Telecommunications) and BRITE (Advanced Manufacturing Technology). These European Community sources of R&D support are likely to be more important in the future than they have been in the past.

NOTES

1 Some technologies may be worth supporting because they would constitute an insurance policy, in the event of certain contingencies. For example an oil importing country may support the development of alternative energy technologies in case oil prices rose to very high levels. If the relevant oil price scenario does not in fact occur then the technologies may not be exploited. However the *ex ante* risk that oil prices might rise justifies the support providing the alternative energy technologies could have been exploited if oil prices reached the necessary level.

2 A more detailed description of DTI Science and Technology policies can be found in *Science and Technology Report 1985–86, Department of Trade and Industry*, copies of which can be obtained from the Department of Trade and Industry, Ashdown House Library, 123 Victoria Street, London SW1E 6RB.

3 The Laboratory of the Government Chemist, the National Engineering Laboratory, the National Physical Laboratory and the Warren Spring Laboratory, which is responsible for research into air pollution, recycling and handling of materials, and metals extraction, among other matters.

4 See the DTI Memorandum submitted to the House of Lords Select Committee on Science and Technology, *House of Lords Paper* 71–vi, Session 1985–86, 19 February 1986. The proportions quoted exclude support for aerospace and the funding of research establishments.

5 See the DTI's *Science and Technology Report* for 1984–85.

6 Since this paper was presented a major new collaborative programme, LINK, was announced which is designed to promote strategic scientific research directed towards the development of innovative products, processes and services by industry, increased exploitation of academic science by industry, and improved links between industry, higher education, the various Research Councils, and other research establishments. The scheme, which is to be funded by all Government Departments with a major R&D spend, aims to generate extra expenditure on R&D of at least £400m over the next five years.

3 The importance of technology policy*

HENRY ERGAS

I Introduction

How do countries' technology policies differ? What impact do these differences have on innovation performance and, more generally, on industrial structures? These questions are the central concerns of this paper.

Innovation involves the use of human, technical and financial *resources* for the purpose of finding a new way of doing things. As an inherently uncertain process, it requires *experimentation* with alternative approaches, many of which may prove technically unsuccessful. Even fewer will survive the test of *diffusion*, where ultimate economic returns are determined.

The capitalist system's historical success as an engine of growth arises from its superiority at each of these levels: generating the resources required for innovation, allowing the freedom to experiment with alternative approaches and providing the incentives to do so.[1]

Though relying primarily on market forces, the system has interacted with government at two essential levels. The first relates to the harnessing of technological power for public purposes. Nation-states have long been major consumers of new products, particularly for military uses;

* An earlier version of this paper was delivered to a conference organized by the National Academy of Engineering of the United States in Washington DC on 14 February 1986.

The author thanks Bruce Guiles of the National Academy of Engineering; Rolf Piekarz of the National Science Foundation; Professor David Encaoua, of the *Direction de la Prevision, Ministère de l'Economie, des Finances, et de la Privatisation*; Christian Sautter, Inspecteur Général des Finances; and P. D. Henderson, H. Fest, J. Shafer, D. Blades, and many other colleagues at the OECD for their valuable comments on earlier drafts of this paper. Special thanks are also given to the author's colleagues Rauf Gönenç, Andreas Lindner, Anders Reutersward, and Barrie Stevens for generously providing data and advice. However, the author wishes to stress that unless otherwise indicated, the views expressed in this paper are attributed only to himself in a personal capacity and not to any institution.

and the need to compete against other nation-states provided an important early rationale for strengthening national technological capabilities. Whether this rationale persists as the primary motive for government action is a major factor shaping each country's technological policies.[2]

The second arises from the system's dependence on its social context. The development and diffusion of advanced technologies requires a system of education and training as a basis for supplying technology and skills; a legal framework for defining and enforcing property rights; and processes such as standardization which reduce transactions costs and increase the transparency and efficiency of markets. These are, at least in part, public goods: the benefits of investment in education are appropriated by a multitude of economic actors; those of the system of property rights are even more widely spread. The way these public goods are provided, and the role industry plays in this respect, also differ greatly from country to country.[3]

This paper examines the interactions between the technological system and government policy in six industrialized countries: the United States, the United Kingdom, France, Germany, Switzerland, and Sweden. It pays particular attention to the relation between innovation policy and industrial structures. The countries examined are placed in two groups.

Technology policy in the US, the UK and France remains intimately linked to objectives of national sovereignty. Best described as 'mission oriented', it focuses on radical innovations needed to achieve clearly set out goals of national importance. In these countries, the provision of innovation-related public goods is only a secondary concern of technology policy.

In contrast, technology policy in Germany, Switzerland and Sweden is primarily 'diffusion oriented'. Closely bound up with the provision of public goods, its principal purpose is to diffuse technological capabilities throughout the industrial structure, thus facilitating the ongoing and mainly incremental adaptation to change.

Every taxonomy involves a loss of information. The one proposed in this paper does not escape this general rule. Thus, the US has important policies – for example, in agriculture or in medical research – which would fit well into a diffusion-oriented mould; equally, Germany and Sweden have major mission-oriented programmes. But the focus of policy does differ in the two groups; and this allows a clearer examination of the relation between technology policy and innovation performance.

These differences in policy stance – though not as sharp as they may at first appear to be – do turn out to be of some importance in shaping patterns of technological evolution. But it is the central hypothesis of this paper that policies are a *facilitating* rather than *explanatory* factor. The critical variables lie in how industry responds to the results and signals of efforts to upgrade national technological capabilities. In turn, this depends to a substantial extent on the environment in which industry operates. Technology policies cannot, in other words, be assessed independently from their broader economic and institutional context.

A central feature of this context is a country's *technological infrastructure* – its system of education and training, its public and private research laboratories, its network of scientific and technological associations. However, the effectiveness of this infrastructure depends not only on its internal functioning, but also on the way a country's factor and product markets respond to innovation opportunities.

Overall, this suggests that, even within the framework of a market economy, the process by which innovations are generated, selected and imitated will differ according to the features of each country's institutional and economic environment – features which will shape the net social return on investment in innovation. In exploring these features, and their relation to countries' technology policies, this paper follows the broad grouping set out above: Part II examines 'mission-oriented' countries, namely the US, the UK and France; Part III, the 'diffusion-oriented' countries, namely Germany, Switzerland and Sweden; Part IV presents a synthesis of similarities and differences, and analyses their broader implications for economic performance, while Part V discusses conclusions for policy formulation.

II   The 'mission-oriented' countries (US, UK, and France)

Mission-oriented research can be described as big science deployed to meet big problems.[4] It is of primary relevance to countries engaged in the search for international strategic leadership, and the countries in which it dominates are those where defence accounts for a high share of government expenditure on R&D (Table 3.1). Though it has also been used in these countries to meet perceived technological needs in civilian markets (for example, in nuclear energy or telecommunications), the link to national sovereignty provides its major rationale.

The dominant feature of mission-oriented R&D is *concentration*. First and most visibly, this refers to centralization of decision-making. As its name implies, the goals of mission-oriented R&D are centrally decided and clearly set out, generally in terms of complex systems meeting the needs of a particular government agency. Specifying these needs and supervising project implementation concentrates a considerable amount of discretionary power in the hands of the major funding agencies.

Table 3.1. *Share of defence-related R&D in government expenditure on R&D, 1981*

Country	%
US	54
UK	49
France	39
Sweden	15
Switzerland	12
Germany	9
Japan	2

Source: OECD.

Table 3.2. *Public funding for R&D in the high, medium and low-intensity R&D industries[a] as respective percentages of total public funding* (approximate estimates)

Country	High	1980 Medium	Low
United States	88	8	4
France	91	7	2
United Kingdom	95	3	2
Germany	67	23	10
Sweden	71	20	9
Japan	21	12	67

[a]   Defined as industries whose ratio of R&D expenditure to sales is respectively more than twice (high intensity) between twice and one-half (medium) and less than one-half the manufacturing average.
Source: OECD.

Concentration also extends to the range of technologies covered. Virtually by its nature, mission-oriented research focuses on a small number of technologies of particular strategic importance – primarily in aerospace, electronics and nuclear energy. As a result, government R&D funding in these countries is heavily biased towards a few industries which are generally considered to be in the early stages of technology life-cycle (Table 3.2).

The scale of mission-oriented efforts also limits the number of projects and restricts the number of participants. At any point in time, only a small share of each country's firms will have the technical and managerial resources required to participate in these programmes; and these are likely to be among the country's larger firms. The concentration of government R&D subsidies on a small number of large firms is therefore also a feature of the countries in this group.

Overall, mission-oriented programmes concentrate decision, implementation and evaluation. A few bets are placed on a small number of races; but together, these bets are large enough to account for a high share of each country's total technology development programme.

This raises two obvious questions: first, how successful are the bets in terms of their own objectives? And second, do they have any effect on the efficiency with which the many other races are run – that is, on technological capabilities more broadly diffused through the industrial structure? We will consider these questions in turn.

II.1   Direct effectiveness

There are enormous difficulties involved in attempting cost-benefit analyses of major mission-oriented programmes.[5] Three criteria for evaluating success can nevertheless be established: first, are stated product development goals being met? Second, is this being done within the original parameters of time and cost? And third, are any objectives set for commercial markets being achieved?

No country's programmes perform extremely well when put against these criteria. On balance, the UK effort has probably been the least successful, while that in France and the US has at least generated a mixed record. Three factors seem to be critical in differentiating success from failure:

First, do the agencies involved have the technical expertise, financial resources and operating autonomy required to design and implement the programme – and the incentives to ensure that it succeeds?

Second, are relations with outside suppliers such as to provide appropriate incentives and penalties – and do they allow for experimentation with alternative design approaches?

Third, can agencies be prevented from expanding their 'missions' indefinitely – and in particular from moving into areas for which their capabilities and structures are inappropriate?

The answers to these questions have differed in each of the three countries.

United Kingdom   The UK's major difficulties arise from the pervasive lack of incentives in its system of mission-oriented R&D.[6] The British system of public administration – with its emphasis on anonymity, committee decision-making and administrative secrecy – ensures that individual public servants have little interest in 'rocking the boat'. The emphasis on internal and procedural accountability also makes government reluctant to devolve major projects to reasonably autonomous entities, so that responsibilities are tangled, decision-making is cumbersome and the organizational and cultural context is inappropriate for developing new technologies. At the same time, the propensity of British agencies to form 'clubs' with their suppliers – within which each supplier is treated on the basis of administrative equity, rather than commercial efficiency – weakens whatever incentives suppliers may have to seek an early lead, while also ensuring that the resources available are so thinly spread as to be ineffectual. Finally, the reluctance to build penalty clauses into development contracts, and to terminate unsuccessful projects (particularly when this would jeopardize the viability of an indigenous supplier), aggravates an inherent tendency to cost-overruns.

France France's relative success arises in considerable part from the great political legitimacy, operating autonomy and technical expertise of its end-user agencies, combined with the strong incentives for success built into the highly personalized nature of power and careers in the French public administration.[7] Particularly over the last decade, there has also been an effort to increase the competitive pressures bearing on suppliers, notably through tighter controls on costs, recourse to penalty clauses and by easing previous market-sharing arrangements. The effects of these moves have been heightened by improved financial and operating control within the agencies themselves.

However, the French system has two major weaknesses. First, resource constraints have usually prevented experimentation with alternative design approaches, and the number of suppliers involved in each major project has typically been small.[8] Second, though compared to the United Kingdom there has been a reasonable willingness to run down (if not terminate) failures, the system has been highly vulnerable to goal displacement as a sequel to success: agencies which have successfully accomplished a mission perpetuate themselves by designing new missions, frequently in areas which have little to do with their original function. This 'Frankenstein' effect is particularly noticeable in the energy and communications fields, where agencies have sought to expand their power base by diversifying their operations, generally into markets for which their technological capabilities and organizational structures are totally inappropriate. As a result, success in one period has in several cases been followed by failure in the next; and the system has had few mechanisms for reallocating resources smoothly.[9]

United States   Seen purely in terms of the efficiency with which projects are designed and implemented, the United States is intermediate between the UK and France; but it has over them the great advantage of scale.[10] This has three important dimensions. First, US agencies draw on a much larger pool of external technological expertise both in selecting and implementing projects – and have much better mechanisms for doing so, notably in the field of university research. Second, particularly in the defence area, funding for mission-oriented programmes in the US rarely falls short of the critical mass required to complete the development stage, and usually has a higher continuity than programme-funding elsewhere. Third, the scale of funding is such, and the range of qualified suppliers so wide, that some experimentation almost invariably occurs with alternative design approaches and philosophies, even if only in the very early steps of programme conception. Thus, even the relatively small sums spent by the US Department of Defense on its DARPA programmes are large relative to total defence R&D in the UK and France.

The US may also benefit from the high degree of accountability inherent in its system of Congressional scrutiny. This has generated strong pressures for terminating unsuccessful projects, notably in the civilian sector (SST and Synfuels being prime examples), but seems to exercise much less control on the defence sector. This has the incidental effect that while military programmes may be allowed to continue too long, some largely civilian programmes are run down too early. It has been argued that this places an excessive burden of financing projects with a high 'public goods' content on the private sector (the safety and decommissioning of nuclear power plants may be cases in point).[11]

Any overall assessment of the direct effectiveness of mission-oriented research must therefore be mixed; but the immediate returns on the research do appear to be higher in the US and France than in the UK. However, even in the US the products directly conceived by mission-oriented programmes account for a very small share of the economy;[12] the extent to which technology generated in these programmes spreads to other areas of activity is therefore a major component of its overall impact.

II.2   Secondary effectiveness

There are relatively few studies of the extent of these secondary effects or of the pace at which they occur. Those studies which there are come to

Table 3.3. *Share of
government-financed R&D carried out
within the government sector*

	1983 (%)
France	46.8
United Kingdom[a]	38.9
Germany	31.6
United States[a]	25.7
Switzerland[a]	24.7

[a] 1981.
Source: OECD.

widely differing conclusions, frequently reflecting individual authors' views of the desirability of defence spending. None of the studies draws international comparisons. Two broad statements can nonetheless be advanced on the basis of the existing material: first, in every country, the direct spinoffs – in the sense of immediate commercial utilisation of the results of mission-oriented research – are very limited;[13] secondly, the indirect spinoffs – arising mainly from improvements in skills and in technical knowledge transferable from the mission-oriented environment to that of commercial competition – appear to occur both in greater number and more rapidly in the United States than in the UK or France.[14]

This, it can be argued, is partly due to the differences in the way programmes are designed and implemented. But the impact of these differences is compounded by differences in countries' economic structure and scientific and technological environment.

The role of programme design   Four factors distinguish the way mission-oriented programmes are designed and implemented in the US from their counterparts in the UK and France.

The first is the more limited direct role of the public sector in mission-oriented R&D in the United States. In general, the US government carries out a low share of its research in-house; the bulk of it is contracted to outside sources (Table 3.3). Even the management of national laboratories has been separated to a considerable extent from the public sector and devolved to universities or to private companies. Problems of technology transfer from the public to the private sector therefore concern a smaller share of government-funded R&D than is the case in France or the UK.

Second, mission-oriented research in the United States involves a greater number and diversity of agents. It is true that within the private sector, most government research and procurement contracts go to a small number of suppliers. But the sums flowing to university research and to small and medium-sized businesses are large in absolute terms.[15] Thus, the number of small firms receiving twenty per cent or more of their total R&D finance from government sources is nearly ten times larger in the US than in the UK or France, Moreover, insistence in defence procurement on second-sourcing of key components ensures a fairly broad diffusion of technological capabilities.

The effects of this dispersion are compounded by a third factor, namely greater US willingness to disseminate the results of mission-oriented programmes.[16] Despite obvious security concerns, US defence R&D programmes have generally either made their results public or at least made them known to a wider circle than that immediately involved in the programme. This has a particular bearing on the 'public good' type information inherent in these results – such as measurement standards, properties of materials or even identification of unsuccessful approaches to solving given technical problems.

A greater US willingness to disseminate results probably involves an element of bowing to the inevitable: given the number and range of participants, results will sooner or later be known. However, other factors have also been at work: the widespread dissemination of results has been considered important in securing ongoing political approval for the programmes; it has also been seen as a way of preventing contractors from consolidating a 'first mover advantage' relative to competitors; and, especially in the universities, it has been facilitated by a research community which (with the notable exception of the Vietnam war period) has not questioned the legitimacy of the programme themselves – so long as their results could be fed into the system of 'publish or perish'!

The situation in the UK and France differs in this respect from that in the US for three reasons: first, once programmes are set up and running there is little external political pressure in favour of disseminating results; second, the members of the programme 'club' themselves have little interest in seeing results publicized and they tend to count more heavily in dissemination decisions; and third, the external environment – and notably that in the universities – has been perceived as probably hostile and possibly untrustworthy. As a result, the information generated by mission-oriented programmes has tended to remain confined to a small circle of participants.

Finally, the US government moved somewhat earlier than its counterparts in France and the UK to encourage commercialization of the results

Table 3.4. *Number   of   research scientists and engineers per 1,000 of the labour force, 1981*

US	6.2
Japan	5.4
Germany	4.7
UK	3.9
Norway	3.8
France	3.6

Source: OECD.

Table 3.5. *Diplomas giving access to higher education as percentage of age group*

Japan (1981)	87
Sweden (1982)	82
United States (1980)	72
Germany (1982)	26
Denmark (1980)	25
France (1983)	28
Italy (1981)	39
United Kingdom (1981)	26
Finland (1980)	38
Austria (1978)	13
Netherlands (1981)	44

Source: OECD.

of government-financed R&D. NASA, and a number of other agencies, have long had specific units concerned with technology transfer. As regards government-financed R&D in the private sector, the 1980 Patent Law Amendments Act established a uniform policy allowing contractors – and notably small businesses, universities and non-profit laboratories – to own inventions resulting from federal R&D funding. The assurance this Act provides of clear title to Government-funded inventions has greatly facilitated patent licensing by universities and other federal contractors to industry, as well as encouraging industry involvement in federally supported university research.

Differences in the environment   Economic actors in the US therefore have greater direct or indirect access to whatever may be transferable in the outcomes of mission-oriented programmes. At the same time they are well placed to exploit these results for commercial purposes and have substantial incentives to do so.

A lower degree of crowding out   To begin with, the sheer size of the US scientific and technological system means that mission-oriented programmes probably 'crowd out' other research efforts to only a limited extent. This size differential is particularly marked in terms of the stock and flow of research manpower: the share of R&D scientists and engineers in the US labour-force is one-third greater than that in the UK and France (Table 3.4); the share of secondary students going on to university training in the US is about double that in France or the UK (Table 3.5); and the proportion of those students choosing scientific or engineering training is reasonably responsive to market circumstances.[17] To this difference in endowment must be added the effect of inflows of scientists and engineers from overseas: in 1982 foreign-born scientists and engineers accounted for fully 17 per cent of all scientists and engineers employed in the United States.

Accessibility and mobility of scientific know-how   The US stock of human and technological capital, in addition to being relatively abundant, is also more easily accessible. It is, in the first place, accessible through contract research, both with private research firms and with universities. Though the share of university research financed by industry in the United States is not high, the links between universities and industry have traditionally been strong[18] – far stronger, at least, than in France or the United Kingdom, both these countries lagging even by European standards in this respect.[19] These links take several forms: active efforts by US universities to commercialize their technological skills; widespread consulting for industry by university scientists and engineers; frequent co-authorship of journal articles by researchers in industry and academia; and sizeable gifts of equipment by industry to university research facilities.[20]

The operation of the US labour market also promotes the accessibility of its stock of human and technological capital. In general, the US labour force is more mobile between employers and regions than the labour force in Europe: average job tenure is about 20 per cent lower in the United States than in France or the United Kingdom; the share of the labour force crossing regional boundaries each year is – at about 3 per cent – double that in Europe. Moreover, US scientists and engineers are almost as mobile as other segments of the labour force: their average job tenure is only about 15 per cent higher than the average. In contrast, mean tenure in France with a given employer is nearly 40 per cent higher for highly qualified staff than for the labour force as a whole.[21]

Differences in labour mobility are even greater as regards movement from university to industry. Some 2 to 3 per cent of all US scientists and engineers move from academia to industry or vice versa every year; the figure for France can be estimated at well below 0.5 per cent.[22] The civil service status of public sector researchers in France makes movement difficult and eliminates incentives to move.

Competition in factor and product markets   High levels of mobility of scientists and engineers in the United States ensure that technological capabilities generated by mission-oriented research are rapidly diffused among firms; but they do not ensure that they will rapidly be exploited. This in turn hinges on the intensity of competition in product markets, which encourages firms to innovate. Three factors distinguish the US in this respect: the receptiveness of capital markets to innovation efforts; the extent of the threat of new firm entry; and the incentives to innovation arising from a large and unified market.

Capital markets   in the United States are distinguished from those elsewhere largely by two features: the depth and breadth of equity markets; and the availability of venture capital finance for start-up companies.[23] It can be argued whether these institutions have proved appropriate for financing long-term market share strategies; but – perhaps because they provide a low-cost means for realising capital gains – they appear to do reasonably well at providing concurrent finance for a broad range of innovation efforts. Certainly the balance of evidence remains that they are effective mechanisms for the monitoring and diversification of innovation-related risks and opportunities.

The functioning of capital markets reinforces the degree of competition in US *product markets* in two important respects. To begin with, the widespread availability of venture capital – together with a range of other environmental factors which reduce the costs of setting up and dissolving businesses – increases the threat of entry by new companies. This is reflected in rates of creation and disappearance of new manufacturing firms, which are nearly twice those in France.[24] Ideas not exploited by large companies are likely to be tried out quickly by a new entrepreneur. This is of particular importance in the early stages of a new technology, when a large number of alternative design approaches are being explored.[25]

Moreover, an active market for corporate control provides an effective means of liquidating new firms which do poorly and incorporating into larger concerns the activities of those which do well. At the same time, the takeover market reduces the risks associated with entry by diversification: large US firms have tended to enter new markets by buying smaller firms already operating in those markets, knowing that if the venture failed it could be disposed of.[26]

The effects of potential competition are compounded by the far greater supply in the United States of potential entrants into advanced technology markets. Over 15,000 firms in the United States have R&D laboratories; this compares to about 1,500 in France and 800 in the United Kingdom. The number of firms with some technological capability in any given area is likely to reflect this differential. This provides the United States with a very large seed bed capable of responding quickly to the 'focusing' effects of innovations and acting as an incubator for potential entrepreneurs. It also provides a very large number of firms capable of acting as a 'fast second' – moving into a new market as its attractiveness is established and as the appropriate technological approach becomes clearer.

The size of the US market   The nature of competition on the US market also intensifies firms' interest in new product areas, notably as a technology approaches the stage where mass marketing becomes essential. Three factors are of particular relevance. First, because of the importance of economies of scale in a relatively homogeneous market, firms vie for leadership in the transition to mass production and marketing.[27] Second, reliance on *de facto* or proprietary standards provides the firm whose product emerges as a dominant design with a considerable advantage. Third, the US market appears to be highly sensitive to 'perceptual' product differentiation, which tends to favour early entrants to the mass marketing and production stage.[28]

Each of these factors can create first-mover advantages, compounding the benefits the United States derives from having a greater number of potential first-movers. As a result, the two basic components of the 'swarming' process – by which firms flock to an emerging market – tend to operate particularly rapidly in the United States: the *experimentation* stage, in which a range of alternative design approaches is explored, frequently by smaller firms; and the transition to *mass commercialization*, as the technology matures to the point of market acceptability. Pre-eminence in both of these stages increases the likelihood that US firms will be well placed to spot an emerging dominant design.

II.3   The link to performance

Our discussion of the countries in this group can be summarised as follows. In the *United Kingdom*, mission-oriented research has tended to yield few direct benefits while possibly crowding out a substantial share of commercial R&D. The indirect spin-offs have been low, creating a 'sheltered workshop' type of economy: a small number of more or less directly subsidised high technology firms, heavily dependent on and oriented to public procurement; and a traditional sector which draws little benefit from the high overall level of expenditure on R&D.[29]

In *France*, the mission-oriented research efforts have themselves been reasonably successful. This has created export markets for France, notably in the large weapons-importing countries of the third world and in other countries where state-to-state trading is important. However, the spin-offs from these efforts have been relatively limited, so that French industry has become increasingly dualistic in its access to, and reliance on, advanced technology. This has been most visible in France's shifting pattern of international trade. Exports of high skill intensity products, though rising, have concentrated to a growing extent on third world markets, reflecting the predominance of state-to-state trading; while in trade with the advanced countries – where products related to public procurement are of much less importance – the relative skill intensity of French exports has tended to diminish. The centralized and concentrated nature of mission-oriented research has therefore led to an increasingly polarized pattern of specialization.[30]

The situation of the *United States* is more complex. While the direct effectiveness of mission-oriented programs is no higher than in France, the results of these programs tend to diffuse particularly rapidly through the US economy. This is a result of three features: the wide range of economic actors capable of exploiting these results for commercial purposes; the low level of the obstacles they encounter in seeking to do so; and the strength of the incentives for rapid exploitation to occur. The mission-oriented stage of research in the US remains highly centralized; but its results are more rapidly carried over into the decentralized experimentation of the commercial market.

Particularly in recent years, this has generated advantages which may be cumulative at the level of the firm but are not at the level of the product. More specifically, while US firms appear to retain many of their established strengths, US production sites have proved considerably better at the experimentation stage than at the follow-on to mass production.[31] This partly reflects the macro-economic circumstances associated with the over-valuation of the dollar, but more fundamental factors may also be at work.

Historically, the United States has lacked a system for training craftsmen, while possessing an abundance of higher skilled (white collar) and lower skilled or unskilled workers.[32] At the same time, the structure of blue collar earnings in the unionized parts of US industry (with low differentials between trainee wages and those of craftsmen) and high labour mobility have discouraged employer investment in transferable skills.[33] Combined with a large and unified national market, this pushed US manufacturing firms into two directions: pioneering mass production techniques which made little use of craft labour; and developing organizational innovations intensive in their use of managerial or supervisory staff – such as multi-plant production, multi-divisional management and the multinational firm.

The advantage superior mass production techniques gave US production sites has tended to erode over time, for at least three reasons. First, in an increasingly integrated world economy, being located in the world's largest single market is of diminishing importance as a determinant of competitiveness. Second, the quality of the US labour force – and particularly that part with only a high school degree or less – has probably declined relative to that overseas, and notably relative to that in Japan.[34] Third, classical mass production techniques on 'Taylorist' lines may be of diminishing effectiveness as the variability and differentiation of products increases, as product workmanship becomes a more important factor in consumer choice and as new technologies for 'mid-scale' production become available.[35]

These factors place US manufacturing industry at a clear disadvantage but they have less impact, if any, on the service sector. As a result, US firms tend to reap the advantages of innovative capabilities in manufacturing mainly at the early stages of the product life cycle (or, if the dollar is low enough, in products which are mature); while in services the gains from innovation have been consolidated further downstream as markets grow. Given a reasonably flexible and open economy, this pattern is reflected in the structure of trade; so that resources have tended to cluster around emerging and/or science-based industries.

In this sense, the United States comes closest to the classical product cycle model, abandoning mature industries in favour of activities with better growth prospects.[36] A system of mission-oriented research, which helps ensure that the frontiers of these activities are constantly being explored, may provide a useful source of ongoing stimulus to this process. It therefore has a certain degree of coherence relative to the US economy. Whether this process would not occur of its own volition – that is, even in the absence of mission-oriented research – remains an open question.

III   The 'diffusion-oriented' countries (Germany, Switzerland and Sweden)

Diffusion-oriented policies seek to provide a broadly based capacity for adjusting to technological change throughout the industrial structure. They are characteristic of open economies where small and medium-sized manufacturing enterprises remain an important economic and political force; and where the state, bearing the interests of these firms in mind, aims at facilitating change rather than directing it.[37]

The primary feature of these policies is *decentralization*. Specific technological objectives are rarely set at a central level. Central government agencies play a limited role in implementation, preferring to delegate this stage either to industry associations or to cooperative research organizations dominated by industry. Whatever funds are disbursed tend to be fairly widely spread across firms and industries, with the high technology industry obtaining a far lower share than in the mission-oriented countries.

Given this degree of decentralization, the precise boundaries of technology policy are often difficult to identify. Switzerland, for example, would certainly deny having a 'technology policy' in the sense in which France has one. A more fruitful framework is to view technology policy in these countries as an intrinsic part of the provision of innovation-related public goods: notably in the fields of education, product standardization and cooperative research. These countries' specific feature is the importance they attach to the organization and high quality of the provision of these goods, and the decentralized mechanisms they have developed for supplying them.

III.1   The economic and institutional framework

The priority accorded to the provision of public goods has its origin in these countries' process of industrialization. Two interrelated features distinguished this process: an emphasis on 'education push', notably through innovations in higher education and in the training of engineers;[38] and an early specialization in the chemical and electrical industries on the one hand and in mechanical engineering on the other.[39]

This early pattern of specialization fed back into the demand for innovation-related public goods.

The chemicals and electrical industries were distinguished from the start by the closeness of their links to the science base.[40] They needed a high quality university system, capable of training scientists for industry, of monitoring scientific developments world wide and of providing external support to the emerging industrial research laboratories. This in turn depended on developing an increasingly efficient and effective school system, which could prepare and select candidates for higher education. The Lutheran tradition of universal literacy and broadly-based instruction provided an ideal basis for this evolution.[41]

The chemicals and electrical industries therefore acted as a politically powerful and well organized lobby for education and for academic research. Being highly concentrated and largely cartellised, they were fully capable of mobilizing in their collective interest.[42] But the needs of the mechnical engineering industries were rather different. First, while chemicals and electricals were science-based, mechanical engineering relied on learning-by-doing and on the tacit, unformalized know-how of skilled craftsmen. Second, while chemicals and electricals tended to be concentrated, mechanical engineering was not, mainly because a high level of decentralization was more efficient in monitoring the type of team production required to maintain the quality of workmanship.

For decentralization to persist, the engineering industry had to resolve three major problems. First, it had to be able to draw on an external pool of skilled labour, since no single small or medium-sized firm could efficiently rely on its internal labour market alone. Second, it had to reduce the transactions costs involved in the decentralized production of components which are close complements from an economic viewpoint – e.g. nuts and bolts. Third, it had to find ways of keeping firms up to date with technological developments, ensuring that the fruits of technical advance accumulated and were appropriated at the level of the industry as a whole, rather than primarily or solely at the level of the firm.

Mechanical engineering was therefore an active lobby for three policies: comprehensive vocational education; product standardization; and cooperative research. It mainly sought these on the basis of provision by industry associations rather than by government; and, particularly in Germany and Switzerland, this coincided with a governmental practice of according quasi-public status and functions to private bodies, originally so as to regulate markets.[43]

As it has evolved in these countries, the overall system of public policy affecting technological capabilities has therefore had three key features.

Vocational education   The most significant feature is probably the depth and breadth of investment in *human capital*, centering on the dual system of education (see Tables 3.6, 3.7 and 3.8.) This involves comprehensive

Table 3.6. *Higher education engineering qualifications*

	First-degree level	Per million population	Below first-degree level	Per million population
Germany (1981)	7,000	110	16,000	260
United States (1982)	80,000	350	—	—
Japan (1982)	74,000	630	18,000	150

Source: NEDO and MSC.

Table 3.7. *Percentage of a generation entering higher education*

	Entrants to further education as percentage of generation (around 1980)	Approximate growth %			
		1965–75		1970–80	
		U	FE	U	FE
Japan	62	153	170	45	50
United States	62	−2	40	−10	10
Sweden	25	—	85	—	—
Germany	20	58	60	20	27
Denmark	33	136	—	23	—
France	34	—	—	—	—
Italy	25	—	130	—	8
Belgium	—	—	—	9	—
Finland	10	19	24	61	—
Netherlands	26	39	—	12	—
United Kingdom	29	15	—	12	43

Note: U = Universities, FE = Further Education.
Source: OECD.

secondary education based on streaming into a high-quality university system which is paralleled by an extensive system of vocational education.[44]

As far as its educational component is concerned, this system is characterized by: very high retention rates (more than 85 per cent of 17-year-olds are in the education and training system; this compares with around 60 per cent in the UK and 70 per cent in France); a relatively high level of per capita expenditure on education at all levels (over the last decade, the elasticity of total public educational expenditure with respect to GDP has been around five times higher in Switzerland than in the United States, starting from a base where Swiss expenditure per pupil was already a higher share of per capita GDP); and finally far-reaching

Table 3.8. *Distribution of students in upper secondary education (full-time and part-time enrolments) around 1980–82*

	General education	Vocational and technical
Japan	70	30
United States	76	24
Germany	21	79
France	40	60
Italy	34	65
Netherlands	40	60
United Kingdom	57	43
Switzerland	25	75
Austria	17	83
Belgium	44	56
Denmark	37	63
Finland	50	50
Sweden	30	70

Source: OECD.

certification: only some 10–15 per cent of the age cohort leave school with no leaving certificate or qualification whatsoever, compared to 20 per cent in the US and as much as 40 per cent in France and the UK.

Particularly in the German-speaking countries, the skill certification of large parts of the youth cohort occurs through the system of apprenticeship-based vocational education. Over 50 per cent of 17-year-olds in Germany and Switzerland are enrolled in apprenticeships, compared to around 10 per cent in France and the UK. These high rates of participation are encouraged both by a substantial differential between trainee wages and those of skilled craftsmen,[45] and by a well-organized and extensive system for training apprentices. Thus, apprenticeships are highly structured programmes of several years duration, involving a combination of enterprise training and college education and culminating in standardized formal examinations. Moreover, completion of apprenticeships is only one stage in skill training: the classification of examination-certified vocational skills forms a continuum from the craftsman to the most highly trained engineer, and movement along this continuum is a relatively standard feature of working life.[46]

There is a high level of industry involvement throughout this system. As regards the general education sector, the main links are between industries and universities (these will be discussed below). But the core of industry involvement is in vocational education. The apprenticeship system is jointly financed and controlled by employers (acting mainly through industry associations) and local education authorities, with trade unions also providing an important input. Industry associations play a major role in defining and revising curricula and in monitoring the system's effectiveness. Combined with the emphasis on formal, written examinations, this ensures that the skills acquired are highly transferable between employers and can be adapted to improvements in the industry's technology base.

Overall, this structure of investment in human capital yields two outcomes: a university system capable of keeping up with the frontiers of science, though not necessarily pioneering their exploration; and a very high level of intermediate skills in the working population.[47] The fact that these skills are certified through a standardized system of examinations erodes the advantages which internal labour markets would otherwise have had in terms of information about individual workers' skills, and hence tends to favour smaller firms. In turn, the ongoing nature of certification encourages relatively high levels of mobility for skilled craftsmen with work experience, providing a further channel for the inter-firm diffusion of technology.[48]

Standards   An emphasis on reducing transactions costs also pervades the second important feature of these countries, namely the system of *industrial standardization*. Of particular importance to the engineering industries, the German system of industrial standardization is unique in the range of intermediate goods and components it covers, the volume of detail it specifies (notably in terms of performance) and the legal status of its norms. This system emerged as part of a conscious effort to promote rationalization in decentralized industries.[49] Though it operates as a quasi-public authority, the system is almost entirely funded and administered by industries. While the budget of the German standards operation (DIN) is two-and-a-half times that of its French counterpart (AFNOR), the share of this budget provided by all levels of government is less than half that in France.[50] To this must be added the considerable investment German industry makes in providing technical support for the standardization process.

The immediate impact of the standardization system is to reduce transactions costs by providing clearly specified interface requirements for products. At the same time, it fulfills a quality certification function, which is especially important for industrial components. But its indirect effects are perhaps even greater.

In particular, the standardization process itself – and notably the preparation of new standards and the ongoing review of existing ones –

provides an important forum for the exchange of technical information both within each industry and with its users and suppliers. Though this information is ultimately rendered public in the published specifications, the long lead-times involved in drafting standards, and the relatively small share of the total information generated which is contained in the published standard, ensure that the exchange process operates as a local public good, the primary beneficiaries being the firms most actively involved in industry associations. The density of these information flows also ensures that by the time a new standard is announced, German firms are in a position to adopt it. The system of industrial standardization, in other words, functions as a means of placing ongoing pressure on firms to upgrade their products, while providing them with the technical information required to do so.

Cooperative R&D   A concern with assisting a decentralized industrial structure to adjust to changing technologies also underlies the third feature of these countries' policies, namely the role of *cooperative research*.[51] This takes two major forms.

The first is close industry–university links. These have traditionally been of particular importance to the chemical industry, and they remain a dominant characteristic of Germany, Switzerland and Sweden. Thus, 15 per cent of university research in Switzerland is funded by industry – the highest share in the OECD and more than three times higher than in the US, France or the UK. The links go well beyond the chemical sector, as the close ties between the EFTZ in Zurich and the Swiss mechanical and electrical engineering industries attest. Similar links can be found in Sweden, notably between the Technical Universities and the large science-based firms. A specific feature of the German system is the role in cooperative research of the three large non-profit research organizations and in particular of the Fraunhofer Gesellschaft, whose 22 research centres have become increasingly involved in providing technical support to small and medium-sized firms.

The second major form of cooperation in R&D centres on industry-wide cooperative research laboratories. These account for a considerably higher share of total R&D expenditure in Scandinavia than elsewhere. Thus, in Norway, even the largest firms have only very small in-house research units, and most industrial R&D is contracted out to cooperative laboratories. In Sweden, an extensive network of industry or technology-specific laboratories is jointly funded by industrial firms and by the State Board for Technical Development (STU). In addition to ongoing programmes aimed at the entire population of an industry, these laboratories carry out contract research for individual firms.

Similar arrangements exist in Germany and (though on a smaller scale and with considerably less government funding) for certain industries in Switzerland.

The most immediate impact of the availability of these outside sources of research expertise, is probably on the cost-effectiveness of R&D. To begin with, they permit sharing of costly instrumentation and research facilities, as well as allowing firms to draw occasionally on specialists whom they could not afford to employ on a full-time basis. In this sense, their role is similar to that played by the larger US technical consultancies (for example Arthur D. Little or Batelle) in providing support to smaller laboratories.

This role may, however, be secondary over the longer term. Rather it can be argued that the important function of cooperative research is really two-fold. The first is *technology transfer*. Universities and cooperative research centres inevitably have a higher content of research relative to development than have the laboratories of relatively small firms. This higher research intensity allows them to generalize and hence transfer the results of individual development projects from firm to firm, thus providing a degree of economies of scope to innovation programmes across an industry or activity as a whole.

The second is *technology focusing*. The process of setting research priorities for the system encourages firms to pool their perceptions of major technological threats and opportunities. This in turn feeds back into the internal R&D planning.

However, the effective discharge of these functions requires that firms have a certain degree of in-house R&D capability, which they then complement through recourse to external sources. Thus the evidence for Germany suggests that the most intensive users of contract research are small and medium sized firms with an internal research unit – on average, these firms spend on external (contract) research an amount equivalent to 30 per cent of their in-house R&D spending.

The role of policy: an example.   It has therefore been a major concern of policy-makers, particularly in Germany to ensure that an in-house R&D capability exists which can complement other forms of R&D. The Federal Ministry of Economics has in recent years helped finance a scheme providing a partial subsidy for the employment of research scientists and engineers in small and medium sized firms. Assessments suggest that the programme has been a considerable success, with about 10 per cent of the eligible firms participating. The scheme is worth examining because it provides a particularly good example of German diffusion-oriented policies, and notably of what are referred to as 'indirect specific' programmes, i.e., government programmes which are specific to a particular industry or technology but which are implemented through a trade or industry association rather than by a government department. Three features stand out.[52]

The first is that the funds involved are small. In total, 1985 expenditure on the R&D employment subsidy was around 420 million DM — less than 1 per cent of German expenditure on R&D. Moreover, the funds are thinly spread, going to around 7,000 firms; of these, a third have fewer than 50 employees.

The second is the decentralized process of implementation. The major responsibility for administering the project lies not with the funding agency, but with the AIF – the German Federation of Industrial Research Associations – which groups some 90 non-profit industrial R&D associations, which in turn represent 25,000 firms in 32 industrial sectors. The AIF – 70 per cent of whose funds come from industry – operates some 60 research laboratories, employing 4,000 scientists and engineers.

Though the AIF has operating responsibility for the project, a low level of discretionary decision-making is involved. Eligibility criteria are clearly set out; and the decision as to whether a firm is eligible is relatively straightforward. The risks of discrimination against particular firms are therefore low. However, being administered by the AIF provides the scheme with high visibility among industrial associations, and over 50 per cent of the firms participating in the scheme learned about it from trade associations or local Chambers of Industry and Commerce

Decentralized implementation is closely related to the third feature of the scheme, namely the uncomplicated nature of its administrative formalities. The application forms do not call for any particular expertise – 90 per cent of participants completed these forms without any external assistance. This limits the fixed costs involved in participating, and further reduces the risks that the programme will degenerate into a privileged club.

Defence R&D   The importance accorded to the diffusion of technological skills has even affected these countries' not insignificant activities in the armaments field. Thus, Sweden has placed great emphasis on actively promoting and to some extent organizing the diffusion of defence-related technological skills into the commercial sector. By law, no Swedish company may have more than 25 per cent of its business in defence, so that defence contractors are forced to develop civilian operations.[53] Specific policies have also been implemented to increase the technical capabilities of subcontractors to the larger companies involved in defence work, with financing provided by the Swedish Industrial Development Fund.

III.2 The effectiveness of the system

The diffusion-oriented countries are therefore characterized by policies which encourage widespread access to technical expertise, and which reduce the costs which small and medium-sized firms face in adjusting to change. In essence, the policy framework serves to increase the capacity for absorbing incremental change without threatening the basic structure of industry.

From this point of view, the policies have indeed been successful. It remains a striking feature of these countries that industrial production is more decentralized than elsewhere, notably in mechanical engineering; and that, while providing the benefits of highly focused management, decentralization does not prevent coordination of interdependent decisions and the reaping of economics of scale and scope. Though firms in these countries are smaller than their competitors' overseas, higher levels of specialization minimize any relative cost disadvantage.[54]

The system has also functioned effectively in promoting adjustment to incremental change. New skills are transmitted rapidly through labour training and re-training, as well as by inter-firm labour mobility; the standardization system itself provides an ongoing flow of technical information; and industry associations and cooperative research institutes allow for inter-firm economies of scale in R&D while focusing firms' attention on emerging technologies.

However, two major concerns have been expressed.

To begin with, the system as it has evolved is geared to the *existing* industries, which basically set the technology agenda; that is, they determine the direction of research, dominate the process of standardization and have a large role in the training and education policies. Entirely new industries and technologies may find it difficult to capture the attention they deserve.

Secondly, even within the existing industries, the decentralized, 'bottom-up', approach leads to a strong emphasis on movement *along* technological trajectories, while reducing the visibility of and preparedness for major shifts in trajectories.

These features – concentration on established industries, a focus on moving along set technological trajectories – are apparent in the evolution of these countries' external trade, which has been distinguished by three trends.[55]

The first is that the diffusion-oriented countries have tended to consolidate and even sharpen their traditional patterns of specialization. They have indeed retrenched in the areas where their original performance was poor but without moving into entirely new areas of activity. Rather, their performance has remained strong in the areas where they have traditionally specialized; and *within* these product areas they have tended to become stronger across the board. As a result, their net exports are highly concentrated in 'product clusters', mainly in products for which world demand is growing relatively slowly; so that improved performance has required a long-term gain in market share.

Secondly, this gain in market shares has occurred in products with unit values well above the average for their product category. For engineering products, around 85 per cent of Swiss exports, 75 per cent of German exports and 65 per cent of Swedish exports in 1970 had unit values above the average for their disaggregated product category; this compared with around 35 per cent for France and the UK. Specialization in the higher-quality segments of markets has tended to increase over time.

Thirdly, and most recently, this pattern of specialization has been seriously threatened by competition from Japanese firms, which have used electronics-based technologies to challenge the European countries' traditional predominance in mechanical engineering. Lags in adjusting to shifts in technological trajectories have led to major losses of market share.

These lags arise less from a lack of technological capabilities, than from the conservatism inherent in industry-wide decision-making processes. The Swiss watch industry and the German machine-tool industry provide striking examples in this respect.

In both cases, the research community associated with the industry was aware of the impact electronics would have – and, in fact, made important contributions to the technology. But research awareness could not be translated into industrial action – partly because of complacency among firms, but also because there were few prospects for adjusting without drastic changes in the industry structure. These changes could not be fitted into the consensus-centred decision-making process; so that both industries severely lost market share to their Japanese competitors.

However, once the loss in market share had begun to occur, the industries were relatively well placed to respond. The basic technological skills had been accumulated; the mechanisms for transferring them to industry were in place. Particularly the German machine-tool industry – which benefited in the early 1980s from the effective devaluation of the DM relative both to the US dollar and to the Yen – succeeded in reversing its loss of market share and making a quick though painful transition to the new technology.

The criticism that the system slows adjustment to entirely new opportunities, while reinforcing specialization in the traditional areas of activity, may therefore have some foundation. However, as these cases bear out, the system's capabilities for adjustment – albeit delayed – should not be underestimated. An ongoing response to the Japanese challenge will require important changes in certain aspects of the institutional context: thus, it has been argued that the apprenticeship system should provide a broader range of generic skills, which could be complemented through continuing vocational education. (The Swedish educational reform, which has somewhat reduced the vocational component of secondary education, clearly goes in this direction.)[56] But given these changes, the diffusion-oriented countries should remain important actors on the world industrial scene.

IV   Shifting and deepening: an attempt at synthesis

IV.1 Directions for research

In recent years, economists have made significant progress in analysing technological advance as an evolutionary process – that is, a process of experimentation, selection and diffusion.[57] The work done provides a convenient analytical structure for synthesizing the arguments presented above and for examining their implications for overall economic performance.

A central concern of recent analyses has been the mechanisms by which innovation shapes market structure, notably in terms of its impact on concentration and on the extent of the barriers to potential competition. The general assumption has been that this relation operates more or less similarly from country to country; but the data presented above suggest that this is not the case. Rather the material reviewed suggests important differences between countries along three dimensions:

— Who *appropriates* the gains from technological advantage? Is it the innovating firm alone or is it the firm and a broader group (for example, its suppliers)?

— To what extent are these gains *cumulative and sustainable* over time? Where does this process of skill accumulation occur – in the individual firm, in the industry, or in the industrial structure as a whole?

— How much *flexibility* is there in responding to innovation? Does flexibility occur through adjustment by existing firms or through shifts in the firm population?

The material reviewed also suggests that differences in each of these respects affect the evolution of each country's industrial structure.

Table 3.9. *Technology systems and industrial structures*

	US	France	Germany
Appropriation	Firm	State	Firm + industry
Skill accumulation	Labour market	Technocracy	Industry + research system
Flexibility	Mainly by entry and exit	Determined through the political system	Adaptation to incremental change; low inter-sectoral flexibility
	Shifting		Deepening
Industrial structure and trade pattern	Product cycle	Dualism	Inherited specialization

In essence, this relation operates through the balance between two (not necessarily alternative) ways of increasing the efficiency with which resources are used: *shifting*, which involves the transfer of resources from old to new uses; and *deepening*, which involves improving their productivity in existing uses.

The greater the mobility of technical, managerial, and financial resources, the greater the contribution which shifting is likely to make to overall growth. Conversely, the greater the extent to which assets are firm- or industry-specific, the greater the importance of deepening for long-term competitiveness. This relation can be highlighted by re-examining three of the countries in our sample; these countries (the US, France and Germany) can be considered to be roughly representative given the similarities between the UK and France, and between Switzerland, Sweden and Germany.

A broad and schematic characterization of the three countries in terms of shifting and deepening is set out in Table 3.9, which summarizes many elements of the discussion above, and can be analysed as follows.

The *United States* can be considered as a paradigmatic case of shifting. An extremely large applied research system, operating at the frontiers of technology, continuously generates potential new areas of commercial activity. Adjustment to these opportunities involves competition between firms on the open market for mobile technical and managerial skills and financial assets. The ease with which these resources can be bid out of existing uses is such as to discourage those productivity-enhancing investments in skills and capabilities which, being specific to a particular firm or activity, can only be justified through longer-term commitments. However, high mobility also ensures that entirely new areas of endeavour are rapidly exploited, first in the domestic market and then through world sales.

In *France*, the transfer of resources to new activities does occur, but largely (though not solely) through major state-initiated programmes aimed both at public and private markets. The technical elite, which is a more or less integral part of the state apparatus, is the essential repository of technological skills and plays the key role in designing and implementing programmes. However, the concentration of power in this elite and the limited diffusion of skills and capabilities outside of its area of activity has two consequences. Firstly, the 'shifting' is confined to those parts of the economy directly affected by the large public programmes; secondly, the rest of the economy lacks the resources (and often the incentives) to 'deepen' its competitive advantage.

Germany, in contrast, is a paradigmatic case of deepening. Skills and resources appear to be highly industry-specific and their development follows paths largely charted by the industries themselves. Relations between firms, between firms and their employees, and between firms and the financial system have traditionally involved long-term commitments which favour investment in activity-specific capabilities. At the same time, high levels of education, industrial standardization, and cooperative research provide powerful mechanisms for diffusing capabilities throughout each industry, so that progress is made across a broad front. The pattern of industrial capabilities is largely inherited, yet it is constantly renewed by 'doing what one has always done, but better'.

IV.2 Implications for overall economic performance

But what does one shift between and along what does one deepen? And what implications does the balance of shifting and deepening have for overall economic performance?

The concept of a technological trajectory provides a helpful building block in exploring these questions. A technological trajectory can be defined as a path of technological development, drawing on a given set of basic scientific principles and propelled by an internal dynamic of improving performance in terms of a few key design criteria.[58]

At the risk of considerable simplification, evolution along this path can be characterized as following an S-shaped curve (Figure 3.1):

  — The emergence phase (*E*) involves experimentation between alternative design approaches, as attempts are made to identify approaches with the greatest promise for subsequent developments;

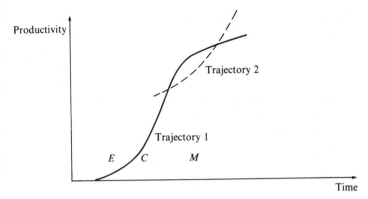

Fig. 3.1   Improvements in key design parameters

— In the consolidation phase (*C*), the concentration of R&D on
  a few critical parameters, within the framework of a broadly
  set design approach, allows rapid improvements both in
  performance and in cost;
— The maturity phase (*M*) occurs as the most easily exploited
  opportunities have been fully utilised, while entirely new
  design approaches, possibly based on a quite different
  applied science base from that of the original trajectory,
  emerge as substitutes in a growing range of uses.

The development of vacuum tube technology illustrates these processes and their pattern of evolution over time.[59] After an original phase
of fairly open experimentation Lee de Forest's triode tube set an
underlying structure for the workable amplification of small electrical
signal voltages. Subsequent progress in tube technology, though yielding
dramatic improvements in performance, concentrated on a relatively
small number of variables, such as the energy efficiency of the cathode,
extending tube life and reliability, and automating the manufacturing
process. However, the development of solid-state semiconductor technology from the late 1940s on dramatically cut across this path of
improvement; and transistor-board devices rapidly established themselves as a more reliable and space-saving alternative to the vacuum
tube, with enormous potential for cost-reduction through progressively
larger-scale integration and automated manufacturing and testing.

As the technology developed, so the structure of the industry changed.
In the early days of the vacuum tube industry, the field was relatively
open to competition. With many differing approaches to tube design,
manufacturing and application, overall profitability in the industry was
probably low, since the small number of 'hits' was more than offset by

high initial development costs and a large number of 'misses' (de Forest himself suffering repeated bankruptcies). Profitability only increased once the basic technology had stabilized and patents and proprietory know-how blockaded entry, weakening price competition, improving R&D focus and allowing cost reduction as output grew. The industry's consolidation phase was dominated by a tight-knit oligopoly, involving some of the largest, most technologically-advanced firms of its day: GE, Westinghouse, RCA and AT&T in the US; Marconi, Siemens and Philips in Europe.

Large size and (for the time) huge R&D budgets did not allow these firms to transfer their dominance to the emerging market for solid-state devices. These drew on an applied science base quite different from that they had learnt to master over the years. However, the vacuum tube industry did not disappear, for four reasons: initial uncertainty about the capabilities of solid-state devices slowed the process of substitution; the emergence of solid-state competition encouraged manufacturers to bring forward improvements in tubes; rapid growth occurred in a number of applications where there were no practicable substitutes for tubes (notably television receivers); and new tubes were developed for applications requiring frequencies unsuitable to solid-state technologies. Overall, substantial opportunities persisted in the industry forty years after its technological base had been basically superseded; but these seemed to rely on a progressively narrower and more vulnerable base.

Three broad conclusions can be drawn from this account:

— The emergence phase of a technological trajectory is not usually associated with high overall rates of return on investment, given large R&D costs, the substantial risk of failure and the intensity of competition.
— It is in the consolidation phase that the greatest improvements are made in product cost and performance, and that the largest scope exists for supra-normal profits.
— As improvements in critical parameters become more difficult to achieve, the maturity phase creates new challenges for the industry, with the development of substitute products intensifying competition and increasing the importance of capturing the least vulnerable niches.

Clearly these conclusions do not have the force of general laws; nor can one indiscriminately aggregate from the level of individual industries to that of national industrial structures as a whole.[60] Nonetheless, they suggest several hypotheses of interest:

— The overall performance of an industrial structure specializing in the emergence phase is likely to depend on: (a) its capacity to experiment on a broad front, thus increasing the probability of success; an important factor in this respect is proximity to a pool of sophisticated customers, who can rapidly distinguish promising from less promising alternatives; and (b) the extent to which it can carry successes over from the emergence to the consolidation phase. However, there is no *a priori* reason for expecting such an industrial structure to show a high rate of growth of real incomes or of productivity, at least as conventionally measured.[61]

— Conversely, an industrial structure specializing in the consolidation phase can expect to capture substantial gains in productivity and per capita income. Whether these will persist over time will, however, depend on its capacity (a) to exploit the results of successive emergence phases without having fully borne their costs; and (b) to transfer resources from one technological trajectory to another, as the maturity phase sets in.

— Finally, to succeed, an industrial structure pursuing technological trajectories into the maturity stage will require high levels of efficiency both in R&D and in applications engineering, allowing it (a) to obtain a maximum of performance improvements out of a given path of development, thus slowing the substitution process; and (b) to retain profitability by specializing in the product segments least vulnerable to intensified competition. Nonetheless, it seems reasonable to suppose that the long-term performance of such an industrial structure will be constrained by the gradual slowing of market growth and the thinning out of technological opportunities.

These hypotheses merge rather naturally with the country analysis presented above.

Thus, the predominance of 'shifting' type behaviour in the *US* economy corresponds to specialization in the emergence phase of technological trajectories. The overall returns to this pattern of specialization are maximized by (a) the scale on which experimentation occurs, increasing the probability of success; (b) the sophistication of the US market (including its public procurement component) which accelerates the process of selection among competing alternatives; (c) the rapidity with which break-throughs in the non-commercial parts of the technological system diffuse into the sphere of commercial experimentation; and (d) the existence of a substantial pool of large US firms capable of transferring the results of experimentation in the US market into world sales.

However, the inherent characteristics of this phase of technological evolution limit the rate of growth of per-capita incomes to which it can give rise; and these limits have been accentuated by the declining competitiveness of US sites (though less so of US firms) in the mass production operations characteristic of the consolidation phase.

The 'imperfect shifting' which, it has been argued, is a major feature of *France's* technological system, limits the returns obtained from concentrating on the emergence stage of technological trajectories. High levels of investment in R&D are incurred so as to establish a presence in this stage; but the scale of experimentation may still be too small to achieve a reasonable chance of success across the board. Even when successful outcomes are obtained, numerous factors slow their transfer from the mission-oriented environment to that of commercial exploitation, and hence the prospects for going from emergence to consolidation.

The growth of French incomes over time has therefore depended heavily on sectors such as motor vehicles, tyres and food processing, which are outside – and only weakly linked to – the core technological system. However, performance in these sectors has proved difficult to sustain. This is at least partly because the decline of traditional industries and the implicit protection accorded high technology activities has forced other sectors to bear a disproportionate share of unfavourable macroeconomic developments.

At the other extreme, the 'deepening' processes characteristic of *Germany's* industrial structure are associated with far-reaching specialization in pursuing technological trajectories into their mature phases. An institutional framework which is, in many respects, uniquely suited to this pattern, has allowed German industry to fully exploit the higher value-added segments of the markets in which it operates; but the experience of the last decades has highlighted some of the risks this pattern of specialization entails.

In particular, it creates vulnerability on two fronts:

— Up-market, from competitors operating in the same product markets, but exploiting new technological trajectories as they enter the consolidation phase. These competitors are well placed to provide rapid rates of increase in cost-performance ratios – as Japanese firms have done in numerically controlled machine tools; and

— Down-market, from competitors whose technological

capabilities may lag behind, but whose factor costs are substantially lower.

The slowing of total factor productivity growth as technological opportunities along the original trajectory diminish, combined with the rationalization pressures arising from greater rivalry on world markets, may make rising living standards more difficult to achieve. This could endanger the high degree of social consensus which underpins the diffusion-oriented countries' industrial model.

Seen overall, this discussion suggests that there are different paths to happiness, as countries' institutional structures and social arrangements facilitate specialization in differing stages of technological evolution. Each of these stages has advantages and disadvantages in providing for the growth of real incomes, but countries also differ in the extent to which they succeed in securing the greatest benefits from any given pattern of specialization.

Over the longer term, it is these differences in efficiency which may be most important. Consider France and Germany: the French state has encouraged specialization in technologies' emerging phase, while German industry has largely retained its traditional pattern of specialization. However, the disparities in performance between these countries arise less from this difference in specialization than from the efficiency with which the potential economic gains implicit in each pattern of specialization are exploited. In other words *where* one is on a technological trajectory may be less important than the efficiency with which the advantages of a particular location are pursued. This, in turn, depends on institutional features (broadly defined) which may be more or less appropriate for a given pattern of specialization.

V   Policy implications

The dominant feature of national technological systems is *diversity*. This partly reflects differences in policy stance between countries but many other factors are also at work. Examination of these factors suggests several conclusions on the scope and limits of technological policy.

The first and most fundamental, is the dependence of technology policy outcomes on their economic and institutional environment. The policies pursued in the UK or France do not differ greatly from those of the United States; but the outcomes do. The reasons for this lie partly in the details of policy design, and in the manner in which policies are implemented. But deeper and more pervasive factors are of far greater significance.

In part, the United States' advantage arises from the very size of its scientific and technological system. This ensures that mission-oriented research crowds-out commercial R&D to only a limited extent; and that there is a huge stock of firms and individuals capable of absorbing and commercializing the results of mission-oriented research. But this advantage of size is accentuated by other features of the US system.

In particular, new technological capabilities spread rapidly in the US economy, both through the direct transmission of ideas – for example, between industry and university – and through the high mobility of technologically skilled personnel. Moreover, lower entry barriers into US industry, combined with pressures which encourage firms to be among the early entrants into new product markets, accelerate the transformation of technological advances into commercial innovations.

In France, by contrast, several factors slow the transfer of the technological advances generated by mission-oriented research into the commercial sector. These include the paucity of contacts between universities and industries, the low mobility of scientists and engineers, the pervasive obstacles to the entry of new firms, and the protective atmosphere of government procurement in which larger firms prefer to remain.[62] Those differences mean that in the United States the results of government-supported R&D diffuse quickly into the commercial sector of the economy, while in France, and even more so the UK, they remain more or less confined to their sector of origin.

The importance of diffusion

This suggests a second conclusion, which is that the key problem of technology policy (as distinguished from science policy) lies less in generating new ideas than in ensuring that they are effectively utilised. The 'high-technology industries', however defined, are inevitably a small share of total output; taken on its own, even predominance in these industries will have a limited impact on overall living standards.[63] Rather, long term growth mainly depends on the capacity to deploy technological capabilities across a broad range of economic activities.

There are a number of ways in which this goal can be achieved. In the United States, technology diffusion is largely a market-driven process, which relies on high levels of mobility of human and financial resources and the existence of a marketplace for ideas. In Germany and Switzerland, in contrast, organized social mechanisms for promoting technology diffusion play a more important role – these include the apprenticeship system, the system of industrial standardization, and the network of cooperative research.

Seen purely in institutional terms, these experiences are not easily transferable between countries. Japan borrowed heavily from overseas in designing its institutional framework, but at an early stage of industrial development. It is questionable whether policy-makers in the UK or France could quickly set up processes of industry-wide technological cooperation akin to those which developed over a long period of time in the German-speaking countries. The institutional mechanisms for technology diffusion must inevitably reflect broader features of a country's economic, social, and even political environment. However, there are some common elements to the countries with a record of success in technology diffusion; these elements can provide some useful overall indications for technology policy. Three such elements emerge from this study.

Promoting diffusion; investment in human capital

The first is the role of *investment in human capital* as a factor favouring the diffusion of technology. This has both a flow and a stock dimension. The flow of newly trained personnel into the active population allows the continuous upgrading of skills and capabilities. At the same time, the better educated the labour force is, the greater will be its capacity to adjust to sophisticated new techniques. Higher levels of education are also likely to make this capacity more widespread, both throughout industry and throughout the active population.[64]

Countries whose investment in human capital lacks depth or breadth may be among the pioneers in generating new technologies, given a sufficiently strong scientific elite. But as far as using these technologies is concerned, they will be disadvantaged on two counts: an inadequate rate of expansion and/or replenishment of the skill base at the margin; and difficulties in adjusting the existing stock to the demands of technological change. Moreover, their difficulties are likely to persist or even mount over time: because the production of human capital is highly intensive in human capital and because the lags involved in correcting deficiencies in the human capital stock can be extremely long.[65]

Policy decentralization

A second factor in promoting diffusion relates to the design of technology policies. Whether those policies actually promote the best utilization of technological recovery appears to be closely related to the range of actors they involve – that is, to their degree of *decentralization*.

This, it can be conjectured, occurs for three reasons. First, centralized programmes frequently concentrate resources on the wrong areas; in both the UK and France, for example, excessive resources have been devoted to projects which are technologically glamorous but not economically relevant.[66] Second, the concentration of resources on a small number of projects itself increases the risk of costly failures, particularly when the projects being supported each involve a high level of risk. Finally, even if successful in terms of their immediate objectives, large, centralized projects usually pose considerable problems of technology transfer once the R&D phase is completed.

There are different ways in which programme decentralization can be achieved. In the United States, the very scale of the defence R&D programme is such that a fairly high level of dispersion of funds is almost inevitable; but conscious policy choices – such as the emphasis on second-sourcing and the support of R&D by new and small firms – are also significant. In Germany, Switzerland and (to a lesser extent) Sweden, the delegation of policy-setting and implementation functions to industry associations and regional bodies averts the risks inherent in centralized, bureaucratic decision-making.

But abstracting from these differences, a number of similarities emerge. The risks of placing too many eggs in one basket (and choosing the wrong basket at that) can be reduced by making support policy less *discriminatory* in the range of firms and sectors covered and by placing less emphasis on *discretionary* choices among alternative approaches. This implies a general preference for measures with a fairly high degree of automaticity – for example, tax expenditures; and for the delegation of power and public support to broadly based rather than narrowly based groups – for example to an industry or research association as a whole rather than a more or less formal 'club' of subsidy receivers.

Traditionally, the major argument against non-discretionary policies is that funds may be provided to firms for projects which would have been carried out in any case.[67] Equally, the case against decentralizing decision-making rests on the risk that support programmes will be 'captured' by organized interest groups, who will abuse them to advance narrow sectional concerns. However, experience suggests that the risks of capture are greatest when decisions are highly centralized, since this usually leads to a symbiotic relationship between a small number of policy-makers and a few large firms) and that it is in this situation that public support is most likely to become a permanent feature of the cash flow of a narrow range of privileged firms.[68]

Providing incentives

Finally, even an improved policy framework need not lead to better performance if the *incentives* to make the best use of technological resources are too weak. At a most obvious level, this is a problem of ensuring that firms are exposed to competition: so that ideas are quickly transferred from the research environment to that of commercial use.

The problem of providing adequate incentives merits particular attention in three areas: public research laboratories and other non-profit research institutions, publicly funded commercial R&D, and public procurement. As regards the first of these areas, there should be scope – notably in the UK and France – both for reducing the share of public laboratories in overall government R&D expenditure and for shifting a greater part of their recurrent funding onto a matching grant basis. As regards the second, opportunities should be explored for building incentives for success into the system of public support for commercial R&D – for example, by making access to continuing finance more clearly conditional on past performance. Finally, public procurement – notably of complex technological systems – too often serves to subsidize long-term inefficiency rather than to encourage the best use of resources and capabilities. Dismantling these protective devices may impose some short-term costs; but these are likely to be small relative to the longer-term benefits.

In summary, it is true that the institutional framework of any one country cannot be mechanically transplanted to others. Nonetheless, comparative analysis suggests three priority areas for action:

— easing constraints and rigidities which slow the diffusion of new skills and technical capabilities;
— improving the human capital base while enhancing the efficiency of markets for highly trained personnel; and
— increasing the extent to which technology policy relies on market signals and incentives, rather than on the administrative allocation of resources.

NOTES

1 See especially Rosenberg and Birdzell (1986); an interesting comparison is provided by the (relatively sympathetic) description of the functioning of a socialist economy (and of its difficulties in innovating) in Nove (1983).
2 See for example Earle (1986).
3 This is a key component of the classic 'market failure' argument for public support for R&D; see Antonelli (1982), Freeman (1974), Kamien and Schwartz (1982), Mowery (1983), and Rothwell and Zegveld (1981).
4 See Weinberg (1967).
5 See Hitch and McKean (1960).
6 This description of the UK draws on Carter (1981), Dickson (1983), Hall

(1980), Henderson (1977), Hogwood and Peters (1985), Vernon (1974) and Young and Lowe (1974).

7 This description of France draws on Bauer and Cohen (1981), Cawson *et al.* (1985), Cohen and Bauer (1985), Dupuy and Thoenig (1983), Grjebine (1983), Shonfield (1965), Stoffaes (1983–84) and Vernon (1974).

8 See especially Ponssard and Pouvoirville (1982); the high concentration levels of overall transfers from the state to industry (including public procurement) are discussed in Centre d'Economie Industrielle (no date), Commisariat Général du Plan (1982), and *Le Monde* (1979).

9 On telecommunications see Cohen and Bauer (1985), Darmon (1985), Ergas (1983), and Peterson and Comes (1985). On energy, see specifically Feigenbaum (1985), and Picard *et al.* (1985).

10 This discussion of the United States draws on Fox (1974), Gansler (1980), Nelson (1982), Nelson (1984), Phillips (1971) and Research and Planning Institute Inc. (1980).

11 See Brooks (1983).

12 See Riche *et al.* (1983).

13 Thus Scherer (1982) estimates that in the US only 12% of 1974 defence R&D funding generated technologies which flowed directly to clearly non-defence uses.

14 Secondary effects are examined among others by Ettlie (1982), Henderson (1977), Malerba (1985), Phillips (1971), Rothwell and Zegveld (1981), Scibberas (1978), and Teubal and Steinmueller (1982). An interesting international comparison of secondary effects can be obtained by contrasting US and UK surveys of the effects of defence funding of national semiconductor industries; see Dickson (1983) and Mowery (1983).

15 The role of US government funding in the growth of small firms is discussed in Bollinger *et al.* (1983) and Research and Planning Institute Inc. (1980); a specific programme is described in US Department of Defense (1981–82); a survey is in Ergas (1984). Defence funding of University research and its growing importance is discussed in National Science Board (1986), Chapter 2.

16 Compare Katz and Phillips (1982) and Lavington (1980).

17 See especially Freeman (1971) and (1976), and National Science Foundation (1985). Compare with Wilson (1980).

18 See Ben-David (1968) and Noble (1977).

19 See Ahlström (1982), Ben-David (1968) and OECD (1984).

20 Quantitative indicators in each of these are provided in National Science Board (1983), pp. 106–08, p. 135; and National Science Board (1986).

21 See Pham-Khac and Pigelet (1979) and Stevens (1986). My colleague Anders Reutersward kindly provided mean tenure data for professional staff.

22 Compare National Science Board (1986), pp. 87 and Appendix Table 4–17 and *Le Monde* (1986).

23 See Gönenç (1986).

24 See Arocena (1983); the factors at work are surveyed in Ergas (1984).

25 See Clark (1985), Freeman (1974) and Nelson and Winter (1982).

26 See Scherer and Ravenscraft (1984).

27 See Ergas (1984); a fascinating case study is National Academy of Engineering (1982). The role of scale economies in intensifying rivalry in the transition to mass production is clearly brought out by recent literature on strategic competition; see for an excellent survey Kreps and Spence (1985).

28 See especially Schmalensee (1982). Advertising-related product differentiation also appears to be a particularly significant factor in explaining persistent profitability in US industry; see Geroski (1985) and Mueller (1985).

29 Aspects of this pattern are highlighted in Prais (1981). Robson *et al.* (1985)
examines the diffusion of technology in the UK; see also Pavitt (1981), and
the analysis of the UK's trade structure in Orléan (1986).

30 In addition to the references in Note 7 above, see analyses of France's trade
patterns presented in Lafay (1985), Orléan (1986) and Vellas (1981).

31 See Lipsey and Kravis (1985). The results of this study conflict with those of
Buckley *et al.* (1984); the latter finds a sharper decline in US firms' overall
share of revenues and profitability.

32 See Floud (1984), National Manpower Council (1954) and Stevens (1986) and
references therein.

33 See Glover (1974), Mitchell (1977) and Ryan (1984).

34 See Murray (1984), pp. 96–112.

35 See Ergas (1984).

36 The classic formulation of this process is Vernon (1966); for empirical analysis
of US trade patterns see *inter alia* the (contrasting) results set out in
Hatzichronoglou (1986), Lafay (1985), Leamer (1984) and Vernon (1979).

37 The general characteristics of these countries are explored in Katzenstein
(1985a) and (1985b).

38 See Ahlström (1982).

39 On Germany and Switzerland see Henderson (1975) and Milward and Saul
(1977). On Scandinavia see Heckscher (1984), and Hildebrand (1978).

40 See among others Beer (1959), Freeman (1974), Liebenau (1985), Rosenberg
(1976) and Rosenberg and Birdzell (1986).

41 See Sandberg (1979).

42 See Forman (1974) and Schröder-Gudehus (1972).

43 See Berger (1981) and Katzenstein (1985a).

44 The general characteristics of these educational systems, and international
comparisons, are set out in Stevens (1986); see also Prais and Wagner (1983a)
and (1983b) and Worswick (1985).

45 See especially Jones and Hollenstein (1983).

46 Thus a recent survey reports that in Germany 45% of labour force participants with vocational training at a higher school level undertook continuing
training during the period 1974–79; see Sonder-forschungsbereich (1986).

47 According to population census estimates, some 50% of the civilian labour
force in Germany and Switzerland has completed an apprenticeship; see
OECD (1986).

48 See especially Maurice *et al.* (1982). See also Glover and Lawrence (1976),
and Office fédéral de l'industrie, des arts et métiers et du travail
(1980).

49 The classic study is Brady (1934).

50 Estimates provided in Laboratorio di Politica Industriale (1982); the literature on standardization is reviewed in Ergas (1984).

51 A general review of the role of cooperative research is in Mowery (1983);
however, the conclusions the article draws are too narrowly based on UK
experience. I am indebted to my colleagues in the Science, Technology and
Industry Directorate of OECD for assisting me in compiling the information
presented here.

52 See especially Meyer-Krahmer *et al.* (1983). My colleague Andreas Lindner

provided me with particularly useful information of the subjects discussed in this section.
53 See Gansler (1980), pp. 245–57.
54 See George and Ward (1975), Prais (1981), and Pratten (1976). Particularly useful case studies are Aylen (1982) and Daly and Jones (1980).
55 This discussion draws on Aglietta and Boyer (1983), Leamer (1984), Ohlsson (1980) and Orléan (1986). A particularly useful discussion of the balance between shifting resources among competing uses, as against increasing their productivity in existing uses, is in Carlsson (1980).
56 See Hodenheimer (1978).
57 See Nelson and Winter (1982), Rosenberg (1976) and Dosi (1982).
58 Useful overviews are in Antonelli (1982), Dosi (1982), Kamien and Schwartz (1982) and Bollinger et al. (1983).
59 On the vacuum tube, see especially Maclaurin (1949), Sturmey (1958) and Baker (1971). On the transition to solid-state devices see Webbink (1977).
60 Some of the caveats in this respect are set out in Ergas (1983). See also Clark (1985).
61 See Ergas (1979).
62 The fact that France, and to a lesser extent the UK, have lagged in applying competition policy to their respective national industries has also presumably been a factor reducing the pressure on firms to innovate.
63 See Nelson (1984) and Riche et al. (1983).
64 A useful case study in this respect is provided by Hartmann et al. (1983).
65 This is nicely set out in Sandberg (1979).
66 See Pavitt (1981) and Hindley (1983).
67 See Whiting (1976).
68 See, for examples, Bauer and Cohen (1981), Cawson et al. (1985) and Cohen and Bauer (1985); and more generally, Young (1974).

REFERENCES

Aglietta. M. and R. Boyer (1983), *Poles de Compétitivité, stratégie industrielle et politique macro-économique*, Paris: working Paper CEPREMAP No. 8223.
Ahlström, Göran (1982), *Engineers and Industrial Growth*, London: Croom Helm.
Antonelli, C. (1982), *Cambiamento Tecnologico e Teoria dell'Impresa*, Torino: Loescher Editore.
Arocena, J. (1983), *La Création d'Entreprise*, La documentation Française.
Aylen, J. (1982), 'Plant size and efficiency in the steel industry: an international comparison, *National Institute Economic Review*.
Baker, W. J. (1971), *A History of the Marconi Company*, New York: St Martin's Press.
Bauer, Michel and Cohen, Elie (1981), *Qui Gouverne les groupes industriels?* Paris: Editions du Seuil.
Beer, J. J. (1959), *The Emergence of the German Dye Industry*, Urbana: University of Illinois Press.
Ben-David, Joseph (1968), *Fundamental Research and the Universities*, Paris: OECD.

Berger, Suzanne D. (ed.) (1981), *Organizing Interests in Western Europe*, Cambridge: Cambridge University Press.
Bollinger, Lynn, Katherine Hope and James M. Utterback (1983), 'A review of literature and hypotheses on new technology-based firms', *Research Policy*, **12.**
Brady, R. (1934), *The Rationalization Movement in German Industry*, Berkeley: University of Californa Press.
Brooks, H. (1983), 'Towards an Efficient Public Policy: Criteria and Evidence', in H. Giersch (ed.), *Emerging Technologies*, Tubingen: J. C. B. Mohr (Paul Siebeck).
Buckley, Peter J., John H. Dunning and Robert D. Pearce (1984), 'An Analysis of the Growth and Profitability of the World's Largest Firms, 1972 to 1977', *Kyklos*, **37.**
Carlsson, Bo (1980), *Technical Change and Productivity in Swedish Industry in the Post-War Period*, Stockholm: The Industrial Institute for Economic and Social Research (Research Report No. 8).
Carter, Charles (ed.) (1981), *Industrial Policy and Innovation*, London: Heinemann.
Cawson, Alan, Peter Holmes and Anne Stevens (1985), *The Interaction Between Firms and the State in France: The Telecommunication and Consumer Electronics Sectors* (mimeo), Trinity Hall, Cambridge.
Centre d'Economie industrielle (not dated), *Quelques réflexions à propos des mécanismes de transfert Etat-Industrie mis en oeuvre en France et en Allemagne* (mimeo), Les Milles.
Clark, Kim B. (1985), 'The interaction of design hierarchies and market concepts in technological evolution', *Research Policy*, **14.**
Cohen, Elie and Michel Bauer (1985), *Les grandes manoeuvres industrielles*, Paris: Pierre Belfond.
Commissariat Général du Plan (1982), *Aides à l'industrie* (mimeo), Paris: Commissariat Général du Plan.
Daly, Anne and Daniel T. Jones (1980), 'The Machine Tool Industry in Britain, Germany and the United States', *National Institute Economic Review*.
Darmon, Jacques (1985), *Le grand dérangement: La guerre du téléphone*, France: J.-C. Lattès.
Dickson, Keith (1983), 'The influence of Ministry of Defence funding on semiconductor research and development in the United Kingdom', *Research Policy*, **12.**
Dosi, Giovanni (1982), 'Technological paradigms and technological trajectories', *Research Policy*, **11.**
Dupuy, François and Jean-Claude Thoenig (1983), 'Sociologie de l'administration française', Paris: Armand Colin.
Earle, E. M. (1986), 'Adam Smith, Alexander Hamilton, Friedrich List: the Economic Foundations of Military Power', in P. Paretz (ed.), *Makers of Modern Strategy*, Princeton: Princeton University Press.
Ergas, Henry (1979), 'Biases in the Measurement of Real Output under Conditions of Rapid Technological Change', OECD (Expert Group on the Economic Impact of Information Technologies, Working Party on Information, Computer and Communications Policy).
(1983a), *Telecommunications Policy in France* (mimeo).
(1983b), 'The Inter-Industry Flow of Technology', Paris: OECD (Workshop

on Technological Indicators and the Measurement of Performance in International Trade).

(1984a), *Why do Some Countries Innovate More than Others?*, Brussels: Centre for European Policy Studies (CEPS Papers No. 5).

(1984b), 'Corporate Strategies in Transition', in A. Jacquemin (ed.), *European Industry: Public Policy and Corporate Strategy*, Oxford: Oxford University Press.

Ettlie, John E. (1982), 'The commercialization of federally sponsored technological innovations', *Research Policy*, **11**.

Feigenbaum, Harvey B. (1985), *The Politics of Public Enterprise: Oil and the French State*, Princeton: Princeton University Press.

Floud, Robert (1984), *Technical Education 1850–1914: Speculations on Human Capital Formation* (mimeo), London: Centre for Economic Policy Research.

Forman, P. (1974), 'Industrial Support and Political Alignments of the German Physicists in the Weimar Republic', *Minerva*.

Fox, J. Ronald (1974), *Arming America: How the U.S. Buys Weapons*, Cambridge: Harvard University Press.

Freeman, C. (1974), *The Economics of Industrial Innovation*, Harmondsworth: Penguin.

Freeman, R. B. (1971), *The Market for College Trained Manpower*, Cambridge, Harvard University Press.

(1976), *The Overeducated American*, New York: Academic Press.

Gansler, Jacques S. (1980), *The Defense Industry*, Cambridge: The MIT Press.

George, Kenneth D. and T. S. Ward (1975), *The Structure of Industry in the EEC: an International Comparison*, Cambridge: Cambridge University Press.

Geroski, P. A. (1985), *Do Dominant Firms Decline?* University of Southampton (Discussion Papers in Economics and Econometrics No. 8509).

Glover, R. W. (1974), 'Apprenticeship in America: an Assessment', *Proceedings of the Industrial Research Association*.

Glover, I. and P. Lawrence (1976), 'Engineering the Miracle', *New Society* (30 September).

Gönenç, Rauf (1986), 'Changing Investment Structure and Capital Markets', in H. Ergas (ed.), *A European Future in High Technology?* Brussels: Centre for European Policy Studies.

Grjebine, André (1983), *L'état d'urgence*, Paris: Flammarion.

Hall, Peter (1980), *Great Planning Disasters*, Berkeley: University of California Press.

Hartmann, Gert, Ian Nicholas, Arndt Sorge and Malcolm Warner (1983), 'Computerised Machine-tools, Manpower Consequences and Skill Utilisation: A Study of British and West German Manufacturing Firms', *British Journal of Industrial Relations*.

Hatzichronoglou, Thomas (1986), 'International Trade in High Technology Products: Europe's Competitive Position', in Henry Ergas (ed.), *A European Future in High Technology?* Brussels: Centre for European Policy Studies.

Heckscher, E. F. (1984), *An Economic History of Sweden*, Cambridge: Harvard University Press.

Henderson, P. D. (1977), 'Two British Errors: Their Probable Size and Some Possible Lessons', *Oxford Economic Papers*, **29**.

Henderson, W. O. (1975), *The Rise of German Industrial Power, 1834–1914*, Berkeley: University of California Press.
Hildebrand, K.-G. (1978), 'Labour and Capital in the Scandinavian Countries in the Nineteenth and Twentieth Centuries', in P. Mathias and M. M. Postan (eds), *The Cambridge Economic History of Europe: The Industrial Economies – Capital, Labour and Enterprise: Britain, France, Germany and Scandinavia*, Cambridge: Cambridge University Press.
Hindley, Brian (ed.) (1983), *State Investment Companies in Western Europe*, London, Trade Policy Research Centre.
Hitch, C. J. and R. N. McKean (1960), *The Economics of Defense in the Nuclear Age*, Cambridge: Rand Corporation and Harvard University Press.
Hodenheimer, A. J. (1978), *Major Reforms of the Swedish Education System*, Washington: World Bank Staff Working Paper No.290.
Hogwood, Brian W. and B. Guy Peters (1985), *The Pathology of Public Policy*, Oxford, Clarendon Press.
Jones, Ian and Heinz Hollenstein (1983), *Trainee Wages and Training Deficiencies: An Economic Analysis of a 'British Problem'* (mimeo. Industry Series No. 12), London: National Institute of Economic and Social Research.
Kamien, M. I. and N. L. Schwartz (1982), *Market Structure and Innovation*, Cambridge: Cambridge University Press.
Katz, B. and A. Phillips (1982), 'The Computer Industry', in R. Nelson (ed.), *Government and Technical Progress*, New York: Pergamon Press.
Katzenstein, Peter J. (1985a), *Corporatism and Change: Austria, Switzerland and the Politics of Industry*, Ithaca, New York: Cornell University Press.
(1985b), *Small States in World Markets: Industrial Policy in Europe*, Ithaca, New York: Cornell University Press.
Kreps, David M. and A. Michael Spence (1985), 'Modelling the Role of History in Industrial Organization and Competition', in George R. Feiwel (ed.), *Issues in Contemporary Microeconomics and Welfare Analysis*, London: Macmillan.
Laboratorio di Politica Industriale (1982), *Materiali di discussione* (mimeo), Bologna: Laboratorio di Politica Industriale.
Lafay, Gérard (1985), 'Spécialisation française: des handicaps structurels', *Révue d'Economie Politique*, 95.
Lavington, Simon (1980), *Early British Computers: The Story of Vintage Computers and the People who built them*, Manchester: The Digital Press.
Leamer, Edward E. (1984), *Sources of International Comparative Advantage: Theory and Evidence*, Cambridge: MIT Press.
Le Monde (1979), 'Le Rapport Hannoun souligne la forte concentration et la faible efficacité des aides publiques à l'industrie' (27 Sept.).
(1986), 'M. Jean-Jacques Duby quitte le CNRS' (6 Feb.).
Liebenau, Jonathan (1985), 'Innovation in pharmaceuticals: Industrial R&D in the early twentieth century', *Research Policy*, 14.
Lipsey, R. E. and I. B. Kravis (1985), *The Competitive Position of U.S. Manufacturing Firms*, Cambridge MA: National Bureau of Economic Research Working Paper No. 1557.
Maclaurin, W. R. (1949), *Invention and Innovation in the Radio Industry*, New York: Macmillan.
Malerba, Franco (1985), 'Demand structure and technological change: the case of the European semiconductor industry', *Research Policy*, 14.
Maurice, M., F. Sellier and J.-J. Sylvestre (1982), *Politique d'Education et*

Organisation Industrielle en France et en Allemagne, Paris: Presses Universitaires de France.

Meyer-Krahmer, Frieder, Gisela Gielow and Uwe Kuntze (1983), 'Impacts of government incentives towards industrial innovation', *Research Policy*, **12**.

Milward, A. S. and S. B. Saul (1977), *The Development of the Economies of Continental Europe, 1850–1914*, Cambridge: Harvard University Press.

Mitchell, J. P. (1974), 'New Directions for Apprenticeship Policy', *Worklife*, U.S. Department of Labor.

Mowery, David (1983a). 'Innovation, market structure, and government policy in the American semiconductor electronics industry: A survey', *Research Policy*, **12**.

(1983b), 'Economic Theory and Government Technology Policy', *Policy Sciences*, **16**.

Mueller, Dennis (1985), *Persistent Performance among Large Corporations* (mimeo), Brussels: Centre for European Policy Studies.

Murray, C. (1984), *Losing Ground: American Social Policy, 1950–1980*, New York: Basic Books.

National Academy of Engineering (1982), *The Competitive Status of the U.S. Auto Industry* (Committee on Technology and International Economic and Trade Issues, Automobile Panel), Washington: National Academy Press.

National Manpower Council (1954), *A Policy for Skilled Manpower*, New York: Columbia University Press.

National Science Board (1983), *Science Indicators 1982*, Washington: National Science Foundation.

(1986), *Science Indicators – The 1985 Report*, Washington: National Science Foundation.

National Science Foundation (1985), *Science and Engineering Personnel: A National Overview*, Washington: National Science Foundation.

Nelson, Richard R. (ed.) (1982), *Government and Technical Progress*, New York: Pergamon Press.

(1984), *High Technology Policies: A Five Nation Comparison*, Washington: American Enterprise Institute for Public Policy Research.

Nelson, Richard R. and S. G. Winter (1982), *An Evolutionary Theory of Economic Growth*, Cambridge: Harvard University Press.

Noble, D. F. (1977), *America by Design*, Oxford: Oxford University Press.

Nove, Alec (1983), *The Economics of Feasible Socialism*, London: George Allen and Unwin.

OECD (1979), *Policies for Apprenticeship*, Paris: OECD.

(1984), *Industry and University: New Forms of Co-operation and Communication*, Paris: OECD.

(1986), *Changes in Working Patterns and the Impact on Education and Training: Human Resources Policies and Strategies in Germany*, Paris: OECD.

Office fédéral de l'industrie, des arts et métiers et du travail (1980), *Politique concernant le marché du travail en Suisse: caractéristiques et problèmes. Vol. 1*, Berne.

Ohlsson, Lennart A. (1980), *Engineering Trade Specialization of Sweden and other Industrial Countries*, Amsterdam: North Holland Publishing Co.

Orléan, A. (1986), 'L'insertion dont les échanges internationaux', *Economie et Statistique*.

Pavitt, K. (1981), 'Technology in British Industry; A Suitable Case for

Improvement', in Charles Carter (ed.), *Industrial Policy and Innovation*, London: Heinemann, pp. 88–115.

Peterson, Thane and Frank J. Comes (1985), 'An Electronics Dream that's Shorting Out', *Business Week* (March 4).

Pham-Khac, K. and J.-L. Pigelet (1979), *La Formation et l'Emploi des Docteurs es Sciences*, Paris: Dossier du Centre d'Etudes et de Recherches sur les Qualifications.

Phillips, A. (1971), *Technology and Market Structure: A Study of the Aircraft Industry*, Lexington: Heath Lexington Books.

Picard, Jean-François, Alain Beltran and Martine Bungener (1985), *Histoire(s) de l'EDF: Comment se sont prises les décisions de 1946 à nos jours*, Paris: Bordas.

Ponssard, J.-P. and G. de Pouvoirville (1982), *Marché Publique et Innovation*, Paris: Economica.

Prais, S. J. (1981), *Productivity and Industrial Structure*, Cambridge: Cambridge University Press.

Prais, S. J. and K. Wagner (1983a), 'Some Practical Aspects of Human Capital Investment: Training Standards in Five Occupations in Britain and Germany', *National Institute Economic Review*.

(1983b), *Schooling Standards in Britain and Germany: Some Summary Comparisons Bearing on Economic Efficiency*, London: National Institute Discussion Paper No. 60.

Pratten, C. F. (1976), *A Comparison of the Performance of Swedish and U.K. Companies*, Cambridge: Cambridge University Press.

Research and Planning Institute Inc. (1980), *Case Studies Examining the Role of Government R&D Contract Funding in the Early History of High Technology Companies*, Cambridge, Mass.: Research and Planning Institute Inc.

Riche, Richard W., Daniel E. Hecker and John U. Burgan (1983), 'High technology today and tomorrow: a small slice of the employment pie', *Monthly Labor Review*.

Robson, M., J. Townsend and K. Pavitt (1985), *Sectoral Patterns of Production and Use of Innovations in the UK: 1945–1983* (mimeo), Centre for Science, Technology and Energy Policy (Economic and Social Research Council).

Rosenberg, Nathan (1976), *Perspectives on Technology*, Cambridge: Cambridge University Press.

Rosenberg, Nathan and L. E. Birdzell Jr. (1986), *How the West Grew Rich: The Economic Transformation of the Industrial World*, New York: Basic Books.

Rothwell, Ros and Walter Zegveld (1981), *Industrial Innovation and Public Policy*, London: Frances Pinter.

Ryan, P. (1984), 'Job Training, Employment Practices and the Large Enterprise: The case of Costly Transferable Skills', in P. Osterman (ed.), *Internal Labour Markets*, Cambridge: MIT Press.

Sandberg, Lars G. (1979), 'The Case of the Impoverished Sophisticate: Human Capital and Swedish Economic Growth before World War I', *The Journal of Economic History*, **39**.

Scherer, Frederic M. (1982), 'Inter-industry technology flows in the United States', *Research Policy*, **11**.

Scherer, Frederic M. and David Ravenscraft (1984), 'Growth Diversification: Entrepreneurial Behavior in Large-Scale United States Enterprises', *Zeitschrift für Nationalökonomie*, Supplement 4.

Schmalensee, Richard (1982), 'Product Differentiation Advantages of Pioneering Brands', *American Economic Review*, **72**.

Schröder-Gudehus, B. (1972), 'The Argument for the Self-Government and Public Support of Science in Weimar Germany', *Minerva*, pp. 537–70.

Scibberas, E. *et al.* (1978), *Competition, Technical Change and Manpower in Electronic Capital Equipment: A Study of the U.K. Mini-Computer Industry*, Brighton: Science Policy Research Unit.

Shonfield, A. (1965), *Modern Capitalism*, Oxford: Oxford University Press.

Sonder-forschungs-bereich (1986), *3 Report*.

Stevens, Barrie (1986), 'Labour Markets, Education and Industrial Structure', in Henry Ergas (ed.), *A European Future in High Technology?*, Brussels: Centre for European Policy Studies.

Stoffaes, Christian (1983–84), *Politique Industrielle*, Paris: Les Cours de Droit.

Sturmey, S. G. (1958), *The Economic Development of Radio*, London: Duckworth.

Teubal, Morris and Edward Steinmueller (1982), 'Government policy, innovation and economic growth', *Research Policy*, **11**.

U.S. Department of Defense (1981–82), *Defense Small Business Advanced Technology Program*, Washington: U.S. Department of Defense.

Vellas, F. (1981), *Echanges Internationaux et Qualification du Travail*, Paris: Economica.

Vernon, Raymond (1966), 'International Investment and International Trade in the Product Cycle', *Quarterly Journal of Economics*, **80**.

(1974), *Big Business and the State: Changing Relations in Western Europe*, London: Macmillan.

(1979), 'The Product Cycle Hypothesis in a New International Environment', *Oxford Bulletin of Economics and Statistics*, **41**.

Webbink, D. W. (1977), *The Semiconductor Industry*, Washington: Government Printing Office.

Weinberg, Alvin M. (1967), *Reflections on Big Science*, Oxford: Pergamon Press.

Whiting, A. (ed.) (1976), *The Economics of Industrial Subsidies*, London: HMSO.

Wilson, R. A. (1980), 'The Rate of Return to Becoming a Qualified Scientist or Engineer in Great Britain, 1966–1976', *Scottish Journal of Political Economy*, pp. 41–62.

Worswick, G. D. N. (ed.) (1985), *Education and Economic Performance*, Aldershot: Gower Publishing Co.

Young, Stephen, with A. V. Lowe (1974), *Intervention in the Mixed Economy*, London: Croom Helm.

4 The value of patents as indicators of inventive activity

ZVI GRILICHES, ARIEL PAKES and
BRONWYN H. HALL*

I Introduction

In this paper we present an overview of a series of studies pursued at the
NBER during the last decade which used patent statistics to study
different aspects of the economics of technological change. It consists of
five substantive sections: a description of our firm level data; a report on
the relationship between R&D expenditures and the level of patenting; a
report on the relationship between patents, the stock market value of
firms, and their R&D expenditures; a summary of work on the estimation of the value of patent rights based on patent renewal data; and a
description of the use of patent data to estimate the importance of R&D
spillovers. A brief set of conclusions closes the paper.

II The NBER R&D data base and the growth of US firms in the 1970s

A major achievement of the NBER project has been the development
and construction of a large data set covering the economic and technological performance of most publicly traded US manufacturing companies
from the early 1960s through the early 1980s. It is the result of a detailed
match of publicly available sales, employment, investment, R&D, and
balance sheet information from the Compustat tapes (based on company
10–K filings with the SEC) with data acquired from the US Patent Office
on patents issued to all organizations between 1969 and 1982. Three
major tasks had to be accomplished to make these data useable: (1) The
Patent Office data on the number of patents granted to various organizations had to be matched with our list of manufacturing corporations.

* We are indebted to our collaborators for many contributions to the work discussed here
and to the National Science Foundation (SOC78–04279, PRA79–13740, PRA81–08635,
and PRA85–12758) and the NBER for financial support.

Table 4.1. *The distribution of patents applied for by year of application, 1970–82, and time to year of grant*[a]

Year of Application	0	1	Percent Granted Years Later 2	3	4	5+	Total in Current Panel
1969	0	11	66	20	2	1	100
1970	0	18	62	17	2	1	100
1971	0	17	61	18	2	2	100
1972	0	28	57	11	2	2	100
1973	0	37	50	10	2	1	100
1974	1	42	48	6	2	1	100
1975	1	42	46	8	1	2	100
1976	2	42	47	6	2	2	100
1977	1	42	41	12	2	2	99
1978	1	24	57	15	2	1	99
1979	0	22	60	15	2	1	97
1980[e]	0	22	53	20	3	2	75
1981[e]	0	17	50	27	—[b]	—[b]	17
1982[e]	0	15	52	—[b]	—[b]	—[b]	0

1969–70 based on a sample of 100,000 patents from the 1969–79 OTAF on patents granted. 1971–82 based on the complete 1984 OTAF tape.
[a] Based on the 1982 OTAF. 1984 information not incorporated yet.
[b] Not computable.
[e] Estimated.

(2) The balance sheet items in the Compustat record had to be converted from historical to either current replacement or constant dollar prices. And (3) detailed sales price indexes had to be imported into these files to allow the computation of output and productivity measures for these companies.

To assemble our data set we started with the population of firms listed in the 1978 Compustat Industrial Tape, to which we added those firms that still existed in 1976 from the Research Tape, firms in the Compustat Over-the-Counter tape and firms in the Compustat Full Coverage tape. This yielded an approximate total of 2,700 manufacturing firms in 1976. (See Cummins *et al.*, 1985 and Bound, *et al.*, 1984 for a description of this sample and the Appendix for more detail on the match procedures). We then matched to this firm data set the detailed information on patents granted from the Office of Technology Assessment and Forecast (OTAF) tapes and found that approximately two-thirds of these firms received at least one patent between 1969 and 1982.

A preliminary analysis of aggregate trends in these data revealed

Table 4.2. *Statistics for the 1976 cross section: trimmed data*

Industry	NFIRMS	AVEPLANT	AVESALES	AVEEMP	NRNDFIRM	AVERND	AVERATIO	NPATFIRM	AVEPAT
Food & kindred products	182	178.7	585.7	8.9	62	5.4	0.005	46	5.8
Textile & apparel	188	55.2	137.8	4.3	49	1.9	0.018	33	5.9
Chemicals, excl. drugs	121	503.2	693.6	9.1	92	18.6	0.021	67	39.0
Drugs & medical inst.	112	116.6	301.7	6.8	96	14.4	0.045	64	28.2
Petroleum refining & ex.	54	3,200.1	4,622.8	20.0	26	34.9	0.005	25	72.0
Rubber & misc. plastics	98	122.4	214.8	5.3	59	5.9	0.016	35	12.2
Stone, clay & glass	81	186.1	243.6	5.3	31	7.0	0.019	26	22.4
Primary metals	103	499.6	488.5	8.6	39	7.7	0.013	44	14.6
Fabric. metal products	196	57.8	131.0	2.6	102	1.8	0.011	77	5.4
Engines, farm & const. equip.	64	186.9	457.3	8.8	51	10.2	0.016	42	25.7
Office, comp. & acctg. eq.	106	288.2	352.9	8.3	94	21.6	0.061	42	39.0
Other machinery, not elec.	199	40.8	116.1	2.8	149	2.3	0.021	111	5.8
Elec. equip. & supplies	105	155.0	405.5	10.7	77	11.2	0.023	56	34.3
Communication equipment	258	31.8	89.9	2.5	199	3.4	0.040	110	13.3
Motor veh. & transport eq.	105	464.2	1,233.6	22.2	59	49.2	0.012	48	25.0
Aircraft and aerospace	37	237.4	754.1	15.6	26	32.7	0.042	17	39.0
Professional & sci. equip.	139	73.4	130.5	3.3	118	8.0	0.051	65	16.0
Lumber, wood, and paper	163	204.2	260.4	4.7	64	2.8	0.007	49	6.9
Misc. consumer goods	100	81.6	232.5	5.2	44	1.8	0.013	41	5.2
Conglomerates	23	1,174.3	2,202.3	50.1	13	43.3	0.014	20	37.3
Misc. manuf., n.e.c.	148	36.3	89.3	2.1	29	0.7	0.027	16	2.1
All firms	2,582	230.9	417.2	6.8	1,479	10.5	0.027	1,034	19.1

NFIRMS = Total number of firms in industry.

AVEPLANT = Average gross plant in millions of dollars.

AVESALES = Average sales in millions of dollars.

AVEEMP = Average employment in thousands.

NRNDFIRM = Number of firms with nonzero R & D.

AVERND = Average R & D expenditure in millions of dollars for firms with nonzero R & D.

AVERATIO = Average R & D to sales ratio for firms with nonzero R & D.

NPATFIRM = Number of firms with nonzero patents.

AVEPAT = Average number of patents for firms with nonzero patents.

Source: Bound *et al.* (1984).

changing lags due to fluctuations in the delays at the Patent Office in processing the applications. Because patents are recorded by date granted while we are interested, primarily, in patent counts by date of application, such delays have implications for the completeness of our series in the later years.

Table 4.1 provides a distribution of US patents by date granted and by date applied for and shows both the degree of completeness of the data at any point of time and the fluctuations in the lag between the application and granting dates. About 97 percent of all patent applications which will be ultimately granted are granted within the first four years of the application date (but only about 70 to 80 percent are granted within the first three years). Hence, our sample of patents by date of application extends effectively only through 1979.

In Bound et al. (1984) we looked primarily at the cross-sectional aspect of these data. We found that about two-thirds of our sample were granted at least one patent between 1965 and 1979 and that the smaller firms (less than ten million dollars in sales) account for a slightly larger fraction of patents than of R&D or sales. The industries with a higher than average ratio of patents to R&D were the chemical, drug, petroleum, engine, farm and construction machinery, electrical equipment, and aircraft industries. Although technology based, firms in the communications equipment and computer industries patent less than the average of firms doing the same amount of R&D. (See Table 4.2).

Turning to the scale question, we found very little evidence that larger firms or firms doing more R&D were more productive in patenting (Figure 4.1). The answer to this question is clouded by conflicting results from alternative specifications of the relationship of patenting to R&D and by the sheer diversity of the firms in our sample. For the larger firms in our sample patenting is approximately proportional to R&D. The smallest firms do seem to show somewhat more patenting per R&D dollar but they are a far more selected group, owing to the way we chose the sample. (A small firm has to be in some sense more than usually successful to be listed on one of the stock exchanges.)

To look at time series aspects of our data, we have focused on a sub-sample of manufacturing firms (excluding foreign-owned firms and wholly-owned subsidiaries) which (1) existed in 1976 and (2) had at least three years worth of good data on our major variables of interest: sales, book value, and market value. This yielded a subset of about 1,900 firms for which we have constructed detailed market value data and revalued their physical assets in current prices. About 1,600 of them have data on sales, market value, and book value of plant for the eight year period 1972–80. They accounted for about one trillion dollars of sales in 1976

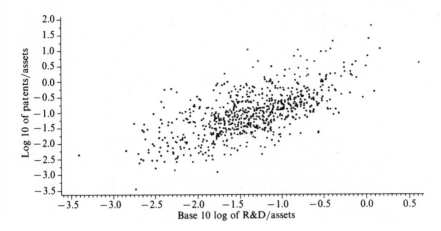

Fig. 4.1 Log of patents/assets vs log of R&D/assets (patents/assets in number per million dollars)
Source: Bound *et al.* (1984)

and employed approximately sixteen million workers. Although we sacrifice the pre-1972 history of R&D for some of these firms in enlarging the sample, this sample is more representative of the whole of US manufacturing and we have the complete patenting history since about 1967 for these firms. They account for about fifteen billion dollars of R&D in 1976 (approximately 88 percent of the total of company-financed R&D reported by the National Science Foundation) and received about nineteen thousand patents. These are the basic data that were used subsequently by us in various analyses of market value, R&D, patenting, and productivity. They were recently updated to 1981–82 and the Quarterly Compustat Tape was used to recompute market values and the stock market rate of return for the fiscal rather than the calendar year to make these variables more comparable to the other data in the record.

Table 4.3 gives some more information on this panel. If we want consistent and continuous data from 1972 through 1980, we have relatively 'clean' data on 968 firms, 525 of which were performing R&D consistently while 235 reported no R&D effort throughout this period. Two things stand out from this table: (1) the R&D firms both grew faster throughout this period, in terms of employment, and had a higher growth in productivity, deflated sales per employee, than non-R&D firms. And (2), there is much variation across industries in this experience. Employment in R&D performing firms grew at about two percent per year while non-R&D firms were hardly growing at all (0.2 percent per year).

Table 4.3. *Average growth rates in the US, 1973–80, at the company and industry level*

Industry	Number of Firms			Growth rates (per cent per year)							
				Employment				Deflated Sales per Employee			
	Total Sample	Non R&D	R&D Sample	Firms Total Industry	Total Sample	Non R&D	R&D Sample	Firms Total Industry	Total Sample	Non R&D	R&D Sample
Total	968	235	525	0.7	1.3	0.2	1.9	0.4	1.2	0.8	1.6
1. Food, etc.	63	22	22	-0.2	2.0	2.0	1.2	2.3	2.0	2.0	2.2
2. Chemicals & Rubber	91	6	71	0.7	1.2	—	1.4	-0.2	0.9	—	0.7
3. Drugs	52	3	44	1.0	3.5	—	4.0	1.5	0.3	—	0.4
4. Metals	135	50	50	-0.5	0.4	-0.5	0.2	-1.3	-0.8	-1.9	0.1
5. Machinery	113	10	82	2.3	2.8	-0.1	2.7	-0.4	0.0	-0.6	0.2
6. Electrical Equipment	140	10	106	2.2	2.6	0.9	2.4	5.1	4.3	5.1	4.4
7. Transport Equipment	63	10	34	-0.5	0.4	—	0.4	-0.9	-0.1	—	0.3
8. Instruments	46	0	39	—	5.2	—	4.7	—	2.6	—	3.0
9. Other	265	124	77	0.6	-0.1	0.5	0.0	0.0	1.2	1.6	1.2
a. Stone, Clay &	39	11	15	—	-1.5	-0.1	-1.4	—	0.5	-0.1	1.1
b. Lumber, Wood &	93	49	27	—	1.5	2.4	1.0	—	0.3	-0.4	0.9
c. Misc Consumer Goods	60	27	23	—	0.5	1.1	-0.8	—	0.9	1.1	0.8

Averages not shown for samples with 10 or less firms.
See Griliches-Mairesse (1983, 1985) for sources and methodology.

If one looks at the same numbers industry by industry, the results are less clear. Only in three out of the eight industries where comparisons can be made, was the growth in average employment unequivocally higher for R&D firms. Nevertheless, this implication is confirmed by a more detailed look at the growth in employment of individual firms during the 1976–79 period by Bronwyn Hall (1985). For a larger sample of 1,524 firms she finds that employment growth is related positively and significantly to R&D intensity (the logarithm of R&D expenditures per employee in 1976) with a coefficient of 0.018 (0.03) and moreover, that the effect of an R&D dollar on employment growth is higher than of a similar conventional investment in physical assets. Inclusion of 20 industry dummy variables and an adjustment for selective mortality between 1976 and 1979 leave these conclusions unchanged.

Another interesting aspect of Table 4.3 is its indication that the overall industry growth rates (of both employment and productivity) are lower than the average rates experienced by the firms in our sample. In part this reflects the selectivity of our sample. To be present in 1976 a firm, other things equal, must have been growing faster before 1976. To survive to 1980 also required above average growth. These issues of selective mortality have been investigated by Addanki (1986) and Hall (1985) Addanki shows that firms that existed between 1976 and 1984 were small on average and less R&D intensive, though with slightly more patents per R&D dollar. The major difference between the numbers at the aggregate and the firm levels arises from differences in weighting. Because the firm level averages are unweighted, they are dominated by the small firms which survived throughout the whole period. They did indeed grow faster (see Hall, 1985). The average firm in the sample was, therefore, during this period growing faster than the corresponding industry total.

The data sets we have constructed contain a large number of interesting variables only some of which have been explored in our own work. The major available variables are: gross and net value of plant in historical, constant, and current prices, total sales in current and constant prices, operating income, dividends, market value of the firm, number of employees, investment and R&D expenditures in current and constant prices, inventories, advertizing and pension expense, number of patents received by date of grant and date of application, stock market rate of return (calendar and fiscal year), and the various relevant price indexes used in the construction of the 'constant price' series. These data are a major research asset which is also available for use by others.

III   Patents and R&D

Much of our work was devoted to using the assembled patent data to study the R&D process and its contribution to economic growth. This is one way of assessing the usefulness of such statistics as indicators of inventive activity. Our work in this area can be divided, roughly, into four categories: (1) Characterizing the cross-sectional and time series relationship between R&D expenditures and successful patent applications. (2) Using patent renewal data to infer the distribution of patent right values, obtain a measure of their quality and estimate their rate of obsolescence. (3) Using stock market valuation data and data on R&D and patents to study the effectiveness of patents as an indicator of inventive activity. And, (4), using patent statistics in constructing and validating measures of R&D spillovers.

Our first papers in this area were based on an earlier, smaller (but longer) sample of firms. Pakes and Griliches (1980, 1984a) estimate something like a patent production function, focusing especially on the degree of correlation between patent applications and past R&D expenditures and on the lag structure of this relationship. Their main finding is a statistically significant relationship between R&D expenditures and patent applications. This relationship is very strong in the cross-sectional dimension. It is weaker but still significant in the within-firm time-series dimension (Table 4.4). Not only do firms that spend more on R&D receive more patents, but also when a firm changes its R&D expenditures, parallel changes occur in its level of patenting. The bulk of the relationship in the within-firm dimension between R&D and patent applications appears to be close to contemporaneous. The lag effects are significant but relatively small and not well estimated (Table 4.5) The significant coefficient for R&D five years back indicates, however, the probability of a long unseen 'tail' to the effect of past R&D on the level of patenting. Pakes and Griliches interpret their estimates as implying that patents are a fairly good indicator of differences in inventive activity across firms, but that short-term fluctuations in their numbers within firms have a large noise component in them. They also find that, except for drug firms, there has been a consistent, negative trend in the number of patents applied for and granted relative to R&D expenditures during their period of observation, 1968–75.

In analyzing the relationship between patents and R&D we encountered a number of serious substantive and econometric problems. The first and, at least in retrospect, most important problem is that the size or value of the 'output' associated with a particular patent varies enormously over different patents. We shall come back to this problem

Table 4.4. *Patents and R & D: selected statistics associated with estimating the equation*[a] $\ell n\ P_{it} = \sum_{j=0}^{5} \beta_j\ \ell n\ R_{it-j} + u_{it}$,
$(N = 121, T = 8, NT = 968.)$

	Total	Between	Within
Variance in $\ell n\ P$	2.41	2.24	0.17
Variance in $\ell n\ R$	1.72	1.68	0.04
$\bar{R}^2$ In $P\ (\sum \beta\ \ell n\ R)$	0.66	0.69	0.33 (0.23)
Lowest, median and highest R^2 across 7 industry groupings	0.74, 0.82, 0.95	0.77, 0.87, 0.97	0.11, 0.28, 0.49 (0.06, 0.16, 0.47)

[a] The values in parentheses are based on partialling out time trends from both ℓn P and ℓn R. 'Between' results are based on 8 year averages of all the variables across the 121 firms. 'Within' results are based on the annual deviations from each firm's own average ℓn P and ℓn R. The industry groupings are Chemicals except Drugs, Drugs, Machinery except Office and Computers, Office and Computers, Electronic Components and Communications Equipment, Instruments, and Other. $\bar{R}^2$ – adjusted partial squared multiple correlation coefficients. Adjusted for degrees of freedom and the included common trend (in the total and within dimensions).
Source: Pakes and Griliches (1980).

Table 4.5. *Patents and R & D: coefficients of the within-firms equation*
$(N = 121,$ degrees of freedom $= 837)$[a]

Coefficient of		
R_0	0.56	(0.07)
R_{-1}	−0.10	(0.09)
R_{-2}	0.05	(0.09)
R_{-3}	−0.04	(0.09)
R_{-4}	−0.05	(0.10)
R_{-5}	0.19	(0.08)
Sum	0.61	(0.08)

[a] See Table 4.4 for definitions. Standard errors in parentheses.
Source: Pakes and Griliches (1980).

below and present some estimates of its magnitude and its consequences for our work. The second is that patents do not represent all of the output of R&D. Only a fraction of it is patentable or patented. Moreover, this fraction may vary considerably over industry, firm, and time. We tried to control for such differences in the firms' propensity to patent by using covariance (fixed-effects) techniques, estimating conditionally on the overall patenting performance of the firm, or treating them as unobservables in a multi-equation context. We also included year effects as a partial solution to the problem of the changing effectiveness of patents as a tool of appropriability over time.

Two other problems required the development of new econometric tools: (1) Our large panel is rather short because public reporting of R&D expenditures became prevalent only after 1972. Thus we have only about six to eight years worth of data and this may be too short a time period to elicit a good estimate of the R&D to patents lag structure. And (2), the dependent variable, patent counts, is an integer with many zeroes and is subject to significant heteroskedasticity due to the wide size range of our firms. In Pakes and Griliches (1984b) we suggest a specific procedure for dealing with the first problem: truncation bias in the estimation of distributed lag models in short panels. It is based on an explicit modelling of the unseen pre-1972 R&D history. The integer dependent variable problem was attacked in Hausman, Hall, and Griliches (1984) by extending, developing, and estimating a Poisson-type stochastic specification for our data. (This methodology was also applied in Bound et al., 1984.) The heteroskedasticity and integer problem was also approached via consistent non-linear estimation with robust standard errors.

Our most recent paper on the relationship between patents and R&D (Hall, Griliches, and Hausman, 1986) updates earlier Pakes-Griliches and Hausman-Hall-Griliches work on the patents and R&D relationship using a more recent and larger (but shorter) sample of firms. It uses patenting data for 642 firms for the five years 1975–79, and associated R&D data for the eight years 1972–79, and reaches one positive, one mixed, and two essentially negative conclusions: (1) There is a strong, largely contemporaneous relationship between R&D expenditures and patenting with an estimated elasticity of about 0.3, which does not disappear when one controls for the size of the firm, its permanent patenting policy, or even the effects of its R&D history. (2) There does appear to be a small effect of past R&D history on current patenting, on the order of 0.1–0.2, but given the large randomness in patenting from year to year and the relative shortness and stability of the R&D series, it is not possible to pinpoint the exact magnitude or the timing of this effect.

Table 4.6. *Time series analysis of log R & D*[a]
642 Firms

Lag	Autocorrelations	Partial Autocorrelations	F-test for Equality of the Autocovariances[b]
0	1.0	—	1.54
1	0.987 (0.051)	0.992 (0.002)	1.81
2	0.991 (0.051)	0.054 (0.035)	0.76
3	0.974 (0.051)	−0.009 (0.034)	2.51
4	0.964 (0.051)	0.017 (0.034)	2.75
5	0.960 (0.051)	−0.036 (0.032)	1.22
6	0.959 (0.052)	0.006 (0.032)	0.92
7	0.959 (0.052)	0.055 (0.123)	—

Estimates of Autoregressive Equations for Log R & D: 1975–79[c]

Equation	(1)	(2)	(3)	(4)	(5)
Log R_{-1}	0.995 (0.003)	0.923 (0.040)	0.923 (0.039)	0.915 (0.040)	0.917 (0.040)
Log R_{-2}		0.074 (0.039)	0.082 (0.053)	0.067 (0.040)	0.069 (0.040)
Log R_{-3}			−0.009 (0.034)		
Log P_0				0.028 (0.009)	
Log P_{-1}				0.002 (0.011)	0.015 (0.009)
Log P_{-2}				−0.012 (0.009)	−0.002 (0.009)
Standard error	0.292	0.291	0.291	0.290	0.291

[a] R & D expenditures are in millions of 1972 dollars. The deflator is described in Cummins *et al.* (1985).
[b] These are tests of the stationarity assumption. We have eight estimates of the variance, seven for the first order covariance, six for the second, and so forth. We have added 1/3 to the patents variable before taking the logarithm due to the presence of some zeroes.
[c] All equations contain a separate intercept for each year.
Source: Hall *et al.* (1986)

(3) There does not seem to be any significant feedback from past patenting successes to future R&D expenditure changes above and beyond their contemporaneous correlation. This too may, however, reflect the high noise ratio in our patent data rather than the true absence of such a relationship. (4) An interesting finding that emerged from this study, and also Pakes' (1985) earlier work, has nothing to say about patenting, although it provides one reason why it is difficult to measure this relationship within firms over time: the pattern of R&D investment within a firm is essentially a random walk (or more precisely, a martingale) with a relatively low error variance (Table 4.6). In other words, R&D budgets over this short horizon (eight years) are roughly constant

(in constant dollars) and therefore must be determined by considerations other than short-run patenting successes. (5) More generally, the small number of patents taken out by most of the firms and their intrinsically high variability from year to year makes the use of patent counts as an indicator of inventive activity in the time dimension suspect, especially for small firms. Moreover, the rough constancy of R&D over time makes it rather difficult to make strong inferences about them. This does not mean that there is no interesting information in these data, only that one should not take small annual variations in small numbers too seriously, a point to which we shall return below.

IV   Patents, R&D and stock market values

The second set of studies involving patents and related variables are connected by their use of stock market values or the stock market rate of return as indicators of the success of inventive activity and as the driving force behind the investments in it. The use of stock market values as an output indicator has one major advantage. Because the public-good characteristics of inventive output make it extremely difficult to market, returns to innovation are earned mostly by embodying it in a tangible good or service that is then sold or traded for other information that can be so embodied. There are, therefore, no direct measures of the value of inventions, while indirect measures of current benefits (such as profits or productivity) are likely to react to the output of the firm's research laboratories only slowly and erratically. On the other hand, under simplifying assumptions, changes in the stock market value of the firm should reflect (possibly with error) changes in the expected discounted present value of the firm's entire uncertain net cash flow stream. Thus, if an event does occur that causes the market to reevaluate the accumulated output of the firm's research laboratories, its full effect on stock market values ought to be recorded immediately. This, of course, need not be equal to the effect that will eventually materialize. The fact that we are measuring expectations rather than realizations, however, does have its advantages. In particular, since expectations are a major determinant of research expenditures the use of stock market values should allow one to check whether the interpretation given to the parameter estimates is consistent with the observed behaviour of these series.

Pakes (1985) uses an investment model and modern time series analysis technique to interpret the dynamic relationship between patents, R&D, and the stock market rate of return. In this model, events occur which affect the market value of a firm's R&D program and what one estimates are the reduced form relationships between the percentage increase in this value and current and subsequent changes in the firm's R&D expenditures, its patent applications, and the market rate of return on its stock. His empirical results indicate that about five percent of the variance in the stock market rate of return is caused by the events which change both R&D and patent applications. This leads to a significant correlation between movements in the stock market rate of return and unpredictable changes in both patents and R&D expenditures, changes which could not be predicted from past values of patents and R&D (see Table 4.7). Moreover, the parameter values indicate that these changes in patents and R&D are associated with large movements in stock market values. On average, an 'unexpected' increase in one patent is associated with an increase in the firm's market value of $810,000, while an unexpected increase of $100 of R&D expenditures is, again, on average, associated with a $1,870 increase in the value of the firm. The R&D expenditure series appear to be almost error free in this context. Patents, however, contain a significant noise component (a component whose variance is not related to either the R&D or the stock market rate of return series). This noise component accounts for only a small fraction of the large differences in the number of patent applications of different firms (about 25%), but plays a much larger role among the smaller fluctuations that occur in the patent applications of a given firm over time (about 95%). Similarly, the effect of unexpected increases in patents on market value is highly variable. Nevertheless, there is still some information in the time-series dimension. If we were to observe, for example, a sudden large burst in the patent applications of a given firm, we could be quite sure that events have occurred to cause a large change in the market value of its R&D program; but smaller changes in the patent applications of a given firm are not likely to be very informative. This statement must be modified somewhat when we consider long-term differences in the patents of a given firm (say differences over a 5- or 10-year interval), since a larger fraction of their variance is caused by events that lead the market to reevaluate the firm's inventive output during these periods.

The timing of the response of patents and R&D to events which change the value of a firm's R&D effort is quite similar. One gets the impression from the estimates that such events cause a chain reaction, inducing an increase in R&D expenditures far into the future, and that firms patent around the links of this chain almost as quickly as they are completed, resulting in a rather close relationship between R&D expenditures and the number of patents applied for. Perhaps surprisingly, he finds no evidence that independent changes in the number of patents

Table 4.7. *R & D, patents, and the stock market rate of return*

Coefficient of:	R & D Equation (r_t)			Patent Equation (p_t)		
	Recursive (1)	Autoregressive (2)	Constrained (3)	Recursive (4)	Autoregressive (5)	Constrained (6)
r_t	n.i.	n.i.	n.i.	0.60 (0.11)	n.i.	0.60 (0.11)
r_{t-1}	0.89 (0.05)	0.90 (0.05)	0.92 (0.05)	-0.21 (0.15)	0.34 (0.12)	-0.21 (0.15)
r_{t-2}	-0.06 (0.07)	-0.10 (0.07)	-0.04 (0.07)	-0.13 (0.17)	-0.20 (0.17)	-0.15 (0.16)
r_{t-3}	0.21 (0.07)	0.24 (0.08)	0.14 (0.08)	0 (0.18)	0.16 (0.18)	0.04 (0.17)
r_{t-4}	-0.03 (0.05)	-0.02 (0.06)	-0.03 (0.05)	-0.13 (0.13)	-0.14 (0.14)	-0.15 (0.12)
p_{t-1}	0 (0.02)	0 (0.02)	n.i.	0.45 (0.05)	0.45 (0.05)	0.45 (0.05)
p_{t-2}	0.03 (0.02)	0.03 (0.02)	n.i.	0.30 (0.05)	0.32 (0.05)	0.30 (0.05)
p_{t-3}	-0.05 (0.03)	-0.04 (0.03)	n.i.	0 (0.06)	-0.02 (0.06)	0 (0.06)
p_{t-4}	0 (0.02)	0 (0.02)	n.i.	0.14 (0.05)	0.14 (0.05)	0.14 (0.5)
q_t	0.13 (0.02)	n.i.	0.13 (0.02)	0 (0.06)	n.i.	n.i.
q_{t-1}	0.05 (0.03)	0.05 (0.03)	n.i.	-0.02 (0.07)	0.01 (0.07)	n.i.
q_{t-2}	0.08 (0.03)	0.08 (0.03)	n.i.	-0.04 (0.07)	0.01 (0.07)	n.i.
q_{t-3}	0.04 (0.03)	0.05 (0.03)	n.i.	0.05 (0.07)	0.08 (0.07)	n.i.
q_{t-4}	-0.02 (0.02)	-0.02 (0.02)	n.i.	-0.01 (0.05)	-0.02 (0.04)	n.i.
σ^2	0.035	0.036	0.035	0.203	0.215	0.201
Test statistics:						
T_1	2,196.52	2,205.88		14.00†	9.92	
T_2	1.91	1.52		358.75	335.62	
T_3	7.54†	3.29		0.21†	0.40	

Standard errors are in parentheses. r – log R & D, p – log Patents, q – one period rate of return on the common stock. T_1, T_2, and T_3, are the observed values of the T-test statistic for the joint significance of, respectively, the R & D variables, and the 1-period rate of return. The critical values are 2.39 and 3.36 at 5 and 1 percent, respectively, except as noted †where critical values are 2.23 and 3.06 at 5 and 1 percent, respectively.
Source: Pakes (1985).

applied for (independent of current and earlier R&D expenditures) produce significant effects on the market's valuation of the firm (this is reflected by a lack of an independent effect of lagged p on r in the R&D equation and of q on p in the patent equation in Table 4.7). The data cannot differentiate between different kinds of events that change a firm's R&D level.

In a related paper Mairesse and Siu (1984) analyze the time-series interrelationship between changes in the market value of the firm, sales, R&D, and physical investment using what they call the extended accelerator model. This paper follows the Pakes paper both in approach and in the use of essentially the same data. It differs by not focusing on patents, instead adding sales and investment to the list of the series whose interrelationship is to be examined. They find that a relatively simple 'causal' model fits their data: 'innovations' in both market value and sales 'cause' subsequent R&D and investment changes without further feedback from R&D or investment to either the stock market rate of returns or sales. There is little evidence of a strong feedback relationship between physical and R&D investment, though there is some evidence of contemporaneous interaction. An interesting conclusion of their paper is that independent changes in sales explain a significant fraction of the changes in R&D (and physical investment) above and beyond what is already explained by changes in the market value of the firm and by lagged movements in R&D itself, implying that by using different variables one might be able to separate out the effects of different kinds of shocks in the R&D process. This finding could, of course, be just a reflection of a substantial noise (error) level in the observed fluctuations of the stock market rate of return, in the sense that not all of the changes in the market value of a firm are relevant to investment decisions.

Ben-Zion (1984) examines the cross-sectional determinants of market value, following an approach similar to that outlined in Griliches (1981). It differs by not allowing for specific firm constants and by including other variables, such as earnings and physical investment, in the same equation. He also finds that R&D and patents are significant in explaining the variability of market value (relative to the book value of its assets), in addition to such other variables as earnings. His most interesting finding, from our point of view, is the relative importance of total patents taken out in the industry as a whole on the firm's own market value. In his interpretation, patents applied for indicate new technological opportunities in the industry, and these overall opportunities may be more important than a firm's own recent accomplishments, though here again this could arise just from the high error rate in the firm's own patent counts as an indicator of its own inventive potential

This set of papers clearly opens up an interesting research area but still leaves many issues unresolved. Like the proverbial research on the characteristics of an elephant, different papers approach this topic from slightly different points of view. Pakes analyzes movements in patents, R&D, and market value; Mairesse and Siu investigate the relationship between R&D, investment, sales, and market value; while Ben-Zion (in his change regressions) looks at R&D, earnings, and market value.

In principle, one would like to use modern time series techniques together with some of the testable implications of recent investment theory to separate out the timing in the relationships between these variables and to consider disturbances processes that intercede between them. One of the conclusions of the Pakes paper, however, was that to separate out successfully the effects of different kinds of events on inventive activity will require a larger model and more indicator variables than were used heretofore. Especially distressing was his inability to distinguish between demand shocks, where demand shocks are loosely defined as events which cause increases in patenting only through the R&D expenditures they induce, and technological or supply shocks which may have a direct effect on patents as well as an indirect effect via induced R&D demand. A model capable of distinguishing between these shocks requires the addition of variables which react differently to such events.

A prototype of such a model is outlined in Griliches, Hall and Pakes (1986), where the results of a replication of some of Pakes' (1985) computations for a larger sample and an expansion of his equation system to add equations for sales, employment, and investment are also reported. They indicate that the addition of the latter variables is helpful, in the sense that fluctuations in their growth rates are related to fluctuations in both the growth rate of R&D and the stock market rate of return and hence should help in identifying the relationships we are interested in. On the other hand, the expansion of the sample to include many small firms with low levels of patenting, deteriorates significantly the informational content of this variable, raising its noise to signal ratio, and making it hard to discern a feedback from the independent variability in patenting to any of the other variables. Thus, at the moment, it does not look as if the data can sustain a model with two separate factors ('market' and 'technological' innovations), even though in principle such a model should be identifiable in this kind of data and with this number of variables.

The difficulties in implementing such models arise to a large extent from the large 'noise' component in patents as indicators of R&D output in the short-run within-firm dimension. While we were aware of the

problem from the beginning, it was the work of Pakes and Schankerman (1984), which we turn to next, and their estimates of the dispersion of patent values which alerted us to its actual magnitude. Using
their numbers Griliches, Hall, and Pakes (1986) estimate that unexpected changes in the present value of R&D output can account only for
about one percent of the variation in the stock market value of a firm
from year to year and that the proportion that is accountable by
unexpected changes in the number of patents is even smaller (less than
0.1 percent). Thus, it is not surprising that it is difficult to use patent
data to separate out demand from supply shocks and follow these
effects over time.

V   Patent renewal data

In many countries and recently also in the US, holders of patents must
pay an annual renewal fee in order to keep their patents in force. If the
renewal fee is not paid in any single year the patent is permanently
cancelled. Assuming that renewal decisions are based on economic
criteria, agents will only renew their patents if the value of holding them
over an additional year exceeds the cost of such renewal. Observations
on the proportion of patents that are renewed at alternative ages,
together with the relevant renewal fee schedules, will then contain
information on the distribution of the holding values of patents, and on
the evolution of this distribution function over the lifespan of the patents.
Since patent rights are seldom marketed, this is one of the few sources of
information on their value. In a series of papers Pakes and Schankerman
(1984), Pakes (1986), and Schankerman and Pakes (1986) present and
estimate models which allow them to recover the distribution of returns
from holding patents at each age over their lifespan. Since the renewal
decision is based on the value of patent protection to the patentee, the
procedure used in these articles directly estimates the private value of the
benefits derived from the patent laws. Estimates of the distribution of
these benefits at an economy-wide level of aggregation, and of
movements in them over the post-1950 period are also obtained.

   In addition, these patent renewal models imply that ideas for which
patent protection is more valuable will tend to be protected by payment
of renewal fees for longer periods of time. This suggests using the patent
renewal data to construct an index of the average value, or quality, of the
ideas embodied in patents, and then using this index to supplement the
quantity-based patent count data in constructing more comprehensive
and accurate measures of the value of patented output. There are two
reasons why an index of the value of patented ideas should prove useful.

First, the average value of patented inventions may differ among groups of patentees or over time periods, so that differences in the number of patents among groups or time periods will provide systematically biased estimates of differences in their value. Second, both small sample case studies and larger sample econometric evidence indicate that the distribution of the value of patented ideas is very dispersed and highly skewed (see below for details). This implies that the 'noise to signal' ratio in the patent count variable as a measure of the value of patented ideas is large. Provided that differently valued patents are renewed for different lengths of time, the renewal data allow us to construct an indicator of the value of patented output with a lower noise to signal ratio than that of the patent count index alone. We illustrate these two uses of the renewal data below.

In Pakes (1986) patent holders are allowed to be uncertain about the sequence of returns that will accrue to the patent if it is to be kept in force. This uncertainty is introduced to allow for the fact that agents often apply for patents at an early stage in the innovation process, a stage in which the agent is still exploring alternative opportunities for earning returns from the information embodied in the patented idea. Early patenting arises in part from the incentive structure created by the patent system, since, if the agent does not patent the information available to him, somebody else might. This incentive is reinforced by the fact that the renewal fees in all countries studied are quite small during the early years of a patent's life.

A patent holder who pays the renewal fee obtains both the current returns that accrue to the patent over the coming period, and the option to pay the renewal fee and maintain the patent in force in the following period should he desire to do so. An agent who acts optimally will pay the renewal fee only if the sum of the current returns plus the value of this option exceeds the renewal fee. It is assumed that the agent values the option at the expected discounted value of future net returns (current returns minus renewal fees), taking account of the fact that an optimal policy will be followed in each future period, and conditional on the information currently at the disposal of the agent. An optimal sequential policy for the agent has the form of an optimal renewal (or stopping) rule; a rule determining whether to pay the renewal fee at each age. The proportion of patents which drop out at age a corresponds to the proportion of patents which do not satisfy the renewal criteria at that age but did so at age $a-1$. The drop out proportions predicted by the model are a function of the model's parameters and of the renewal fee schedule. The data gives us the actual proportion of drop outs. The estimation problem consists, roughly speaking, of finding those values of the model's parameters which make the drop out proportions implied by the model as 'close' as possible to those we actually observe.

The empirical results from the Pakes (1986) paper indicate that patents are applied for at an early stage in the inventive process, a stage in which there is still substantial uncertainty concerning both the returns that will be earned from holding the patents, and the returns that will accrue to the patented ideas. Gradually the patentors uncover more information about the actual value of their patents. Most turn out to be of little value, but the rare 'winner' justifies the investments that were made in developing them. His estimates imply also that most of the uncertainty with respect to the value of a patent is resolved during the first three or four years of its life. Using this result, Schankerman and Pakes (1986) employ a simpler but more detailed model to examine changes in the distribution of patent values over time and the correlates of these changes. The substantive results from these papers imply that the average value of a patent right is quite small, about $7,000 in the population of patent applications in France and the UK. In Germany, where only about 35 percent of all patent applications are granted (about 93% and 83% were granted in France and the UK respectively), the average value of a patent right among grants was about $17,000. The distribution of these values, however, is very dispersed and skewed. One percent of patent applications in France and the UK had values in excess of $70,000 while in Germany one percent of patents granted had values in excess of $120,000. Moreover, half of all the estimated value of patent rights accrues to between five and ten percent of all the patents. The annual returns to patent protection decay rather quickly over time, with rates of obsolescence on the order of 10 to 20 percent per year. Since about 35,000 patents were applied for per year in France and the UK and about 60,000 in Germany, these figures imply that though the aggregate value of patent rights is quite large, it is only on the order of ten to fifteen percent of the total national expenditures on R&D. While these returns (which are the result of the proprietary right created by the patent laws) may, depending on the response elasticity of R&D investments to such incentives, stimulate a large amount of R&D investment, it is clear that other means of appropriating the benefits of R&D must be quite important.

Even though the total number of patent applications fell during the 1970s, one should not take this decline in numbers as implying, necessarily, the exhaustion of technological opportunities. Schankerman and Pakes find that although the numbers of patents per scientist and engineer fell sharply, their estimated 'quality-adjusted' total value of patent rights per scientist and engineer was remarkably stable over the period examined by them (Table 4.8).

Table 4.8. *Estimated indices of quantity, quality and total value of cohorts of patents at five-year intervals between 1955 and 1975*[a]

Index	United Kingdom				France				Germany			
Year	PA	P5	V̄	V	PA	P5	V̄	V	PA	P5	V̄	V
1955	1.00	1.00	1.00	1.00	1.00	1.00	1.00	1.00	1.00	1.00	1.00	1.00
1960	1.24	1.35	0.80	1.08	1.26	1.39	1.14	1.59	1.04	1.08	1.01	1.10
1965	1.56	1.67	0.86	1.42	1.67	1.78	1.49	2.64	1.21	1.04	0.99	1.03
1970	1.72	1.78	0.84	1.49	1.67	1.83	1.68	3.08	1.21	1.01	1.32	1.33
1975	1.45	1.58	1.40	2.18	1.55	1.65	1.86	3.06	1.10	0.99	1.93	1.91

[a] *PA* and *P5* are indices of the number of patents applied for and the number of patents which survive until age 5, respectively. *V̄* and *V* are indices of the mean and total of the estimated discounted present value of patent protection from age five for the patents surviving until age five. The index numbers refer to the cohorts applied for in the year row.
Source: Schankerman and Pakes (1986).

One final point. Disaggregated patent renewal data are gathered by the International Patent Documentation Center (INPADOC). These data would allow one to investigate the returns to patent protection separately by technical field of the patent and by the nationality and type of patentor (e.g., individuals and small business enterprises vs large corporate entities). Issues related to which sectors of a particular economy, and which economies, derive disproportionate benefits from the patent laws lie at the heart of most discussions of cost and benefits of alternative patent systems (see Scherer, 1965, Chapter 16, and the literature cited there.) Moreover, inter-sectoral differences in the patenting and R&D processes are central to the literature on market structure, industrial policy, and technical progress. Thus, future studies using these data could be very interesting and should be encouraged.

VI   The spillover effects of R&D

One of the major unresolved issues in this area of research is the identification and measurement of R&D spillovers, the benefits that one company or industry receives from the R&D activity of another. It is difficult to trace such spillovers without having strong *a priori* notions about who are the potential beneficiaries of whose research. One of the ways we have been trying to approach this problem is by using the detailed information on patenting by type of patent (patent class) to cluster firms into common 'technological activity' clusters and looking whether a firm's variables are related to the overall activity levels of its cluster.

In his thesis and several recent papers, Adam Jaffe (1983, 1984, 1985, 1986) has used firm level data on patenting by class of patent and on the distribution of sales by 4-digit SIC to cluster 500+ of our panel firms into 21 distinct technological clusters and 20 industry (sales orientation) clusters. It turns out that these two clustering criteria lead to different clusterings. Using the technological clusters Jaffe constructed a measure of the total R&D 'pool' available for spillovers (borrowing or stealing) in a cluster. He then looked at three 'outcome' variables: R&D investment ratio for the firm (in 1976), patents received (average number applied for during 1975–77), and output growth between 1972 and 1977. In each of these cases, his measure of the R&D pool contributed significantly and positively to the explanation of the firm level 'outcome' variables even in the presence of industry dummies (based on the sales clustering). Not surprisingly, perhaps, firms in technological clusters with large overall R&D 'pools' invested more intensively in R&D than would be predicted just from their industrial (SIC) location. More interesting is the finding

Table 4.9. *Patent equation estimation results, non-linear two-stage least squares (1976 cross section)*

Dependent Variable: Log of Average Patents Applied for, 1975–77				
	1	2	3	4
Log (R & D) (β_1)	0.940	0.961	0.937	−2.09
	(0.034)	(0.047)	(0.070)	(0.214)
R & D Elasticity				0.871
$\beta_1 + \beta_3 \log (s^T + \delta s^C)$				(0.115)
Log (Pool) (β_2)			0.746	0.551
			(0.164)	(0.179)
R & D-Pool Interaction (β_3)				0.361
				(0.072)
Within-Cluster			0.763	0.670
Premium (δ)			(0.364)	(0.371)
χ^2-statistic for the significance of technological cluster effects	n.i.	53.6	42.1	39.2
Root mean square error	0.943	0.913	0.862	0.923

537 observations. Numbers in parentheses under coefficients are heteroskedasticity consistent standard errors; χ^2 statistics are not corrected for heteroskedasticity. R & D elasticity is calculated for comparison with other equations. For this purpose, the pool variables are evaluated at the mean of the data.
'Pool' = $S^T + \delta s^C$. s^T = weighted R & D of 'others'. s^C − weighted R & D of others within the same technological cluster. n.i. − not included. The 99.5% critical value for χ^2_{20} is 39.9.
Source: Jaffe (1985).

that firms received more patents per R&D dollar in clusters where more R&D was performed by others, again above and beyond any pure industry differences (based on a classification of their sales). (See Table 4.9). Similarly, his analysis of firm productivity growth during the 1972–77 period showed that it was related positively to both the average R&D intensity of the individual firms and the change in the size of the R&D pool available to these firms (Table 4.10). The magnitude and significance of these effects is robust, allowing also for industry-based differences in average rates of productivity growth. In terms of profits, or market value, however, there are both positive and negative effects of neighboring firms' R&D. The net effect is positive for high R&D firms, but firms with R&D about one standard deviation below the mean are made worse off overall by the R&D of others. More generally, the idea of R&D spillovers is made operational by using the information in the patenting patterns of firms to construct a measure of their position in

Table 4.10. *Firm sales growth as a function of conventional inputs, R & D intensity, and R & D spillover measures*

Dependent Variable: Log (Deflated 1977 Sales) – Log (Deflated 1972 Sales)				
	1	2	3	4
ΔLog (Employment)	0.721	0.692	0.690	0.681
	(0.047)	(0.038)	(0.033)	(0.033)
ΔLog (Net Plant)	0.037	0.127	0.138	0.155
	(0.045)	(0.047)	(0.031)	(0.032)
R & D/Sales	1.98	1.45	1.08	1.26
	(0.41)	(0.46)	(0.28)	(0.52)
ΔLog (Cluster Pool Stock)	0.041	0.098	0.158	0.176
	(0.049)	(0.051)	(0.038)	(0.045)
$\Delta(\frac{\text{Out of Cluster Pool Stock}}{\text{Cluster Pool Stock}})$	0.00034	0.00035	0.00011	0.00015
	(0.00029)	(0.00028)	(0.00054)	(0.00052)
F-statistic on Industry Effects	n.i.	6.3	n.i.	2.1
		(18,403)		(18,383)
F-statistic on Technological Area Effects	n.i.	n.i.	5.8	1.9
			(20,401)	(20,383)
R^2	0.618	0.702	0.703	0.732
Root mean square error	0.191	0.172	0.172	0.167

434 observations. Numbers in parentheses under coefficients are heteroskedasticity consistent standard errors, F-statistics are not corrected for heteroskedasticity. n.i. – not included.
F critical values: 0.95   0.99
        (20,400)   1.6   1.9
        (50,400)   1.4   1.6
Source: Jaffe, A. (1985).

'technological space' and of the closeness between them and it is shown that this position has an observable impact on the firm's success.

VII   Summary

In this paper we describe a number of studies whose common denominator is the use of patent statistics to illuminate the process of innovation and technical change. One of the main findings of this project was the discovery of a strong relationship in the cross-sectional dimension. Patents are a good indicator of differences in inventive activity across different firms. While the propensity to patent differs significantly across industries, the relationship between R&D and patents is close to proportional, especially for firms above a minimal size. Small firms do receive a significantly higher number of patents per R&D dollar but this can be explained largely by their being a much more highly selected group. (To be in our sample a small firm must be successful enough to have publicly traded securities.) There is also a statistically significant relationship between R&D and patents in the within-firm time-series dimension, but it is weaker there. The bulk of the observable effect is contemporaneous. There is some evidence that history also matters, that there are some lagged effects, but they seem to be small and difficult to estimate precisely. These findings can also be interpreted as implying some reverse causality: successful research leads both to patents and to a commitment of additional funds for the development of resulting ideas.

Using data on patent renewal rates and patent renewal fees in selected European countries we have estimated the private value of patent rights, their dispersion, and their decay over time. The average value of patent rights is quite small, about $7,000 and $17,000 per patent in France and Germany respectively. It is also very variable and its distribution is quite skewed. While most patent rights were close to worthless, one percent of them had values in excess of $70,000 and $120,000 per patent in France and Germany respectively. These returns were estimated, however, to decline rather rapidly over time, with rates of obsolescence between 10 and 20 percent per year. While the aggregate value of patent rights appears to be quite high, it is estimated to be only of the order of 10 to 15 percent of total national expenditures on R&D. Hence it is unlikely to be the major factor in determining the overall level of such expenditures. Using these newly developed methods of analysis we show that even though the total number of patent applications fell during the 1970s, their estimated 'quality' rose, implying that one cannot take the observed decline in numbers as indicating, necessarily, the exhaustion of technological opportunities. The finding of extreme skewness in the distribution of the value of patent rights has, however, pessimistic implications for the use of patent counts as indicators of short run changes in the output of R&D.

Nevertheless, patent data represents a valuable resource for the analysis of the process of technical change. There are other ways of using them besides simply counting them. It is possible to use a firm's distribution of patenting by field to infer the position of its R&D programme in 'technological space' and to use this information, in turn, to study how the results of R&D spillover from one firm to another and to illuminate the process of strategic rivalry that the firm finds itself in. If, as is now happening also in the US, patent renewal information were to become available at the individual patent and firm level, one could use these data together with information on patent citations to construct more relevant 'quality weighted' inventive 'output' measures. Even without going that far, the currently available patent data can be used to study longer-run interfirm differences in levels of inventive activity and as a substitute for R&D data where they are not available in the desired detail.

Appendix: The Compustat–OTAF patents match

In accomplishing this match the major problem we faced was that the OTAF tapes do not have CUSIP numbers (the identifying corporation code on the Compustat Tapes). They list only the names of individuals and organizations, of which there were 66,000 or more distinct ones and among which we needed to find our 2,700 firm names. The work that had to be done is described in more detail in Cummins *et al.* (1985). Basically, we had first to find all (or most) of the subsidiaries of our 2,700 companies and enter all of their distinct names, 16,000 of them, into the computer; write and run a lexicographical search and match computer program that would assign OTAF names to the Compustat firms; check the results manually; investigate the many discrepancies and resolve various conflicts. The first round of the match yielded about 4,500 OTAF organizations to associate with 1,500 of our firms. After checking the list of patenting organizations with at least five patents in the 11 year period from 1969 through 1979 we found that approximately 8,000 organizations remained which were not matched to the firms in our sample. Based on a sample, about a third of those appeared to be foreign firms and another third remained unidentified after looking them up in the 1981 Directory of Corporate Affiliations. To reduce the number of firms which had to be investigated by hand, we restricted the sample of unmatched organizations to those with more than 50 patents in the 11 year period or at least five patents in the period 1975 to 1977. Of these 900 organizations, a third were matched to our sample or otherwise disposed of. The remaining largest unmatched organizations turned out to be agencies of the US Government, several privately-held companies, and a few service companies which obtained patents for inventors.

REFERENCES

Addanki, S. (1986), 'R&D, Innovation and Mergers', Harvard University, Ph.D. Thesis.

Ben-Zion, U. (1984), 'R&D and Investment Decisions and Their Relationship to Stock Market Values and Sales: Preliminary Results', in Z. Griliches (ed.), *R&D, Patents, and Productivity*, Chicago: University of Chicago Press.

Bound, J., C. Cummins, Z. Griliches, B. H. Hall, and A. Jaffe (1984), 'Who Does R&D and Who Patents?', in Z. Griliches (ed.), *R&D, Patents, and Productivity*, Chicago: University of Chicago Press.

Cummins, C., B. H. Hall, E. S. Laderman and J. Mundy (1985), 'The R&D Master File: Documentation', September, unpublished.

Griliches, Z. (1981), 'Market Value, R&D, and Patents', *Economics Letters*, 7. (Reprinted in Z. Griliches (ed.), *R&D, Patents, and Productivity*, Chicago: University of Chicago Press, 1984.)

Griliches, Z., B. H. Hall and A. Pakes (1986), 'Is There a Second (Technological Opportunity) Factor?', unpublished.

Griliches, Z. and J. Mairesse (1983), 'Comparing Productivity Growth: An Exploration of French and U.S. Industrial and Firm Data', *European Economic Review*, 21, pp. 89–119.

(1985), 'R&D and Productivity Growth: Comparing Japanese and U.S. Manufacturing Firms', NBER Working Paper No. 1778.

Hall, B. H. (1985), 'The Relationship Between Firm Size and Firm Growth in the U.S. Manufacturing Sector', NBER Working Paper No. 1965, December.

Hall, B. H., Z. Griliches and J. A. Hausman (1986), 'Patents and R&D: Is There a Lag?', *International Economic Review*.

Hausman, J., B. H. Hall and Z. Griliches (1984), 'Econometric Models for Count Data with an Application to the Patents–R&D Relationship', *Econometrica*, 52(4), July.

Jaffe, A. (1983). 'Using Patent Class Data to Measure Technological Proximity and Research Spillovers Among Firms', Harvard University, unpublished.

(1984), 'The Effects of Market Demand, Technological Opportunity and Research Spillovers on R&D Intensity and Productivity Growth', NBER Working Paper No. 1432.

(1985), 'Quantifying the Effects of Technological Opportunity and Research Spillovers in Industrial Innovation', Ph.D. Thesis, Harvard University.

(1986), 'Technological Opportunity and Spillovers of R&D: Evidence from Firms' Patents, Profits and Market Value', *American Economic Review*, 76.

Mairesse, J. and A. Siu (1984), 'An Extended Accelerator Model of R&D and Physical Investment', in Z. Griliches (ed.), *R&D, Patents, and Productivity*, Chicago: University of Chicago Press.

Pakes, A. (1985), 'On Patents, R&D, and the Stock Market Rate of Return', *Journal of Political Economy*, 93, No. 2, April.

(1986), 'Patents as Options: Some Estimates of the Value of Holding European Patent Stocks', *Econometrica*, 54, July.

Pakes, A. and Z. Griliches (1980), 'Patents and R&D at the Firm Level: A First Report', *Economics Letters*, 5, 377–81.

(1984a), 'Patents and R&D at the Firm Level: A First Look', in Zvi Griliches (ed.), *R&D, Patents, and Productivity*, Chicago: University of Chicago Press.

(1984b), 'Estimating Distributed Lags in Short Panels with an Application to the Specification of Depreciation Patterns and Capital Stock Constructs', *Review of Economic Studies*, 51, No. 165, April.

Pakes, A. and M. Schankerman (1984), 'The Rate of Obsolescence of Knowledge, Research Gestation Lags, and the Private Rate of Return to Research Resources', in Z. Griliches (ed.), *R&D, Patents, and Productivity*, Chicago: University of Chicago.

Schankerman, M., and A. Pakes (1986), 'Estimates of the Value of Patent Rights in European Countries During the Post-1950 Period', *Economic Journal.*

Scherer, F. M. (1965), *Industrial Market Structure and Economic Performance*, 2nd edition. Rand McNally College Publishing Company, Chicago.

5 Learning to learn, localized learning and technological progress

JOSEPH E. STIGLITZ[1]

There is a well known saying that 'Consistency is the Hobgoblin of small minds'. If this be true, then economics has been well endowed with minds that are not small.

Among Adam Smith's many contributions to economics, two that perhaps stand out are his 'invisible hand' conjecture and his discussion of the role of specialization. Modern day economists applaud him for both of these insights; but when they have come to formalize the former conjecture, in the shape of the Fundamental Theorem of Welfare Economics, they have made assumptions concerning convexity which essentially preclude the existence of specialization, or are in any case inconsistent with the arguments put forward by Adam Smith for the advantages of specialization within his famous pin factory.

This chapter takes seriously the notion of economic specialization. The advances in living standards over the past two centuries have been accompanied by – perhaps caused by – increasing specialization, and it is essential to understand the nature of specialization if we are to understand the development of modern economies. One must understand both what are the returns to, and the limits of, specialization.

There appear to be two basic sources of economies of specialization. (a) Many of the costs associated with the performance of a task are fixed costs – in particular, the costs associated with learning how to perform the task well. These costs are, in part at least, *individual specific*; that is, while R&D may develop general procedures for performing some task, which can be transmitted to all workers, there is a fixed cost of transmitting that information to each worker, and each worker must use up a certain amount of time and energy absorbing this information. Moreover, no matter what one is taught, much has to be learned by oneself; the attention that any individual can give to any one task – to improving one's skill in it – is reduced when there are many tasks being performed. (b) There may be *switching* costs; these costs can again be related to learning – or, more precisely, to forgetting. When one does not perform a task, one forgets the best way of doing it, and it takes a while to relearn the best way of doing it; indeed, switching costs may be sufficiently high that individuals who are assigned many tasks have little time to improve their performance in any one of them; all of their energy is spent re-attaining levels of performance previously attained.[2]

In this chapter, we wish to push the notion of specialization one step further: the past half century has been marked not only by greater specialization in production, but also by greater specialization in *learning*. Within a corporation, there are individuals whose primary function is to think of better ways of performing tasks, and within our society there are organizations (corporations) whose niche is to think of better products and better ways of producing pre-existing products. Learning is an activity which in some ways is much like producing; there are gains to be had by having individuals and institutions specialize in learning. Just as, by specializing in production, one learns how to produce better, so too, as a result of specializing in learning, one learns how to learn better.

The frame of mind which is associated with asking 'how can this task be performed better?' is fundamentally different from the frame of mind which is associated with asking 'how am I supposed to perform this task?' And there are better (and worse) ways of going about learning about how to perform a task better.

We do not need, for the purposes of this chapter, to enquire into the micro-micro economics of this process of learning how to ask the right questions, learning the methods by which such questions can be answered, etc. Central to our concern are certain properties of this learning process and their consequences.

The objective of this chapter is to explore some of the implications of the fact that the ability to learn has to be learned, that the skills associated with learning are, like other skills, specialized. We are concerned both with the micro-economic implications – its consequences, for instance, for firm decision making – as well as its macro-economic consequences.

The importance of technological progress for understanding growth processes has, of course, been recognized, at least since the work of Solow (1957).[3] Among the questions which motivated the research programme of which this is a part[4] is: why is it that the growth rates and income levels of various countries have not converged faster than they have? (Indeed, there is some evidence that for a significant number of LDCs there has been divergence rather than convergence.) Traditional economic theory (Solow, 1956) predicts that in the long run the growth rates in all countries should be related only to the rate of (labour augmenting) technological progress; and differences in levels of *per capita* income should be related to differences in savings rates. Even if LDCs adopt the best practices of the developed countries with a lag, the rate of technical progress will be the same, and differences in levels of *per capita* income will then be related also to the length of the lag in the diffusion of technology.

This is not the only unsatisfactory aspect of modern neo-classical growth theory. It is, for instance, completely ahistorical: the long-run development of the economy seems completely independent of (and unaffected by) major events like war and plagues.

This chapter is divided into three parts. In Part I, we analyse the implications of our theory for micro-economic analysis, while in Part II, we pursue the macro-economic implications. The theory which we develop in this paper has some important policy implications. Part III presents some of these, as well as some speculative remarks concerning the broader implications of our theory.

I   Micro-economic analysis

1.   *Learning by learning and the structure of technology*

All economic analysis begins with an analysis of the central trade-offs: one cannot have more of one good without giving up something else. It is obviously desirable to increase one's learning capacities. What does one have to give up to do this?

1.1 Localized technological progress   To understand what is at issue, we need to make use of a concept introduced some years ago by Atkinson and Stiglitz (1969); localized technological progress. They argued that changes which affect one technology, one way of producing a good, will have limited effects on other technologies. Learning is, in other words, localized.

The degree of applicability of knowledge can, of course, vary extensively. The distinction is sometimes made between basic scientific knowledge, which has a bearing on a large variety of situations, and technical knowledge. The extreme case of technological knowledge is that which is specific to a single production process, which has no spill-overs to other industries or processes. For example, the basic concept of 'weaving' is involved in virtually all textile production, but much of the technical knowledge associated with modern automated factory production is inapplicable to hand-loom technology.[5]

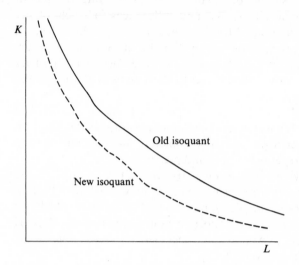

Fig. 5.1   Labour-augmenting technical progress: all techniques affected similarly

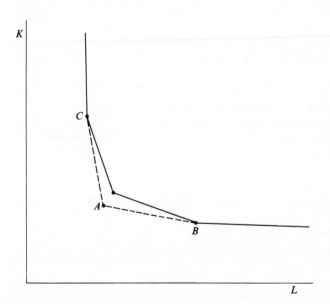

Fig. 5.2   Localized technological progress: no spill-overs

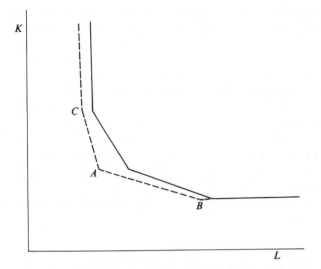

Fig. 5.3   Localized technological progress: slight spill-overs

There are several significant differences between technical and basic knowledge. Technical knowledge is, for example, more subject to obsolescence; the automobile made obsolete much of the accumulated knowledge on efficient horse-shoeing. But the most important difference is that, because technical knowledge is specific to particular processes, improvements in one technique will leave others relatively unaffected. Each successive improvement in the capital-intensive transport technology of automobiles has left the horse and buggy technology essentially unchanged.

We can illustrate the concept of localized technological progress using a variant of the standard isoquant. We typically represent the set of production technologies available by a smooth isoquant (ignoring the potentially important scale effects) as in Figure 5.1; yet we can perhaps better think of there being a discrete set of techniques, as in Figure 5.2, with production at intermediate factor ratios consisting of employing linear combinations of the adjacent techniques. Earlier discussions of technical progress focused on labour or capital augmenting technical progress, which reduced the labour or capital requirements for each technique equiproportionately (Figure 5.1). Localized technical progress emphasizes that changes which alter one technology may have little (or no) effect on other technologies; thus in Figure 5.2, the labour requirement for technology A is reduced, but technologies B and C are left unaffected. In many cases there are spill-overs, with a change in technology *A* having a slight (but far from equiproportionate) effect on technology *B*, and even less effect on more remote technologies (Figure 5.3).

1.2 Localized learning   But just as learning is (partially) localized, learning to learn is (partially) localized: though there are in general spill-overs, that is, some of what one learns about learning to perform one set of tasks has spill-overs for learning about learning to perform another set of tasks; still the spill-overs are not complete; some of learning to learn is localized. Learning how to adapt a computerized textile machine to local conditions (e.g., to the peculiarities of the local yarns) may have few spill-overs for learning how to adapt a hand-loom. There are, however, some spill-overs (for instance, those which arise simply out of the questioning process).

1.3 Learning by doing   To understand how learning to learn and localized learning affects economic decisions, we need to introduce one more concept, learning by doing. There are two major sources of improvements in technology; some improvements are the result of direct expenditures on R&D, while many are by-products of production. The notion that one learns from experience is hardly a new one, but there has been almost no research investigating either why that is so, the processes by which this learning occurs, or its implications for economic theory. (An important exception is Arrow, 1962). The fact that productivity increases as a result of production is referred to as 'learning by doing'.

1.4 Learning by learning   Just as experience in production increases one's productivity in producing, so experience in learning may increase one's productivity in learning. One learns to learn, at least partly in the process of learning itself. Earlier, we emphasized the importance of specialization, and the fact that learning is an activity, like a production activity. By specialization in learning, one may improve one's learning skills.

1.5 The basic trade-offs   The firm makes many decisions which affect its (employees') learning capacities. In this section, we wish briefly to characterize the major trade-offs facing the firm in making these decisions.

First,` a direct consequence of learning by doing is that if the firm increases its production today, it lowers its cost of production tomorrow. There is a value to knowledge, and the firm will accordingly produce beyond the point where price (or if the firm faces a downward sloping demand schedule, marginal revenue) equals (current) marginal cost. There is thus a trade-off between current profitability and future profitability. Myopic rules – based on maximizing current profits – simply will not do.

Secondly, by the same token, if there is learning by learning, it will take into account not only the lower cost next period, but the lower costs which will accrue as a result of the improvement in learning capacities.

Thirdly, the fact that technological progress is localized means that firms cannot be myopic in their decisions concerning the choice of technique. The value of learning, of improving a technique, depends on the extent to which that technique will be used in the future. If some technique will not be used in the future – say, because increasing wages make it unprofitable – then the learning associated with that technique will not be of much value. Firms will thus switch from one technique to another not when they have equal costs at current factor prices, but at some date before that.

Fourthly, the nature of learning, and learning to learn, also implies that myopic rules will not work. To the extent that learning to learn is localized, it strengthens the argument for switching techniques at some date prior to that at which they are equally costly at current factor prices. But the facility to increase learning capacities may differ with different techniques. There exist some technologies in which most of the learning possibilities have been exhausted: technological changes are difficult to come by. Those working on these technologies thus have little opportunity to learn, and technological change will be slow. Firms (governments), recognizing this, may choose technologies which, at current market prices – and indeed, at future market prices – are more expensive than other available technologies, on the grounds that those technologies will in fact enhance learning capacities.

Fifthly, the degree of localization (in effect, the degree of specialization in learning) is, itself, a decision variable, at least to some extent. We previously discussed the distinction between basic and applied research; by allocating more resources to more basic research, one decreases the degree of localization. So too, by assigning workers a variety of tasks, one may enhance the range of their learning capacities, at the cost of reducing their current productivity (because they are less specialized in their current production activities). They may then be more *flexible* in their learning capacities, better able to adapt to a wider variety of circumstances.

1.6 Externalities, learning, and multiple equilibria The extent of spillovers is also affected by other choices. A decision to improve a technology which is very different from those being employed elsewhere (by the firm, or by other firms) is likely to have fewer spill-overs. Though a firm may not take its external benefits to others much into account, it may take into account the external benefits it receives from others. If it is 'near' others technologically, it will receive benefits – in the form of improved technology and improved learning capabilities – which it would not receive if it decided to strike out on its own. The consequence of this is that there may be multiple equilibria; if all but one firm are using technology A, it pays the last firm to use technology A; if all but one firm are using technology B, it pays the last firm to use technology B. One of these equilibria may Pareto dominate the other.

The externalities which are associated with learning and adapting are more pervasive than our analysis thus far has suggested. We referred earlier to the specialization of individuals and organizations: when technological change is low, there is little need for organizations specialized in acquiring and disseminating the kind of information which facilitates such changes; and in the absence of such institutions, it is expensive (difficult) for firms to innovate. The absence of such institutions is thus both a cause and an effect of the lack of technological progress. There may be multiple equilibria to the economy: there may be one equilibrium in which there is little technological change, and another one with more rapid technological change.

The structure of the argument is a familiar one: in the absence of a complete set of markets, there frequently exist multiple (Nash) equilibria to the economy. If individuals consume coffee only with sugar, and consume sugar only with coffee, then in the absence of coffee, there will be no sugar produced, and in the absence of sugar, no coffee will be produced. There can exist a market equilibrium with neither produced, which is inferior to one in which both are produced. The necessity for coordination has often been adduced as a reason for government intervention. For the kinds of example just presented, I have always found such arguments unpersuasive: the interactions are sufficiently 'obvious' that the market can do the necessary coordination just as well as any government bureaucrat. When US Steel decided to construct a steel mill on the southern shore of Lake Michigan, they internalized all these externalities, by simultaneously constructing the railroad and the necessary mines, as well as providing housing and other public goods for their employees.

But the kinds of externalities with which we are concerned in this chapter are *diffuse*; the technological infrastructure that facilitates change and adaptation serves a large number of enterprises. Indeed, by its very nature, what one learns in dealing with the problems of one enterprise has spill-overs which enhance one's capabilities of dealing with another; there is a natural monopoly, limited only by the standard problems associated with diseconomies of scale. Of course, there may be instances of large enterprises, of sufficient scale that much of the 'technological change externalities' may be internalized – that is, even in the absence of the availability in the market of specialized information gathering services, it pays the firm to establish its own specialized internal unit (just as it paid the coffee firm to establish the sugar firm).[6]

2. Implications for micro-economic analysis

In the previous section, we described some of the important characteristics of certain aspects of technological change: much of learning is localized, but there are some spill-overs; the ability to learn, like the ability to produce, can be improved; some learning is a by-product of producing (learning by doing) and, similarly, some improvement in the ability to learn is a by-product of learning (learning to learn). In this section, we review and re-emphasize some of the implications that these properties have for micro-economic analysis. There are four, in particular, to which we would like to call attention:

2.1 Optimality of non-myopic policies We have already noted that decisions concerning the level of production and the choice of technique should be made in a non-myopic way. It should be emphasized that although we have couched most of our analysis in terms of the firm's choice of technique or level of production, the analysis applies with equal force to the firm's decision about which products to produce, or about whether to enter a particular market at all. The firm may decide to produce some commodity, knowing full well that it is likely not to make a profit on that commodity. It anticipates, however, that by doing so it will enhance its learning capacities, enabling it subsequently to produce another commodity at a profit. This seems to have been the case with Japanese chip manufacturers; they lost money on the first kind of chips they produced, but the learning experience enabled them to make a profit on subsequent chips.

In the Appendix we describe in more detail how localized learning combined with learning by doing affect the levels of production and the choice of technique.

2.2 Non-convexities and imperfect competition As Arrow recognized in his early essay (1962), learning by doing gives rise to non-convexities.

These non-convexities are exacerbated by the presence of localized learning and learning to learn effects.

Arrow failed, however, to grasp the full implications of these non-convexities. Non-convexities are important for at least four reasons, two of which we have already noted. First, they imply that specialization is often advantageous. Secondly, and relatedly, they imply that gradual processes of transition from (say) one labour-intensive technique to another, more capital-intensive technology, may not be optimal.

Thirdly, market equilibrium is not likely to be perfectly competitive. Unless there are perfect spill-overs to other firms, these learning by doing and learning to learn effects result in there being a natural monopoly (Dasgupta and Stiglitz, 1985).

2.3 Multiplicity of equilibria   The fourth consequence we have already discussed: the possibility of a multiplicity of equilibria. In Part II we discuss some of the implications of this multiplicity of equilibria for the macro-economic behaviour of the economy.

2.4 The importance of history   Firms' (individuals') ability to learn, as well as their state of knowledge, is critically dependent on past history. A labour shortage may induce firms to shift to a less labour-intensive technology; but subsequently, when the labour shortage is eliminated, the new technology may dominate the one previously used.

Similarly, individuals in a stagnant economy (or who work for a stagnant firm) may have limited capacities to learn. It is worth observing that they may be locked into a low level equilibrium, and not just be there as a result of excessive myopia: given their limited ability to learn, and their high rate of time preference, it may not pay them to make the current sacrifices required to develop technological capacities. It is precisely for this reason that events like wars and plagues may 'force' firms (economies) out of their current equilibrium to another one, in which there are higher rates of technological progress.

II   Macro-economic implications

There are two important macro-economic implications of our analysis. Both follow directly from our micro-economic analysis. The first is just a restatement, for the economy as a whole, of the results of the previous sub-section: history matters. The fact that some technique was employed at some time changes for ever the shape of the production possibilities schedule. And economies with different past experiences may have divergent futures.

Our analysis thus perhaps provides an explanation for the quandary we posed in the Introduction: why is it that growth rates have not converged? For our model is consistent with there being multiple equilibria. Some economies may be caught in a low level equilibrium trap. They employ technologies with limited learning capacity; and because of that they have little surplus to invest, so that they cannot proceed, without great cost, to use more capital-intensive technologies with more learning capacity.

These conclusions are reinforced if learning capacities are in fact learned. For, then, the history of low learning has perpetuating effects. These results hold both in simple descriptive growth models of the Solow variety, in life-cycle models, and in optimal growth models (or in models where it is assumed that there are infinitely lived agents maximizing their intertemporal utility).

Macro-economic trade-offs In Part I we emphasized the trade-offs facing firms; they could, in effect, sacrifice current profits (by producing more than is myopically efficient, or by choosing a technique which did not minimize current costs of production) for future profitability. At the macro-economic level, there are trade-offs as well. It may, for instance, pay society to save more than it would otherwise, in order to move quickly to the more capital-intensive technique which it eventually would like to employ; and, indeed, it may even be worthwhile for the country to experience some unemployment, using more capital-intensive techniques than are myopically desirable, because of the long-run learning benefits associated with the more capital-intensive technique.

This analysis also provides an explanation for why firms may not use more labour-intensive techniques, even in the face of a decline in wages, if they believe that the decline is temporary. The firms must compare the short-run gain of higher current profits generated by switching to more labour-intensive processes with the long-run benefits of learning associated with continuing the use of the more capital-intensive processes.

We establish these results in the next two sections.

3.   *Multiple equilibrium with localized learning*

We first postulate that the rate of labour augmenting technological progress is an increasing function of the capital intensity of the technology. Denoting the rate of labour augmenting technological progress by α we postulate that

$$\alpha = \alpha(k) \quad \alpha' > 0$$

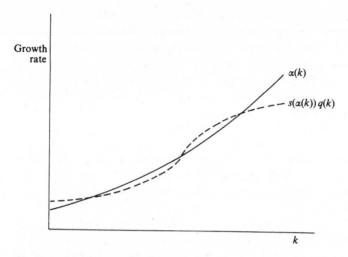

Fig. 5.4   Multiple equilibria
Note: With savings rates increasing with the rate of technological progress, and higher rates of technological progress associated with more capital intensive techniques, there may exist multiple equilibria.

where k is the capital/effective labour ratio. For simplicity, we assume a constant population. k denotes the technique of production.

We further postulate that the savings rate, s, is an increasing function of the rate of growth in income *per capita*; when income is increasing rapidly, one finds it easier to save.[7] Thus,

$$s = s\,(\alpha(k)), s' > 0$$

In steady state equilibrium, the rate of growth of capital must equal the rate of growth of the effective labour supply, i.e.

$$\frac{dK/dt}{K} = \frac{sQ}{K} = s(\alpha(k))q(k) = \alpha(k) \tag{1}$$

where Q is total output, and $q(k)$ is the output-capital ratio for technique k. q is a declining function of k; if s increases rapidly enough, there can clearly exist more than one solution to equation (1) (see Figure 5.4). In the low level equilibrium, savings rates are low because growth rates are low; and growth rates are low because of the low levels of technical progress; and the rate of technical progress is low because firms use technologies with limited potential for productivity increases.

Life-cycle version   One can easily construct a life-cycle version of this model. Consider the simplest version of the life-cycle model, where

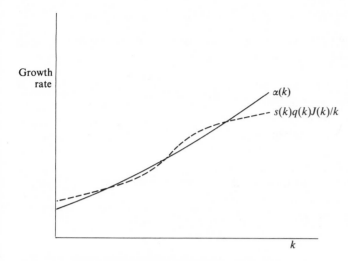

Fig. 5.5   Multiple equilibria in the life cycle model
Note: If savings rates increase with the rate of interest there may be multiple equilibria in the life cycle model.

individuals live for two periods, earning wages in the first, and saving for their retirement. Assume indifference curves are homothetic, so that savings rates are a function only of the rate of interest, which in turn is a function only of k. Steady state equilibrium is described by

$$\alpha(k)k = s(k)J(k)q(k)$$

where now $\alpha(k)$ is the ratio of output per man on technique k at time $t+1$ to that at time t, and $J(k) =$ the share of wages. If savings rates increase with k (decrease with the rate of interest), as they will if the elasticity of substitution between consumption at different dates is low and $J' \geq 0$ (the elasticity of substitution between capital and labour≤ 1), then there can exist multiple equilibria, again with the rate of technological progress higher at the more capital intensive equilibrium (see Figure 5.5).

4.   Long-run equilibrium with learning to learn

In the model of the previous section, previous learning experiences do not affect the ability to learn. To capture this, we postulate that the economy has a particular learning capacity, S, associated with each technology, k. The rate of technological progress, the reduction in labour requirements per unit of output associated with any technology k, is thus an increasing function of S; and it depends on the distance of the technology k from the actual technology being employed at time t, $k^*(t)$.

$$\alpha = b[S(k,t), k - k^*(t),k]$$

Moreover, changes in learning capacity are related to current and past learning experiences.[8]

$$dS(k,t)/dt = -gS + b[S(k,t),k - k^*(t),k] \qquad (2)$$

In steady state, we need only focus on what happens to the technology which we actually employ. Then learning capacities converge (rates of technological progress converge) to $S^*(k)$, where $S^*(k)$ is the solution to

$$b(S,0,k) = gS \qquad (3)$$

(There may not exist a unique solution to (3) for each value of k; for the moment we assume there does, and that

$$db/dk = b_1 S^{*\prime} + b_3 > 0$$

The steady state path of the economy is now described by

$$s[b(S^*(k),0,k]q(k) = b[S^*(k),0,k]$$

It is apparent that this equation is identical in form to (1), with $\alpha(k) = b[S(k),0,k]$. There thus exist multiple equilibria.

The model is, however, not identical to the previous one, because although the set of steady state solutions is the same, the dynamic paths are different. In particular, if an economy has had a low level of S (low previous learning experience), it may not immediately benefit very much from switching to a more capital-intensive technique, since its learning capacity on that capital-intensive technique, in the short run, is extremely limited.

Thus, in this model, history is even more important than in the previous one. It is more likely that a country could be 'trapped' in a low level equilibrium.

5.   *Learning by doing*

In the models of the previous two sections, learning was related to the technique employed, but not to the level of output. We now postulate that the rate of technological change is proportional to the level of output. We focus, in particular, on the rate of technical change in the technology actually being employed. Then

$$\alpha = h(a)m(S,k)Q$$

The rate of technological change increases with output, Q, is a function of the state of learning capacity, S, as well as of the technique, k, and may depend on the labour requirements per unit output, $1/a$. $h(a)$ reflects the fact that if labour requirements have already been greatly lowered, it

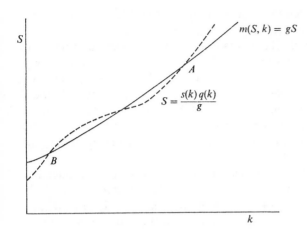

Fig. 5.6   Differing equilibrium growth rates
Note: At different equilibria, not only are techniques chosen different, but rates of growth differ.

may be more difficult to make further improvements. In particular, we now assume that

$$h(a) = a$$

Recalling that the labour supply is fixed, if we normalize it at unity, we can write,

$$Q = a$$

so that

$$a = m(S,k) = s(k)q(k) \tag{4}$$

This equation is exactly of the same form as that analysed in previous sections, with similar results.

If we postulate that S evolves in the manner described in the preceding section, the steady state solutions, in terms of growth rates and equilibrium technologies, will then be the same. Economies with lower levels of experience will never fully catch up; their productivity levels will remain lower, but the relative gaps will not increase.

The steady state paths will correspond to the solutions to (4) and

$$gS = m(S,k) \tag{5}$$

In our previous analysis, we first solved for the steady state S for each value of k. Figure 5.6 presents an alternative diagrammatic depiction of the equilibrium, not requiring the assumption that there exists a unique solution in (5) for S as a function of k.

Again different equilibria are associated not only with different ratios of capital per effective worker, but (more importantly for our purposes) with different rates of technological progress. Thus, if a high learning technology is employed, it can be sustained; and, indeed, the high rate of learning will reinforce itself. Moreover, if there are two stable equilibria, such as A and B, there will be a convergence in growth rates among the developed (high k) economies, but increasing disparities in living standards between these and the low k economies.[9]

Particular events may, moreover, move the economy from one equilibrium to another. An event such as the Black Death, by forcing a change in the technologies of production, may lead to an improvement in the new technology, and an improvement in the economy's ability to learn.

It is possible that the economy be trapped in a low performance equilibrium, even when firms are non-myopic. Given their currently low abilities to learn, it may not pay them to attempt to undertake the technologies with higher learning capacity. There is an intertemporal trade-off. Output today may be lower. On the other hand, if one believes that imperfect capital markets lead firms to use an excessively high discount rate or to be excessively risk averse, then one might argue that there are circumstances in which it will be socially desirable to undertake a switch in technology – perhaps even experiencing transitional unemployment – for the long-run gains to be had.

6.   *Policy implications*

It is not our purpose in this chapter to draw out the full policy implications of those aspects of the technology of technological change which we have emphasized here. We briefly note, however, that our analysis has important consequences, both for the choice of technique and for industrial policies. We have observed, for instance, that myopic rules for the choice of technique in LDCs may be inappropriate. LDCs have often been criticized for using 'inappropriate technologies' that is, technologies which are not cost minimizing at the (shadow) factor prices in their countries. Our analysis says that that view *may* be misguided, for if traditional technologies have less learning potential than the 'inappropriate' technologies, then LDCs may face a trade-off: current output may indeed be lower (unemployment higher) with the inappropriate technologies, but future output may be higher.

But our analysis goes one step further: we argue that future output may be higher not only because of the greater learning potential associated with the newer technologies, but also because of the increased capacity to learn that is engendered by the process of learning. Whether the learning potential of intermediate technologies, given the history of the economy up to now, is significantly lower than that for more advanced technologies is an empirical question which we cannot hope to resolve here. It does seem apparent, however, that the learning potentials in some commodities may be significantly different from those in others. We discuss the implications of this for development strategies in the concluding sections of this chapter.

III   Some speculative remarks

For generations, there have been two conflicting paradigms for development strategies. One has emphasized the importance of the principle of comparative advantage: countries should first find out what their comparative advantage is, and then exploit it. For most LDCs, with their relative abundance of labour, this would entail their pursuing labour-intensive agricultural production and labour-intensive manufacturing. Advocates of this approach preach free market and export oriented policies.

The second paradigm says that there is a natural path of development; that the LDCs should look to those who have been successful along the road to development to discover what that natural path is. Since (at least during the nineteenth century) that path, for the most part, involved heavy industrialization, devotees of this approach (including Stalin) advocated a policy of industrialization. Since the developing country seldom had a short-run comparative advantage in the production of such goods, this development strategy was associated with protectionism and the development of a domestic market (import substitution). Advocates of this view point out the marked increases in output that have often occurred in wartime, when countries have been forced to develop such inward looking strategies.

Neither argument is completely convincing, yet neither is without merit. Our analysis sheds light on both the limitations and the strengths of these views. Optimal development strategies should not, we have argued, focus on current (myopic) comparative advantage, but look at dynamic comparative advantage. At the same time, there is no persuasive reason why the pattern of development of imitators need repeat the pattern of the innovators; indeed, the fact that they are imitators gives them an advantage and a disadvantage. As imitators, they need not expend the resources that the innovators had to spend on R&D; they need not repeat the mistakes that the innovators inevitably make as they experiment with alternative technologies. But as imitators, they cannot capture the rents commonly associated with innovation. The problem of those developing today is thus fundamentally different from that facing those countries which have already developed, and one has to be careful not to learn the wrong lessons from those earlier experiences.

The case against focusing on static comparative advantage is perhaps even stronger than we have made it appear. For many countries, even were they successful in adopting today the best-practices in agriculture, with reasonable assumptions concerning labour/land/capital substitution, and even assuming that they had full access to as much capital as they wished[10] it is doubtful that output per worker would increase enough to move them into the category of the 'developed'. For these countries, if *per capita* output is to increase substantially, there must be industrialization.[11]

But that does not fully resolve either the problem of what the country's long run (dynamic) comparative advantage is, or how to ensure that the country's enterprises pursue it. In ascertaining static comparative advantage, we need only look at current resources and capabilities relative to those of other countries. In ascertaining dynamic comparative advantage, we need to look at future resources and capabilities relative to those of other countries. And these are, at best, conjectural: is there any *a priori* reason why Switzerland should have a long-run comparative advantage in watches?

Those who advocate greater government involvement in the development process have always been attracted to infant industry arguments, and they will be even more attracted to the arguments presented in this chapter. For there is a suggestion that private markets cannot solve these dynamic problems adequately.

Critics of these pro-government advocates have objected to the infant industry argument on the grounds that if it is socially profitable for an industry to develop, it is privately profitable for it to develop: no government subsidy is in fact required.[12][13] Imperfect capital markets may necessitate the government providing loans, but not protection.[14]

Our analysis has provided a criticism of this criticism: to the extent that there are diffuse externalities (which cannot easily be internalized), and to the extent that there are important economies of scale associated with technological progress and learning, there may be scope for government activity.[15] Indeed, our models provide some explanation for the often observed phenomenon that countries in wartime experience enormous growths in productivity.

Recently, Dasgupta and Stiglitz have muddied the waters further: they point out that markets in which learning by doing effects are important are inherently imperfectly competitive;[16] hence in the presence of learning by doing, one cannot rely on the standard welfare theorems to argue that market equilibrium will be efficient.

Their analysis provides, however, a hint of a theory of dynamic comparative advantage, one which can have operational significance for developing countries. There is, in their analysis, a distinct 'first mover' advantage in industries in which learning by doing is important, in contrast to a 'second mover' advantage in industries in which imitation is easy and technical progress requires large expenditures on R&D.

There is, in this perspective, a certain serendipidy in the determination of dynamic comparative advantage: being in the right place with the right idea gives the firm the advantage over followers. Being in a position to take advantage of any learning spill-overs gives neighbouring firms an advantage over more distant firms as 'imitators'.

But the localized nature of technological progress (and of learning to learn) also means that it is not always obvious what it means to be 'first'. That is, it may be possible to develop another technology (say a more labour-intensive one) for producing a commodity, to reduce the costs to using it so that the new technique dominates (at going factor prices) other available techniques.

This chapter has emphasized the importance of learning to learn, of the localized nature of learning, of the non-convexities associated with learning – giving rise to specialization, both among individuals and institutions in learning – and the consequences that these have for the structure of the economy and the rate of technological progress. But there is more to innovation and entrepreneurship: innovation and entrepreneurship reflect a set of mental attitudes and social conventions, which admit – and indeed seek out – alternative ways of thinking and performing. There are other, alternative sets of mental attitudes and social conventions which are antithetical to innovation and entrepreneurship – those which have now commonly become associated with the pejorative term 'bureaucratization' (though in the late nineteenth century and early twentieth century, the term did not have these overtones). In a sequel to this chapter, we explore the nature of social equilibrium, taking into account mental attitudes and social conventions, arguing that there are likely to be multiple equilibria, some of which are associated with stagnation, others with growth and innovation.

The relative importance of these social and attitudinal factors, compared to the technological factors on which we have focused in this chapter, has important implications for the design of development strategies.

Appendix

Learning by doing and localized technological progress

In this Appendix, we present some of the analysis behind the arguments presented in Part I of this Chapter. The Appendix is divided into three parts: in the first we analyse how learning by doing affects the optimal scale of production; in the second, we show how localized learning affects the choice of technique; and in the third, we show how learning to learn further affects the choice of technique.

Localized learning by doing postulates that the input coefficients associated with any technology are a function of the previous history of production. The greater the previous production, the lower the current input requirements. We will focus on the case where the labour input requirement at time t depends solely on cumulative output up to date t,

$$Q^* = \int_{-\infty}^{t} Q(t)dt$$

(Figure 5.7). Thus, denoting output per unit of labour by $a(t)$, we postulate that

$$a(t) = V(Q^*(t))$$
$$\dot{a} > 0 \tag{A.1}$$

Optimal scale

First, we consider the problem of a firm (country) facing a downward sloping demand for its product, with a unique method of production requiring fixed inputs of labour and machines per unit of output:

$$Q(t) = \min\left[a(t)L(t),\, b(t)K(t)\right] \tag{A.2}$$

Machines can be rented at rental r, and labour hired at wage w. The firm faces a demand curve at time t, given by $p(t) = p[Q(t),\, t]$. It will be convenient to use a revenue function,

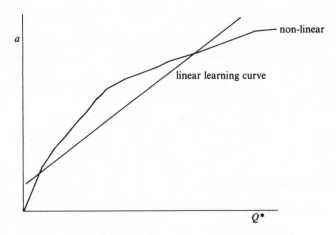

Fig. 5.7   Learning curves

$$R[Q(t), t] = p[Q(t), t]Q(t) \tag{A.3}$$

The traditional static theory of the firm argues that the level of output should be set so that marginal cost (MC) equals marginal revenue ($dR/dQ = R'$), or,

$$R' = \frac{w}{a} + \frac{r}{b} = MC \tag{A.4}$$

But when there is learning by doing, this consistently understates the optimal level of output for the firm.

From (A.1),

$$\dot{a}(t) = V' Q(t) \tag{A.5}$$

Where there is learning, the value of current output, $p(t)$, to the firm includes a term valuing the technical knowledge acquired as a by-product of production:

$$P(t) = R[Q(t), t] - Q(t) \cdot [w/a + r/b] + u(t)\dot{a}(t) \tag{A.6}$$

where $u(t)$ is the value placed on the increase in technical knowledge. u is clearly non-negative, and will be strictly positive for any firms which plans to produce any output using the given technique in the future. The firm will choose Q so as to maximize (A.6), i.e.,

$$R' + uV' = w/a + r/b \tag{A.7}$$

so that for a firm giving a positive value to technical progress, marginal revenue will be less than marginal cost.[17]

Further insight can be obtained if we rearrange terms to write

$$p - MC = (p/\text{elasticity of demand}) - \text{Value of learning} \quad (A.7')$$

Price may thus either exceed or be less than the marginal cost, depending on the value of learning and the elasticity of demand. As the elasticity of demand increases, it becomes more likely that the optimal scale of production will entail a loss, which will have to be financed either by borrowing or by government subsidy.

The extent to which static profit maximization will underestimate the optimal level of output depends on the exact value of u, and how this changes over time. To indicate the general form of solution, we can consider the special case of a firm which expects the wage rate to increase exponentially over time at the rate g,

$$w(t) = w_0 e^{gt} \quad (A.8)$$

and the demand curve to shift upward at the same rate,

$$p(Q,t) = p(Q(t)e^{-gt}) \quad (A.9)$$

Machine rentals are assumed to be constant and the learning curve is linear in cumulative output (V' is constant).

A natural counterpart of static profit maximization in this long run context is the maximization of the present discounted value of profits. The rate of discount is denoted by d (and it is assumed that $d > g$). We can show that a firm following an optimal policy will converge to a steady state where both output and labour productivity are growing at rate g. To see the nature of the solution, it is convenient to introduce trendless variables:

$$\hat{Q}(t) = Q(t)e^{-gt}$$
$$z(t) = a(t)e^{-gt} \quad (A.10)$$

Since $\dot{a} = V' Q$, for a and Q to grow at the same rate, $z(t)$ must approach $V'\hat{Q}/g$.[18] An increase in a results in a savings of labour costs of wQ/a^2. Thus u, the present discounted value of the savings, is given (letting asterisks denote steady state values) by

$$u^* = \frac{w_0 \hat{Q}^*}{dz^{*2}} = \frac{g}{d} \frac{w_0}{z^* V'} \quad (A.11)$$

Hence, from (A.7) (by assumption, R' is a function of q alone),

$$R'^* = \frac{w_0 g}{\hat{Q}^* V'} \left(1 - \frac{g}{d}\right) + \frac{r}{b} = marginal\ cost^* - \underbrace{\frac{g^2 w_0}{d\hat{Q}^* V'}}_{\text{(value of learning)}} \quad (A.12)$$

This then determines the steady state level of output, as shown in Figure 5.8. We assume that a solution to (A.12) exists, and that R' cuts the other

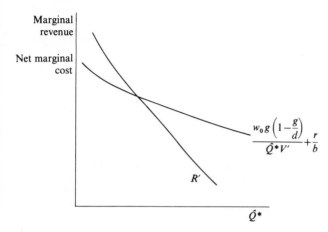

Fig. 5.8   **Steady state output** $= \hat{Q}^* e^{gt}$

curve from above (this is the dynamic equivalent of the condition that the marginal revenue curve cut the marginal cost curve from above).[19]

From (A.12) we can see that the higher the rate of growth, and the smaller the rate of discount, the more will marginal cost exceed marginal revenue – i.e., the greater will be the returns from learning by doing.

The choice of techniques

We now show that where there is localized technical progress, the myopic rule for the choice of techniques no longer obtains. Firms do not necessarily choose the technique which minimizes costs today, but must be concerned with the full dynamic consequences of alternative technique choices.

The firm has a choice of two techniques, with capital and labour coefficients denoted by b_i and a_i, $i = 1, 2$. Localization means that experience gained by using technique 1 affects only a_1 and not a_2, and vice versa. Again the firm seeks to maximize the present discounted value of profits; this means that at any time it maximizes

$$R(Q_1 + Q_2) + u_1 V'_1 Q_1 + u_2 V'_2 Q_2 - Q_1(w/a_1 + r/b_1) - Q_2(w/a_2 + r/b_2)$$

| Revenue | Value of learning | total costs on technique 1 | total costs on technique 2 |

where Q_i is the output produced using the ith technique, V'_i the learning function for the ith technique, and u_i the firm's valuation of the gain in knowledge about technique i. Hence the firm sets

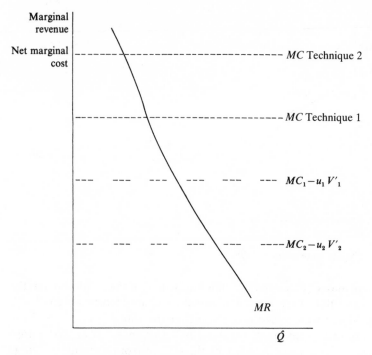

Fig. 5.9   Choice of technique for given $u_1(t)$, $u_2(t)$

$$R' = \frac{w}{a_i} - \frac{r}{b_i} + u_i V'_i, \; i = 1, 2 \text{ with equality if } Q_i > 0 \quad (A.13)$$

In other words, the firm chooses that technique for which Total Marginal Cost (*TMC*), where

$$TMC = w/a + r/b - u_i V'_i$$

is smallest; and will use both techniques (or a linear combination of the two) only if the two values of *TMC* are identical.

Were technical knowledge not specialized to one particular technique, then $u_1 = u_2$, so that if $V'_1 = V'_2 = $ constant, the firm would choose that technique that minimized marginal cost – i.e., it could behave completely myopically. But where technical progress is localized, the firm must worry about the full dynamic consequences of its decisions today. If, for instance, the firm places a sufficiently high value on knowledge about technique 2, then it may use this technique even though it has a higher cost at current factor prices. Notice from Figure 5.9 that this will mean a higher output and lower prices than with the 'static' behavioural rule of equating marginal cost and marginal revenue.

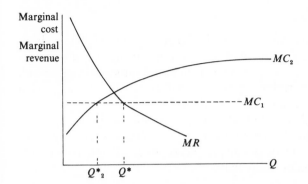

Fig. 5.10 **Learning as a non-linear function of current output:** V'_2 **depends on** Q_2

In the previous part, it was assumed that the gain in technical knowledge as a result of learning was a linear function of current output, but in reality thre may well be a non-linear relation: for a given total past output, experience is higher if spread over a longer period. In this case, it may pay to use both techniques simultaneously. An example of this is the simultaneous construction of both atomic and conventionally-fired power plants. On current factor price considerations, the latter probably dominates the former, but experience with the operation of the atomic plants provides a valuable addition to technical knowledge.[20] The return from learning by doing, however, falls rapidly with the number of plants constructed at one time. In Figure 5.10 we illustrate a particularly simple case, where $V'_1 = 0$, $V''_2 (0) < 0$, and u_1 and u_2 are given. Then the firm will produce Q^*, of which Q^*_2 will be produced by technique 2, and the remainder by technique 1.

We have shown that where there is localized learning by doing, the firm will not necessarily choose the technique that minimizes static costs. To see the implications of this non-myopic rule another way, consider a firm which knows that at some time in the future it will switch from one technique to another (more capital-intensive) one, because it expects wages to rise. When should it make the switch? According to the static myopic rule, the answer is when the marginal costs on the two machines are equal. Our rule, however, says that the switch should be made when the marginal cost on the capital-intensive technique is greater than that on the other. For, assuming that the firm knows that it will not switch back to the less capital-intensive technique, at the switch point the value of additions to knowledge on the second technique is zero, while that on the capital-intensive technique is strictly positive.

Learning to learn

Assume now that there are three technologies. Technology 0 has been well exploited in the past, so that there are no further learning possibilities. Assume, however, that the learning possibilities associated with either of the two other technologies depend in part on the learning which has previously occurred, particularly the learning of the recent past. We postulate that there is, within the firm, a certain learning capacity, denoted by S, and that the amount learned from any experience (either an expenditure on R&D, or as a by-product of production) depends on S. Thus there is learning by doing, with

$$\dot{a}_i(t)/a_i(t) = h(a_i) \, m_i(S)Q_i(t) \tag{A.14}$$

where m_i is the elasticity of learning associated with technology i, and depends on the learning capabilities

$$m = m(S), m' > 0 \tag{A.15}$$

while if technological change occurs as the result of direct expenditures, R,

$$\dot{a} = F(R,S) \tag{A.16}$$

with $F_s > 0$

Further, S itself is a function of previous (and particularly recent) learning experiences, e.g.

$$S = \int (\dot{a}(t)/a(t)) \, e^{-gt} \, dt \tag{A.17}$$

so

$$\dot{S} = -gS + \dot{a}/a$$
$$= -gS + hm(S)Q \tag{A.18}$$

Clearly, the elasticity of learning can differ across technologies. The 0 technology has been postulated to have no learning potential – i.e. $m_0 = 0$. We assume $m_1 < m_2$. Letting the shadow price associated with S be n, in presence of learning to learn and learning by doing we now choose that technique for which

$$MC_i - u_i a_i h_i m_i(S) - nh_i m_i(S) \tag{A.19}$$

is lowest.

Now, we have to take into account not only the value of learning, but of learning to learn. A technology which is inferior currently – and, indeed, might always be inferior – might be utilized simply because of its capacity to generate learning capacity (i.e., u, which is specific to the technique, may be small, but if n, which is associated with all techniques, is large, and $m(S)h$ is large enough, it may be desirable to produce with the given technique).

NOTES

1 This chapter represents in part joint work with Raaj Sah. Section II is based on earlier work done jointly with A. B. Atkinson. Financial support from the Hoover Institution and the National Science Foundation is gratefully acknowledged.

2 An analogy to computers may be instructive. It is as if a separate programme has to be inserted each time a new task is performed; it takes time to input each programme. Several programmes may be stored in core memory, but this may reduce the speed with which the computer functions.

3 Solow's work may perhaps best be thought of as the beginning of a revival of interest in technological progress, which played a pivotal role in, for instance, the work of Schumpeter.

4 In a companion paper, 'Learning to Learn, Technological Change, and the Economic and Social Structure', presented at a UN WIDER conference on 'Debt, Stabilization, and Development', in memory of Carlos Diaz Alejandro (Helsinki, August, 1986), I explore some of the determinants of the social structure which affect the rate of technological progress, and in a sequel, 'Learning to Learn, Technological Change, and Development Strategies', presented at the World Congress of the International Economic Association, Delhi, December 1986, Raaj Sah and I explore some of the implications for the development process.

5 In this perspective, the standard assumptions made in modern growth theory – whereby technological progress shifts the whole isoquant in a uniform way – can be viewed as implicitly assuming that all knowledge is 'basic'.

6 There is a second reason why it may be more difficult for firms to create their own effective information gathering/research units: the differences in styles of management between production firms and research firms are likely to be greater than, say, between the management of a coffee processing firm and a sugar refining firm. These differences themselves need to be explained – e.g., in terms of differences in technology, in the kinds of managerial problems typically faced by these organizations.

7 This conclusion does not fall inevitably from standard micro-economic assumptions; in the standard life cycle model, savings rates are related to the rates of interest as well as to rates of growth in wages.

8 In particular, if we assume that S is a discounted weighted average of previous learning experiences, with the discount factor g, then equation (2) follows.

9 This should be contrasted with the standard Solow model, which, as we have already noted, predicts convergence in growth rates and living standards. Our analysis ignores spill-overs from one economy to another, but a straightforward extension of our analysis allows for these.

10 That is, so that the return to capital, at the given levels of labour and land, was equal to the international real rate of interest.

11 This is not to say that it might not be optimal to pursue a policy of

development of agriculture for a time; but this can be at most a phase within the development process.

12 Moreover, there is no reason to believe that private firms are any less myopic than the government.

13 They have also raised the political economy objection: in fact much of what is originally justified in terms of 'infant industry' protection is maintained long after that justification is defensible. In practice, it seems difficult for governments which turn to protectionist policies to distinguish between industries in which some infant industry argument might at least be debatable and those where it appears (to us academics) as indefensible.

14 Of course, in the presence of uncertainty, loans distort behaviour. Moreover, the ability of governments to give loans at below market rates of interest (i.e., below rates of interest reflecting the true risk of the prospect) makes this instrument every bit as much subject to political abuse as protection, and perhaps more so.

15 We are cautious in suggesting that there is a scope for government activity, for clearly the consequences depend on the precise activities that the government undertakes. Frequently, government activities serve to stifle competition and (indirectly) to suppress learning and innovation, and thus are counterproductive. To the extent, for instance, that government employment diverts individuals who might otherwise have been engaged in entrepreneurial activities into the greater security of civil service employment, and fosters notions that the government should be the bearer of residual risk, government activities may have had an overall deleterious effect on growth potential.

16 Except in the implausible case where there are 100% spill-overs over a large number of firms.

17 This is analogous to Arrow's result that the social return to investment exceeded the private return.

18 $\dot{z} = V'\hat{Q} - gz$; hence $z \to V'\hat{Q}/g$

19 If there is more than one intersection, a global comparison must be made.

20 We are ignoring the problem caused by government intervention in changing the costs to the firms of the two techniques.

REFERENCES

Arrow, K. J. (1962), 'The Economic Implications of Learning by Doing', *Review of Economic Studies*.

Atkinson, A. B. and J. E. Stiglitz (1969), 'A New View of Technological Change', *Economic Journal*, September.

Dasgupta, P. and J. E. Stiglitz (1985), 'Learning by Doing, Market Structure and Industrial and Trade Policies', CEPR Discussion Paper No. 80, October.

Saah, R. K. and J. E. Stiglitz (1986), 'Learning to Learn, Technological Change, and Alternative Development Strategies', paper presented to World Congress of the International Economic Association, Delhi, December 1986, forthcoming in proceedings.

Solow, R. M. (1956), 'A Contribution to the Theory of Economic Growth', *Quarterly Journal of Economics*, pp. 65–94.

Solow, R. M. (1957), 'Technical Change and the Aggregate Production Function', *Review of Economics and Statistics*, **39** (August), pp. 312–20.
Stiglitz, J. E. (1986), 'Learning to Learn, Technological Change, and the Economic and Social Structure', paper presented to UN WIDER conference on Debt, Stabilization, and Development, Helsinki, August 1986, forthcoming in proceedings.

6 Some analytical observations on diffusion policies

PAUL STONEMAN

I Introduction

My intention in this paper is to explore government intervention in the process of diffusion. My definition of diffusion is the process by which a technology already innovated spreads across an economy.[1] Two 'stylized facts' on diffusion can usefully be presented at this stage, (i) diffusion takes time, often many years and (ii) the pattern of market penetration of a new technology often follows some S-shaped path when plotted against time. Much of the diffusion literature is concerned with 'explaining' these two stylized facts, or testing explanatory models to see to what extent they are capable of explaining observed diffusion patterns. I have surveyed such literature elsewhere, see Stoneman (1983a, 1983b, 1986). My reading of this literature is that we do not have one dominant theory or explanation of diffusion that will apply in all situations; we have instead a selection of hypotheses stressing different aspects of economic behaviour that may be more or less important in specific situations. For the majority of this paper I will concentrate on three separate frameworks that emphasise different aspects of behaviour; the first concentrates on 'strategic' behaviour, the second emphasises information and uncertainty and the third stresses differences between potential adopters. Any real world situation is likely to contain elements of all three, but we may learn a considerable amount by considering the frameworks separately.

A theme of much of my recent work on diffusion has been to emphasise that diffusion is not just the result of demand side phenomena but must be considered as the result of supply-demand interaction (see for example, Stoneman and Ireland 1983, Ireland and Stoneman 1986). This will be reflected in the work below. However, the major impact of this extension is its implications for policy analysis. Adding a supply side enables us to characterize welfare optimal diffusion paths and thus allows an evaluation of policies in terms of their welfare impact. It seems to me that in the diffusion field, policy issues for too long have been characterized by a view that 'technological change is good, so faster technological change must be better', and if this paper contributes anything, it is to consider policy in a somewhat more illuminating light. To illustrate the point, we might argue that if the characteristics of the diffusing technology are taken as predetermined, then use of a technology in a given period will be welfare optimal if for the marginal adopters, the benefits obtained from having the technology in that period rather than later (earlier) is equal to the resource cost of supplying it in that period rather than later (earlier). Extensions of use beyond this point would not be welfare improving, and thus faster technological change would not necessarily be better. One does have to be careful however, for in supply-demand models, the profits obtained by suppliers are the prize pursued in the R&D process. Changes (policies) that affect the (expectation) of these profits can affect R&D and thus the nature of the technology to be diffused. In such circumstances one cannot fully rely on conceptualizations of welfare where the technological characteristics are assumed to be given. We do take care below to avoid the trap.

The typical scenario that I have in mind for this piece is one in which industry A produces a new technology embodied in a new capital good that is used by industry B for which the new technology represents a process innovation.[2] When there is more than one firm in industry A we assume that their products are homogeneous, in that as yet I do not have satisfactory methods for dealing with product differentation. The firms in industry A are assumed to do the R&D that generates the new products they sell. Industry B sells a homogeneous product to consumers.

Most of the formal analysis in this paper is kept deliberately simple by considering only two time periods, labelled $t = 1, 2$. This framework allows one to make most of the relevant points without excessive complexity. Multi-period analysis is possible, as previous papers will illustrate, see for example, Ireland and Stoneman (1986), but we do not pursue it here.

The paper is constructed as follows. I initially consider a 'strategic' model in which some positive analysis is pursued, expectations are stressed and the effectiveness of government intervention in a positive sense is explored. Next an information-based model is explored where supplier reactions are stressed, before moving to a differences-based model for a deeper analysis of the welfare implications of policies. The last sections discuss limitations of earlier analysis, the diffusion–R&D link and policy measures not yet covered. In the majority of the paper I concentrate on two types of policies (i) information provision policies, as exemplified by the US Agricultural Extension Scheme and the Microelectronics Applications Project in the UK and (ii) subsidy (and tax) policies as exemplified by UK government treatment of digital computers in the late 1960s. It seems to me that these two characterize most diffusion orientated policies, although others are discussed at the end of the paper.

II   A strategic framework

The modelling framework we consider here is loosely based on the work of Reinganum (1981).[3] The framework abstracts from information problems and differences between potential adopters by considering a world in which all firms are aware of the existence of a new technology and its performance characteristics and all firms in the user industry are the same. The user industry is assumed to be oligopolistic with N producing firms. Entry and exit are ignored and thus N is held constant throughout. The per period profits of a typical firm will be dependent upon the number of firms using the new technology in the period (m_t, $t = 1, 2$). A non-user will make profits in time t of $\pi_0(m_t)$, a user will make profits in time t of $\pi_1(m_t)$. It is assumed that $\pi_1(m_t) - \pi_0(m_t)$ is declining in m, and thus as use extends, the per period profit gain from adoption declines. The new technology is assumed to be supplied at prices p_1 and p_2 in periods 1 and 2 respectively. There is a discount rate r.

Consider the second period first. The equilibrium number of second period users will be m_2 where m_2 satisfies.

$$\pi_1(m_2) - \pi_0(m_2) = p_2 \qquad (1)$$

It is assumed that this second period equilibrium is attained. In the first period the adoption decision has two steps. An adopter must find adoption profitable and also first period adoption must be more profitable than second period adoption. If we use an e superscript to represent a first period expectation of a second period outcome, m_1, the number of first period adopters must satisfy (2) and (3)

$$\pi_1(m_1) + v\,\pi_1(m_2^e) - \pi_0(m_1) - v\,\pi_0(m_2^e) \geqq p_1 \qquad (2)$$

$$\pi_1(m_1) - \pi_0(m_1) \geqq p_1 - vp_2^e \qquad (3)$$

where $v \equiv 1/(1+r)$.

However, given that firms realize that (1) holds then one may assume that $p_2^e = \pi_1(m_2^e) - \pi_0(m_2^e)$ and thus (2) may immediately be rewritten as (3). In equilibrium m_1 will thus be determined by (3) holding as an equality. It is assumed that this first period equilibrium is attained and thus m_1 is determined by (4).

$$\pi_1(m_1) - \pi_0(m_1) = p_1 - vp_2^\varsigma \tag{4}$$

We assume here, and throughout the paper that $N > m_2 > m_1 > 0$, and thus there is a diffusion path. Two special cases of (4) are worth noting; (a) myopia, where $p_2^\varsigma = p_1$ and

$$\pi_1(m_1) - \pi_0(m_1) = rvp_1 \tag{5}$$

and (b), perfect foresight, where $p_2^\varsigma = p_2$ and

$$\pi_1(m_1) - \pi_0(m_1) = p_1 - vp_2^\varsigma \tag{6}$$

As it has been assumed that firms know of and about the new technology, in this modelling framework there is no role for information policies. However, subsidy policies may operate, in some cases, to increase use. Let there be subsidy rates paid to adopters of s_1 and s_2 in the first and second periods respectively and let s_2^ς be the first period expectation of the second period subsidy rate. Such subsidies will reduce the effective cost of second period acquisition to $p_2(1-s_2)$ and from (1) it is immediately clear that a second period subsidy will increase the level of use of the technology in period 2.

Under myopia, it is reasonable to assume that $s_2^\varsigma = s_1$ and (5) can be written as (5a)

$$\pi_1(m_1) - \pi_0(m_1) = rvp_1(1-s_1) \tag{5a}$$

Thus a first period subsidy will increase first period use. Under perfect foresight $s_2^\varsigma = s_2$, and (6) may be written as (6a)

$$\pi_1(m_1) - \pi_0(m_1) = p_1(1-s_1) - vp_2(1-s_2) \tag{6a}$$

Here we may observe that a first period subsidy will act to increase first period use but a second will act to decrease first period use. This is, of course, not surprising. A second period subsidy cheapens second period acquisition making it relatively more attractive; a first period subsidy makes first period acquisition more attractive. The point to be made, however, is that although a subsidy applied in period t makes acquisition more attractive in that period, expectations of future subsidies can reduce usage in the current period. This is not, of course, a startling result, but it has rarely been stressed in diffusion studies.

From the arguments above we may thus deduce that the effects of subsidy on the time path of usage will depend on (a) the relative intertemporal subsidies, (b) the expectations of the relative subsidies, and (c) the absolute size of the subsidies.

One should note before proceeding, however, that in this framework it is assumed that $\pi_1(m_t) - \pi_0(m_t)$, the profit gain from acquisition, declines as m_t increases. There may be a number of technologies for which this assumption is invalid. For example, in telecommunications, benefits might increase as usage extends. Consideration of such technologies raises further policy issues, but we do not consider them here.

III   Information-based models

The literature includes a number of approaches to diffusion that stress the information and/or uncertainty issues involved. Perhaps the most well known is the Mansfield type epidemic learning model, see Mansfield (1968), but more rational models based on Bayesian learning do exist, see Stoneman (1980) and Jensen (1982). I have the impression that implicitly this approach to diffusion underlies a number of policy initiatives in the field. My intention in this section is to argue that if one considers suppliers' reactions (Industry A's reactions) to government policy, then the normal simple expectations as to how government information provision will affect the diffusion path must be re-assessed. Later we will also make some comments on how more complicated learning models have some lessons for us.

The simple learning model, say an epidemic model, basically allows that we have a new technology that is superior to the old (and prices develop so as to keep it so), but limited knowledge on the existence of this technology limits its use. However, knowledge is spread by interpersonal contact. Thus in a two period framework.

$$
\begin{aligned}
m_1 &= \alpha_1 N \\
m_2 &= \alpha_2 N \\
\alpha_2 &= F(\alpha_1, m_1, N) \ F_1 > 0, F_2 > 0, F_3 < 0 \\
0 &\le \alpha_t \le 1
\end{aligned}
\tag{7}
$$

where α_t = proportion of the population who know of the technology in time t, m_t, N as above.

Government information provision policy may directly stimulate α_1 (and thus α_2 indirectly) or α_2, to increase use. Of course given that the technology is superior, welfare would be improved by increased use if the information policy costs are ignored.

My main objection to this simple result is that it takes no account of the industry supplying the goods embodying the new technology or the reaction of that industry to the policy. Consider for example a monopolist supplier. Such a supplier may well provide information to potential buyers through, for example, advertizing. If he does so, he is likely to advertize to the point where the marginal profitability of extra advertizing is zero. A government financed programme of information provision will then have the effect of making the monopolist's marginal advertizing less profitable, and his advertizing will be cut back. The point is that the government provision of information may lead to reduced private provision. Of course the monopolist supplied information may be better/worse, more persuasive or less persuasive than government supplied information or the government's information provision costs may be less/more than those of the monopolist, and thus it is difficult to predict the overall impact of government information provision on the diffusion path, but the point is made. If the supply industry were competitive and suppliers were unable to appropriate the benefit of any advertizing that they undertook, then any information provision by government would be unlikely to be offset by reductions in suppliers' efforts, for they may already be near zero, and the government effort would represent a net addition.

These simple epidemic models are, however, only the tip of the iceberg when information and uncertainty are discussed. In another paper Paul David and I have considered information policies in a model where suppliers use prices to affect information by stimulating m_1, and thus indirectly m_2, and considered the impact of policies of subsidy and information provision in such a model. Here, however, I want to consider an alternative story, one concentrating not on knowledge of existence, but on the perception of characteristics by potential users of the technology.

In Stoneman (1980), diffusion is considered in the following framework. A potential buyer of new technology is assumed to be informed on existence but unsure of the 'true' characteristics of a new technology. A technology is characterized by the mean and variance of its returns. The true mean and variance of the old technology are known. The potential buyer forms expectations of the mean and variance of returns to the new technology by updating priors in a Bayesian way using information gained from earlier use. The buyer is assumed to maximize a utility function defined on the overall mean and variance of returns, made up of a weighted sum of the means and variances of returns to the two technologies, the weights reflecting his level of use of the technologies. In the initial period, given his priors, a certain level of use of new technology will be determined. The experience gained from this use will lead to the updating of the prior and a different optimal level of use in the second period. The Bayesian process ensures that the updated priors will tend over time to the 'true' values of the mean and variance of returns to the new technology.

In such a framework, extra information on existence will not affect the diffusion path. Firms require firm-specific information on 'what the technology can do for them'. The UK government in the Microelectronics Applications Project has had policies of free provision and subsidization of consultancy services. This is more appropriate in this environment, and may be considered to act directly on the priors. Subsidies to new technology will act to increase the (mean) return to the new technology. However

(a)   consultancy arrangements may not act to increase use. If the consultancy leads to a reduction in the prior estimate of the mean return this may reduce usage. This, however, would be welfare improving, for it would reduce the number of 'mistakes' made in adopting new technology.

(b)   The subsidy will act to increase use. The effect, in welfare terms, of this may be two-fold; (i) the increased use will lead to faster learning and thus fewer mistakes later on but (ii) in those cases where the prior expectations of returns are too optimistic it will only act to reinforce errors already made, and this will involve some welfare cost. Even where priors are not too optimistic, one would require, for welfare optimality in the absence of market failures, that the subsidy declines as the 'true' mean and variance of returns to the new technology are approached.

There is, in the above, already a hint that potential adopters may differ from one another. It is to such a framework that we now turn.

IV   Differences-based models

In a variety of papers in conjunction with Norman Ireland, I have explored diffusion paths in models where potential buyers differ from one another. The 'standard' version of these models can be characterized as follows. The population of potential adopters is of size N, and adoption is completed by the acquisition of one unit of a new capital good. There is perfect information on existence and the benefits to be obtained from use of new technology. The benefit an adopter receives from ownership of the new technology is determined solely by his ranking in the population. Thus the Xth ranked adopter will receive $g_t(X)$ in time t, whereas the $X+1^{th}$ adopter will receive $g_t(X+1)$. It is assumed that $g'_t(X) < 0$, and thus the lower the ranking (the higher X), the less is the benefit. Given adopters only buy one unit, and assuming no depreciation, if X_t is the rank of the marginal adopter in time t, then the stock of new capital goods in time t is X_t.

If we allow there to exist subsidy rates of s_1 and s_2 in periods one and two respectively, we may immediately proceed to state that X_2, the extent of use in period 2, the rank of the marginal adopter in period 2, is given by

$$g_2(X_2) = p_2(1-s_2) \tag{8}$$

and X_1, the extent of first period use and the rank of the first period marginal adopter is given by either of two conditions

$$g_1(X_1) + vg_2(X_1) - p_1(1-s_1) = 0 \tag{9}$$

$$g_1(X_1) + vg_2(X_1) - p_1(1-s_1) = vg_2(X_1) - vp_2^e(1-s_2^e) \tag{10}$$

which we call respectively the profitability and arbitrage conditions. In what follows we will interpret $g_t(X_t)$ as reflecting not only the private benefit but also the social benefit received from the use of the new technology by the Xth ranked user.

On the supply side, we assume there are n firms, each of whom has costs, C_1 and C_2, in periods one and two that are invariant with respect to output. It is assumed that these costs fall over time and $C_1 > vC_2$. It will be further assumed that these costs reflect the social cost of resources used in production. Without derivation, I can state under these assumptions that welfare optimal diffusion (where welfare is defined as the difference between the social benefit from use and the social cost of producing the capital goods that embody the new technology), is realised when

$$g_2(X_2) = C_2 \tag{11}$$

and $$g_1(X_1) = C_1 - vC_2 \tag{12}$$

To evaluate policy initiatives, it is clear given our information assumptions that there is no role for information policies. To fully explore subsidies we have to proceed a bit at a time. Let us start by assuming that the supply industry is perfectly competitive, thus $p_1 = C_1$ and $p_2 = C_2$. If $s_1 = s_2 = s_2^e = 0$, and we assume perfect foresight on the part of buyers then (8), (9) and (10) reduce to

$$g_2(X_2) = p_2 = C_2 \tag{13}$$

and, because (10) will dominate (9),

$$g_1(X_1) = p_1 - vp_2 = C_1 - vC_2 \tag{14}$$

which are of course the same as (11) and (12), the welfare optimality conditions. Given this, it is clear that those values of s_1 and s_2 that yield increases in use beyond this point will be welfare suboptimal. Thus using

(8) and (10) given $s^e = s_2$, if $s_2 > 0$, X_2 will increase beyond optimal use, and also, if $p_1(1-s_1) - vp_2(1-s_2) < p_1 - vp_2$, X_1 will extend beyond optimal use. It is also clear that if $s_2/s_1 > C_1/(vC_2)$, then the subsidy programme could decrease first period use. Basically, however, given our assumptions of perfect competition and buyers' perfect foresight, no intervention is necessary or desirable.

If we relax the assumption of perfect competition in capital goods supply our results will change. If the buyers have perfect foresight, a present value maximizing monopolist will price such that marginal revenue, appropriately defined, is equal to marginal costs, appropriately defined. We may state these conditions as that, with zero subsidies,

$$g_2(X_2) + X_2g_2'(X_2) = C_2 \tag{15}$$

and $\quad g_1(X_1) + X_1g_1'(X_1) = C_1 - vC_2 \tag{16}$

Assuming $Xg(X)$ has positive first and negative second derivatives, and that $g'(X) < 0$, it is immediately clear that without subsidy X_1 and X_2 are below their optimal values as defined by (11) and (12). As we have already discussed in earlier frameworks the implications of different intertemporal subsidies we will proceed from here with the simplest case where $s_1 = s_1 = s_2^g = s > 0$. Then with a subsidy rate s, the monopolist will price such that

$$g_2(X_2) + X_2g_2'(X_2) = C_2(1-s) \tag{17}$$

and $\quad g_1(X_1) + X_1g_1'(X_1) = (1-s)(C_1 - vC_2) \tag{18}$

with $\quad p_2 = g_2(X_2)/(1-s) \tag{19}$

and $\quad p_1 = (g_1(X_1) - vg_2(X_2))\dfrac{1}{(1-s)} \tag{20}$

From (17) and (18) it is clear that a positive subsidy could correct some of the underproduction imposed by the monopolisation of the supply sector if $Xg(X)$ has a negative second derivative. However, it is also clear from (17) and (18) in comparison with (11) and (12) that with a *constant* rate of subsidy, the welfare optimum cannot be achieved.

The basic difference between the competition and the monopoly case is that for the former, usage extends to the point where the marginal user receives benefits equal to the (opportunity) resource cost of generating them, and the subsidy pushes usage of technology to users with lower benefits, whereas under monopoly, without subsidy the marginal user receives benefits greater than the cost of their provision and extensions of use beyond this point will still imply users having benefits greater than the cost of their provision.

One could of course consider oligopolistic structures in the supply industry but basically the results will lie between the competition and monopoly cases. Of more interest is to consider the case where buyers of the technology do not have perfect foresight but are myopic. In this case, assuming $p_2^e = p_1$, $s_2^e = s_2 = s_1 = s$, the demand equations are

$$g_2(X_2) = p_2(1-s)$$

and given that under myopia (9) dominates (10),

$$g_1(X_1) + vg_2(X_1) = p_1(1-s)$$

With a perfectly competitive supply industry $p_1 = C_1$, $p_2 = C_2$, and usage in periods 1 and 2 without subsidy will extend to the point where

$$g_2(X_2) = C_2$$
$$g_1(X_1) + vg_2(X_1) = C_1$$

Given that $X_1 \leq X_2$, then $g_2(X_1) \geq g_2(X_2) = C_2$, and it is clear that $vg_2(X_1) \geq vC_2$. By comparison with (12), the level of use of the new technology in period 1 may be seen to be beyond the welfare optimal level. This result basically arises because the reducing cost of the technology ($C_1 > vC_2$) is not taken account of by first period buyers under myopia. Thus with myopia, and competitive supply, use of the technology may extend too far. The obvious solution is a first period *tax*, not a first period subsidy.

With monopolistic supply, and a zero subsidy, X_1 and X_2 will be determined such that the level of use is less than under competitive supply. Although it does not work out quite so neatly in a two period framework, in Stoneman and Ireland (1986) we show in an infinite horizon model that the monopolist facing myopic buyers will price so that the welfare optimality conditions are satisfied. There is thus no need for a tax or subsidy, although a subsidy would extend use of the technology. These results have three important messages:

(1) They stress that the need for and the impact of subsidies will depend upon the structure of the industry supplying the new technology.
(2) They emphasize the welfare aspects of policy, indicating that in some cases policies that extend usage may not be welfare improving and
(3) They emphasize that expectations on the part of buyers are an important factor to consider in analyzing the impact of technology policy.

These results, however, do have some limitations. I wish to concentrate on two of them in the following sections.

(a)   A limited concept of welfare optimality is being considered whereby the availability of the technology is presumed, and

(b)   They are limited to a closed economy context.

The first of these we discuss in the context of the R&D/diffusion linkage. The second we treat here by one sketchy scenario rather than in a complete way. Consider a scenario where the capital good is imported at prices $\bar{p}_1$ and $\bar{p}_2$ and is then purchased by potential users. If we assume that in the rest of the domestic economy prices reflect social cost, then the price of the imports can be allowed to represent the social cost of paying for them.

Then,

$$W = \int_0^{X_1} g_1(X)dX + v\int_0^{X_2} g_2(X)dX - \bar{p}_1 X_1 - v\bar{p}_2(X_2 - X_1)$$

and welfare is maximized where

$$g_1(X_1) = \bar{p}_1 - v\bar{p}_2$$
$$g_2(X_2) = \bar{p}_2$$

If buyers have perfect foresight, then from (13) and (14) use of the technology will extend to exactly this point, and we will have welfare optimality. Under myopia first period use will extend beyond the welfare optimal point and usage will be excessive. The point to make is that the expectations issue is still important. Of course, if elsewhere in the economy there are imperfections implying that $\bar{p}_1$ and $\bar{p}_2$ do not reflect the social cost of providing these machines, or the integrals of $g(X)$ over X do not reflect the social benefit derived from the use of the machines, then these results would have to change.

There are of course many other issues involved in dealing with the open economy case, but as they are not at present really clear in my own mind I do not pursue them further here.

IV   Diffusion and R&D

There are a number of ways in which diffusion and R&D can be linked. One possibility is technological search expenditures by potential adopters, see, for example, Mowery (1983). However, the link I wish to explore is that between the diffusion process itself and the expenditure incurred in inventing and innovating the new technology that is diffused. The link is established because it is the expectations of profits in the supplying industry that are generated during the diffusion process which are the incentive to develop the technology in the first place. To be more dynamic one might argue that the expectation of profits generated by changing the diffusion pattern will provide the incentive to improve a new technology as it matures.

The implications of this link for technology policy arise by two main routes. The first is direct, the second is via expectations.

If, for the sake of argument, we consider that firms undertaking R&D can perfectly forecast profits and policies in the diffusion process, we can establish the direct links quite strongly.

(1)   We showed in the previous section that the welfare optimal diffusion path in that model could be achieved under monopoly supply with myopic buyers or with competitive supply with buyers having perfect foresight. However under the latter regime the suppliers make no profits, under the former the suppliers make maximal profits. Thus under one regime there is no incentive to do R&D, under the other there is a maximal incentive. Without going into details it is clear that this will have implications for both patent and anti-trust policy. The new insight provided here is that the need for a patent policy will depend on the expectations of potential buyers of the new technology.

(2)   When subsidies are discussed it is often not considered that with some monopoly power in the supply of new technology, these subsidies will affect the profit performance of new technology suppliers. This will then impact on the incentives to undertake R&D. In fact it can be argued that not only subsidy but also information provision policies can have this effect. We have thus established a link between diffusion policies and R&D incentives. This raises a common issue in technology policy circles – should financial incentives be given for R&D, or should the incentives be directed at users of new technology with the resulting profit given to suppliers acting as an incentive to R&D?

(3)   The final point to raise in terms of the direct connection is to do with welfare optimality in R&D. When R&D policy is considered, the diffusion pattern is usually ignored, and diffusion is generally considered instantaneous. Judgements are then made on the basis of comparing the cost of R&D to the extent of the advance achieved. Once the link is established some new issues come into play. In particular, as R&D expenditure leads to changes in technology, those changes will affect the diffusion paths and by doing so affect the welfare generated on the diffusion paths. The point is that welfare gains generated by policies directed at R&D may possibly be offset by welfare losses because of the resultant impact on the diffusion path.

With regard to expectations the two following points seem relevant.

(a)   Just as expectations of price reductions can lead to lower levels of use of new technology today, so can expectations of technological improvements. If government policy is to subsidize the

R&D process, this may lead to expectations of price reductions or technological improvements that reduce current demand for a technology.

(b)   We have discussed earlier how expectations of future subsidies or policies can affect the diffusion path. Given the link to R&D, these changes may themselves affect the R&D effort with a consequent feedback on the diffusion path.

I would argue that the way forward, because of the existence of the R&D–diffusion link, in the whole area of technology policy, must be one that treats the process of technological change as a whole – not one treating its three components of invention, innovation and diffusion as separated elements. The comments above are a start in the pursuit of such a treatment.

VI   Some qualifications

The discussions above may seem somewhat definitive in terms of their policy prescriptions, but I consider that a number of cautionary reservations must be made.

(1)   We have considered a number of analytical frameworks separately. When the real world has a combination of forces driving the diffusion process it could well be that in policy terms these forces counteract each other. For example in Stoneman and David (1986) we combine an epidemic and a differences-based model. There, extensions of use in period 1 brought about by policy may involve usage by firms where benefits are less than the costs of supplying those benefits (and thus costly in welfare terms), but the extended usage generates welfare gains by increasing second period knowledge. The two impacts counteract each other.

(2)   The modelling frameworks we have used often make specific assumptions that crucially affect the results e.g. in the differences-based approach we assumed suppliers' costs (C_1 and C_2) were given. If these costs are in fact related to cumulative output (learning by doing), the results would be different, see David and Olsen (1984).

(3)   Our work has concentrated on technologies that are another industry's new processes. We have not considered in any detail innovations that give rise to new consumer products. We cannot guarantee that our results would be unchanged when looking at this other case.

(4)   Although it has been touched upon, the full implications of openness of the economy are yet to be explored.

(5)   The welfare analysis we have undertaken is very much dependent upon assumptions that markets clear and prices reflect opportunity costs. I am in general sceptical of such assumptions. In alternative frameworks

welfare analyses perhaps ought to consider the impact of diffusion on employment. This is an issue I have discussed elsewhere (e.g. Waterson and Stoneman, 1985,) but not one for which I have explored policy issues in any great depth.

(6) The majority of this essay has concentrated on information and subsidy policies. Diffusion policy does of course contain other initiatives e.g. skill and training programmes, demonstration projects etc. Although in many cases these other instruments could be interpreted in terms of subsidies or information packages, it is possible that by so doing we will be missing something. One policy that cannot fit into the subsidy/information framework is government co-ordination of standards. But fortunately others are considering this issue.

(7) The final reservation I state is that the analytical frameworks I have discussed tend to fit into the neoclassical paradigm. Alternative approaches, e.g. Nelson and Winter (1982) may provide different insights and have different policy implications.

VII Conclusions

In this paper I have made an attempt to discuss a number of issues that arise when government policies aimed at speeding up the take-up of new technology are discussed. I have stated a number of reservations in the previous section, but even so, some conclusions ride above these reservations. In particular I wish to stress; (a) that faster take-ups are not necessarily welfare improving; (b) that supply side responses are crucial in determining the impact of any particular policy; (c) that expectations are important, both in terms of how the expectations environment affects the desirability of policy and in how expectations of policies will affect their impact and (d) that R&D and diffusion are inextricably linked, and any policy aimed at either will affect the other. If nothing else is clear, these conclusions suggest that appropriate diffusion policies are perhaps much more difficult to design than often seems to have been suggested in the past, although David (1985) is a notable exception to this general rule.

NOTES

1 At this time I will not extend the analysis to diffusion across national borders.
2 It is not a major step to reinterpret our findings in terms of consumer goods innovation, but this is not a step we take here.
3 Reinganum considers her model to be strategic, which is why I use the label.

However, Quirmbach (1986) argues that the strategic label is misleading. This does not affect our arguments or results.

REFERENCES

David, P. A. (1985), 'New Technology Diffusion, Public Policy and Industrial Competitiveness', paper presented at the Symposium on Economics and Technology, March 17–19, Stanford, Ca., USA.

David, P. A. and T. Olsen (1984), 'Anticipated Automation: A Rational Expectations Model of Technological Diffusion', Centre for Economic Policy Research, Publication No. 24 (CEPR, Technological Innovation Program Working Paper No. 2), Stanford, Ca., USA, April.

Ireland, N. and P. Stoneman (1986), 'Technological Diffusion, Expectations and Welfare', *Oxford Economic Papers*, **38**, 283–304.

Jensen, R. A. (1982), 'Adoption and Diffusion of an Innovation of Uncertain Profitability', *Journal of Economic Theory*, **27**, 182–93.

Mansfield, E. (1968), *Industrial Research and Technological Innovation*, W. W. Norton, New York.

Mowery, D. (1983), 'Economic Theory and Government Technology Policy', *Policy Sciences*, **16**, 27–43.

Nelson, R. and S. G. Winter (1982), *An Evolutionary Theory of Economic Change*, Cambridge, Mass., Harvard University Press.

Quirmbach, H. C. (1986), 'The Diffusion of New Technology and the Market for an Innovation', *Rand Journal of Economics*, Spring, **17**, No. 1, pp. 33–47.

Reinganum, J. (1981), 'On the Diffusion of New Technology: A Game Theoretic Approach', *Review of Economic Studies*, **48**, 395–405.

Stoneman, P. (1980), 'The Rate of Imitation, Learning and Profitability', *Economics Letters*, **6**, 179–83.

(1983a), *The Economic Analysis of Technological Change*, Oxford University Press.

(1983b), 'Theoretical Approaches to the Analysis of the diffusion of new technology', in S. Macdonald *et al.* (eds.), *The Trouble with Technology*, London, Frances Pinter (Publishers) Ltd.

(1986), 'Technological Diffusion – the Viewpoint of Economic Theory', *Ricerche Economiche*, forthcoming.

Stoneman, P. and N. Ireland (1983), 'The Role of Supply Factors in the Diffusion of New Process Technology', *Economic Journal*, Supplement, March, 1983, 65–77.

Stoneman, P. and P. David (1986), 'Adoption Subsidies vs. Information Provision as Instruments of Technology Policy', RES/AUTE Conference Supplement, *Economic Journal*, March.

Waterson, M. and P. Stoneman (1985), 'Employment, Technological Diffusion and Oligopoly', *International Journal of Industrial Organization*, **3**, No. 3, 327–44.

7 International trade and technology policy*

BRUCE LYONS

'Compare the situation of Great Britain at present, with what it was two centuries ago. All the arts, both of agriculture and manufacturers, were extremely rude and imperfect. Every improvement, which we have since made, has arisen from our imitation of foreigners; and we ought so far to esteem it happy, that they had previously made advances in arts and ingenuity . . . The commodity is first imported from abroad, to our great discontent, while we imagine that it drains us of our money: afterwards, the art itself is gradually imported, to our visible advantage: yet we continue still to repine, that our neighbours should possess any art, industry, and invention: forgetting that, had they not first instructed us, we should have been at present barbarians; and did they not still continue their instructions, the arts must fall into a state of languor, and lose that emulation and novelty which contribute so much to their advancement' (David Hume, 1758).[1]

'. . . it may be laid down as a general Proposition, which very seldom fails, That operose or complicated Manufactures are cheapest in rich Countries; – and raw Materials in poor ones . . . No Man can set Bounds to Improvements even in Imagination; and therefore, we may still be allowed to assert, that the richer manufacturing Nation will maintain its Superiority over the poorer one, notwithstanding this latter may be likewise advancing towards Perfection.' (Reverend Josiah Tucker, 1758; as quoted in Hufbauer, 1970).

The international dimension of technology policy is not nearly as new as most of the references at the end of this chapter might suggest. The remarkable coincidence of Hume and Tucker's publication dates in 1758 came nearly 20 years before Smith's theory of the division of labour, almost 60 years before Ricardo's theory of comparative advantage, and over two centuries before what we now call the 'new' technological

* Helpful comments have been received from John Black, Steve Davies, Peter Townroe and several participants at the London conference. As usual, however, the burden of responsibility for any errors rests firmly on the author's shoulders.

theories of international trade were put together in reaction to the Leontief paradox and post-War dollar shortage. Without Ricardo's insight, Tucker's technology gap and Hume's product cycle were each invoked in an attempt to find a theoretical foundation to stave off the prevailing policy of protectionism. It is ironic that technology theories are nowadays more likely to be invoked as a justification *for* protection.[2] A major purpose behind this essay is to provide an understanding of, though not necessarily support for, the protectionist arguments.

The idea of technology-based trade may be old, but a full investigation of the welfare consequences, and thus policy implications, has had to await progress in the technology of economic theory. We are still a long way from a comprehensive understanding, but at least the bounds of our ignorance have been reduced. It is with genuine humility (I refer to none of my own writings below!), and a clear warning not to take any of the policy recommendations too literally, that I offer the following paper.

The theory of economic policy can be either normative or positive. The aim of a normative policy recommendation is to increase some measure of aggregate social welfare.[3] The positive theory of economic policy eschews such worthy objectives, concentrates on the welfare gains and losses of various groups within society, and translates these into political pressure and lobbying activity designed to directly influence actual policy decisions. Whilst it is important to separate the positive from the normative, what makes the international context so interesting is that the two become inter-twined because governments are naturally inclined to look to the national interest (a well defined, if heterogeneous, interest group) rather than maximize global welfare.

The 'selfishness' of national governments introduces crucial areas of conflict into the theory and practice of technology policy that are easily overlooked in the closed economy analyses to be found in so much of the literature (including in this volume). International progress is not as simple as getting backward countries to emulate the USA or Germany or Japan or whatever idyll is currently fashionable. Although the 'technical progress game' is not zero sum, there are many occasions in which one country loses out as another progresses. To ignore such possibilities or to assert that the gains inevitably outweigh the losses would be a dangerous example of ostrich economics. Even if Albanian isolationism has been shown to remove the benefits of trade that Hume first noticed, this is insufficient evidence to argue against protection or in favour of freer trade at the margin. Nor does it say very much about the international consequences of R&D subsidies (an area in which the GATT rules are quite ineffective). In order to tackle such issues, an explicitly international approach is required.

Both the literature and the issues to be discussed are vast. It is therefore impossible to provide a full survey in a short paper. Useful supplementary reviews are provided by Cheng (1984a) and Soete (1985) (see also Roman and Puett, 1982, for a 'business school' review). What I hope to give is an overview which places the various strands in a coherent framework and draws out the implications for technology policy. Section I identifies the main elements which distinguish the distinctively international from the national dimensions of technology policy. Section II outlines the standard technology gap and product cycle models and briefly summarises the empirical literature. Section III moves on to review the more formal international trade literature, which explicitly models social welfare and is thus able to provide some policy pointers. The ways in which technological progress can be harmful to some countries (i.e. immiserizing) are fully discussed. Such possibilities are important for policy makers to understand, but should not necessarily be taken to be the normal state of affairs. Immiserization possibilities are most clearly illustrated by assuming that technological change is exogenous and costless, and this assumption is made throughout Section III. Section IV directly tackles the endogeneity of technology in an open economy, and Section V discusses technology policy when more than one country can be innovative and there are profitable export markets to fight over. Such models provide insight into, for instance, some of the worries that businessmen have over Japanese trade policies.

Finally, it is worth making two general observations. Firstly, the variety of models reviewed reflects not so much disagreement between economists, as the diversity of technology-related issues in the world economy. Secondly, a major gap in this review is that the problem of technologically induced unemployment is hardly touched on. This is because the literature is so sparse, which in turn reflects the lack of a generally agreed theory of unemployment.

I   Distinctively international dimensions of technology

Compare an autarkic economy with one open to international trade and competition. What features are magnified in or unique to the open economy?

(i)   Greater diversity of geniuses[4]

This may simply be a matter of there being more brains at work on the same problem. Alternatively, inventive talent may be inspired by different local environments and the consequent problems revealed (e.g. climate or typical housing stock). In both ways, the sum total of available ideas is magnified in an open economy.

(ii)   Larger market size

The size of the potential market is a key incentive to inventive and innovative activity. A given cost reduction is spread over more units of output and new products can find more potential customers. However, in an open economy inventors are likely to face more competition and, from a simple Schumpeterian viewpoint, this could be a disincentive. The net effects require more detailed modelling and this is taken up in Section IV.

(iii)   Different histories

Differing histories of industrialization give differing experiences and so differing levels of technological attainment to different countries (Arrow, 1962). Legal and institutional differences (e.g. the patent system or lack of it) are influenced by and contribute to such divergences. Furthermore, given that countries have had differing factor prices and factor availabilities, at least at some time in their past, it is almost certain that they will have developed different types of technology. As Atkinson and Stiglitz (1969) have noted, progress based on 'localized' learning does not shift out of the entire production function, but improvements take place only around those technologies in current use. In this way, history can greatly magnify what were once very small, environmentally induced differences.[5] Finally, the history of human capital accumulation, especially that applicable to R&D activity and its exploitation, will result in different capabilities to engage in technological progress. Importantly, such factors can lead to a world in which one country inherits a technological lead over another.

(iv)   Separate governments

When it comes to policy issues, this is what really matters. Two major implications will be investigated. Firstly, if technological progress leads to a change in the *terms of trade*, this leads to a change in the world distribution of income, and the possibility arises of a reduction in the welfare of some parts of the world. Secondly, economists have recently begun to examine a new role for technology policy in *shifting profits* from foreign to domestic firms. The underlying power that governments have is that they can sometimes make more credible commitments than can firms. For instance, in the early stages of the 'race' to make a supersonic passenger aircraft, it soon became clear that there would be room for only one project to make the massive investments required: that project might have been American had it not been for commitments given by the British and French governments that they would stay in the race. A mere promise by the European firms involved, on their own, might not have been sufficient to keep the Americans out because their greater experience at aircraft manufacture could have given them the edge.[6] If governments see fit to intervene, then apart from the usual technology policy instruments (e.g. R&D subsidies, patents, royalties), a new array of implements designed to act initially on international trade, but indirectly also on technology and its consequences, becomes available (e.g. tariffs, quotas, export subsidies).

II   Empirical background

The papers by Posner (1961) and Vernon (1966) provided the original stimulus behind most empirical work on technology and trade. Posner's technology gap, G (measured in, say, years), represents the difference between the time it takes for foreign firms to imitate production, L, and the lag before foreign consumers begin to demand the new innovation, D. Thus, $G = L - D$ and international trade is an increasing function of G. Placing his model in a dynamic setting, Posner implicitly agreed with the Rev. Tucker in arguing that technology gaps can be self-perpetuating as one innovation leads to another. Most simply this may be due to the creation of dynamic enterprises or R&D teams. Alternatively, innovations may be demand-induced and so be cumulative (e.g. fast engines require speed resistant tyres and disc brakes; also the spinning jenny created the need for a weaving innovation, the flying shuttle, to relieve bottlenecks). Posner expected the demand lag, D, to be smaller for processes and capital goods than for consumer goods, as competitive pressures induce firms to search more intensively for new technologies. However, mass communications, particularly television, have probably eroded international differences in consumer tastes, so D has probably been falling for all goods. On its own, the latter trend would raise G, but it is argued below that L has also been shrinking, possibly more rapidly, and largely due to the activities of MNEs. The net effect on G and so on technology gap trade is unclear.

Vernon (1966) takes up the story to develop both the geography of invention and the motives behind and limits to technology transfer. Although primary scientific knowledge is an international public good, the entrepreneurial application of such knowledge requires a local stimulus because it is easier to gather information on latent demand the nearer one is to the potential market. Thus, that country in the world which has the highest per capita income will be the first to satisfy the latent demand for new consumer goods. Furthermore, its high wage costs and abundant capital will also inspire labour saving technologies. Such arguments explain the technological lead of the US at least for the quarter century following the Second World War. Having discussed the characteristics of countries where first innovation takes place, Vernon goes on to explain the imitation lag, L. During the early stages of development, the advanced country retains a comparative advantage in production as its superior labour skills and supply infrastructure permit more efficient experimentation to develop the most efficient technique of production. Proximity to the market also provides essential information fed back from early customers (learning by using).[7] Such advantages are so important that, for instance, even though jet engines were first invented in Britain and Germany, they were first manufactured in the US. Finally, as production becomes more standardized, less advanced countries are able to exploit their lower wages and production moves abroad.

The empirical testing of these models is well reviewed by Stern (1975) and Deardorff (1984).[8] Most of the evidence relates to the US. Hufbauer (1966) found a strong positive relationship between imitation lags and export performance in a large sample of products in the synthetic fibre industry. In many broader based but more aggregated industrial cross-section studies, the main finding is that R&D is a major, and often the major, determinant of US exports. This result can be replicated for West Germany, but the evidence for other countries is scant. A major problem with the interpretation of such results is that, formally, they are hard to distinguish from the 3 factor (including human capital) version of the Heckscher-Ohlin model. However, work by Sveikauskas (1983), together with supplementary case study evidence, supports the view that much US trade is technology based, in new products and between countries operating on different production functions.

Walker (1979) warns against taking Vernon's product cycle too literally. In many progessive capital goods industries (e.g. aircraft, textile machinery), the speed of technological progress is so rapid that production never gets transferred abroad. In other industries, even though technology is transferred, this is not because production has become standardized. The product may be standard (e.g. TV sets), but the process technology continues to develop, often in search of economies of scale.

Walker goes on to correlate a measure of export growth with R&D intensities in an international (OECD) cross-section for various industries. In general, and notwithstanding one or two anomalies, his results are consistent with the view that R&D is more central to export success in the more progressive industries (e.g. aircraft, drugs) than for others (e.g. ships, non-ferrous metals). Pavitt and Soete (1980) and Soete (1981) provide similar, but more detailed, exercises relating per capita exports (and world export shares) to shares of patents taken out in the US. Once more, the technology variable is found to be more correlated with exports in the more progressive industries. Further evidence relating technological and international trading performance is given in a recent study by the OECD (1986). They find that high technology industries have higher growth rates, a disproportionate share of government R&D funds, and higher levels and growth rates of import penetration.[9] Some purely international reasons for government support to 'high tech' industries are given in Section V.

One other recent study (Hughes, 1986) is of interest because it attempts to distinguish, albeit very crudely, skilled labour (SL), technology levels (RD), and technology gap (TG) theories of export performance. A regression analysis, using instrumental variables to account for feedback from exports to R&D, is carried out on a cross-section of UK industries. RD is measured by R&D as a proportion of value added and TG is proxied by the difference between domestic and foreign R&D (US plus France plus Germany plus Japan). She finds that both RD and TG have significant, positive coefficients in the preferred equations. This suggests that R&D intensive industries are more export oriented, even when the home country does not have a technological lead. Of the SL variables, skilled manual labour has a significant positive coefficient, but non-R&D professional and technical staff, like physical capital intensity, is not significant. Hughes finds evidence of simultaneity, but does not report the R&D regression.

A major flaw in all the above work, which concentrates on international trading performance, is that it fails to account for the alternatives to exports as a means of exploiting a technological advantage. Immigration by skilled labour, reverse engineering,[10] licensing, and joint ventures have all been vehicles for technology transfer. However, the role of the multinational enterprise (MNE) has now become paramount.[11] A hint of its importance is given by Horst (1972) and Wolff (1977) who find that US R&D is more closely related to the sum of US exports and overseas production by US MNEs, than it is to exports alone. At least four important empirical questions arise in relation to the transfer of technology. First, how difficult is it to transfer an existing technology abroad? Second, how much adaptation does transfer require? Third, how do the costs of transfer within an MNE compare with market transfers (e.g. licensing)? Fourth, how does the possibility of international transfer affect the incentive to invent?

Teece (1977) provides some useful evidence on the resource costs, excluding royalties, of instruction, learning and de-bugging in 26 instances of technology transfer by US MNEs.[12] Transfer costs ranged from 2%–59% of total project costs, averaging 19%. Local skills and a history of receiving technologies were particularly important in keeping costs down. A country has to be adept in order to adopt. Capital-intensive chemical and petroleum processes were more easily transferred than were machinery technologies. However, one point insufficiently stressed by Teece is that a third of the transfers were to developing countries, and, though he provides no cross tabulation, only in a half of all cases did managers consider international transfers to be more expensive than local transfers (with international transfer being cheaper in half the remaining cases). The costs of technology transfer are high, but the international dimension does not necessarily make it much higher, at least when channelled through MNEs to advanced countries. Without the institutional advantage of MNEs, one would expect that local licensing was easier than international licensing because of lower search and post-transfer communications costs. Some evidence for this is discussed below.

Turning to the degree to which technologies are adapted on transfer.[13] Mansfield, Teece and Romeo (1979) provide survey evidence that US MNEs carry out over 10% of their R&D abroad and for 'practically all firms ... the principal reason is to respond to special design needs of overseas markets' (p. 188). The moral may, therefore, appear to be that a country has to be adept in order to adapt and adopt! But this would be going too far because there is much case study evidence that very little adaptation actually goes on.[14] The implication is that adaptations are costly, so it may be more economical to transfer an apparently inappropriate technology than cater for specific local needs. Alternatively, the receiving country is often chosen to suit the technology and not the other way around.[15]

Technology transfer within an MNE is much quicker and less costly than is an external transfer. Mansfield and Romeo (1980), in a sample of 65 US technologies, show that the mean lag between US innovation and overseas transfer is 5.8 years when channelled through an overseas subsidiary in a developed country, 9.8 years to subsidiaries in developing countries and 13.1 years for licensing or joint ventures.[16] Mansfield, Romeo and Wagner (1979), employ another smallish sample of 30 US firms to show that three-quarters of their product innovations were first exploited abroad by foreign production within the MNE (there were apparently no technology gap exports), while for processes, exports were the favourite channel for initial exploitation. This appears to be because process technologies leak out more easily once transferred and there is a natural reluctance to facilitate such leakages. There was almost no process licensing, but a quarter of products were licensed. The theory developed in Section III suggests that this relative bias in favour of product transfer, while benefitting the firm, may not favour workers in the transferring country.

The final question posed above was on the incentive effects of technology transfer and once more it is Mansfield, Romeo and Wagner (1979) who provide the most direct evidence. On average, one third of the returns to R&D were expected to come from abroad; more from products than processes, more in R&D-intensive firms, and of course more for firms with greater overseas involvement. If transfer to foreign subsidiaries was not permitted, managers estimated that R&D would fall by 16%, and if licensing and the export of innovative capital goods were also not permitted, US R&D would fall by 26%. Managers were not asked to estimate the effect of banning exports of standard products made by innovative technologies, so the full influence of the international economy on US R&D is underestimated. Finally, since the USA has the world's largest home market, the international influence on R&D in the rest of the world is probably much greater.[17]

The overall picture that results from this research by Mansfield and his colleagues is that the international element of the costs of technology transfer is not a great hurdle provided it occurs between similar countries (so little adaptation is required) and is carried out within an MNE. Nevertheless, substantial lags do remain. The possibility of technology transfer is a significant incentive to further technological progress.

The conclusions to this section are presented in the spirit of stylized facts, against which the empirical basis for the following theoretical models can be informally judged.

1. National R&D and patenting efforts are positively related to international export shares, particularly in technologically progressive industries.

2. Within the most developed nations, more R&D-intensive industries have a higher propensity to export.

3. The same developed nations also have a higher propensity to import higher technology products than products arising from less progressive technologies.

4. At the same time as the world market has been growing rapidly, the size of individual R&D projects has also been growing.[18]

5. Imitation (technology transfer) is probably at least as important as invention as a source of technological progress.

6. International technology transfer takes place, continually, but

international differences in productivity testify to the fact that international technologies converge only slowly (and sometimes not at all).

7.   MNEs are the most efficient vehicle for technology transfer.

8.   Technology is not exogenous, and its creation is sensitive to the international environment.

9.   As much of the developed world has approached US income levels, the US has lost its technological hegemony. The product cycle has lost its predictive power and needs replacing with a model of international technological competition.[19]

III   Transcendental technological progress

Almost invariably, technological progress involves the prior investment of real resources. It is a rare occasion indeed when ready-to-produce innovations fall from heaven like the apple on Newton's head (even in Newton's case, he had to work at perfecting his innovatory theory). Learning by doing, inasmuch as it creeps on us unawares, does provide one source of transcendental (zero explicit investment) technical progress. However, inasmuch as we appreciate the investment implied by current production and act to exploit it, the explicit investment element returns.[20] This section investigates the welfare consequences of transcendental technological progress, not because it is empirically very important, but because it provides the simplest backdrop from which to investigate the terms of trade effects of technical change. Such effects are also present when technological progress is costly, but, given the added complexities of endogenous change, it will often be convenient to abstract from them in later sections. It may also be worth mentioning that transcendental technological progress is also the only type permitted in the traditional international trade literature!

The welfare consequences of transcendental progress in an open economy can be approached from either a conventional comparative static or a simplified comparative dynamic viewpoint. The former investigates an exogenous change in the technology of one country and traces its effects both at home and abroad. The latter investigates a steady state of continuous innovation in one economy and technology transfer to another, and considers the consequences of altering the rate of progress in the advanced economy or the rate of transfer to the other. Such models can be thought of as capturing the welfare side of the Tucker-Posner technology gap theory. I proceed by first considering process innovation, then product innovation, before concluding with a few thoughts on the channels of international technology transfer. For simplicity, competitive product and factor markets are assumed throughout, unless explicitly stated otherwise. I shall also take a two nation view of the world and refer to only the Home and Foreign countries; or where one region is assumed to be the more advanced, the North and the less advanced South. Two reservations concerning this dichotomous view of the world require mention at the outset. In practice, each 'nation' is usually a bloc and concerted behaviour within each bloc, which is a feature of some of the policy recommendations in the models to be described, is just not feasible. Secondly, a great deal of technology transfer takes place within a bloc and is sometimes balanced by flows in each direction. Such two-way flows are less likely to result in harm and conflict. Nevertheless, our purpose here is to identify potential problems and application to real examples must be made with appropriate care and caution.

Before moving on I offer an important background proposition that will permeate throughout what follows. International factor price equalization is bound to fail when factor endowments are fixed and international technologies differ. Therefore, unlike in the Heckscher–Ohlin–Samuelson world, trade in products alone cannot substitute for factor or technology movements in assuring global efficiency. This simple point offers the theoretical basis for both international income differences and the incentive for international factor (and technology) movements. On the other hand, if factors (e.g. capital) are mobile, if technological advantage is industry-specific, and if the technically advanced country is big enough to produce the entire world supply, then capital mobility can equalize factor prices so technology transfer becomes irrelevant to factor rewards and economic policy.

(i)   Process innovation[21]

Technical change can take on a large permutation of forms depending on whether it is factor augmenting, product augmenting, product-specific factor augmenting, country-specific or worldwide. The interesting questions concern differential international progress, and important distinctions must be made between progress in the import and export sectors. The main principles involved are fairly general, though the reader may prefer to bear in mind the examples of country-specific, general factor (or product) augmentation in the Heckscher–Ohlin model and industry-specific progress in the Ricardian world.[22] The possibility that technological progress may make the innovating country worse off is highlighted. Next, the theory of technology transfer is developed, and finally a more dynamic model of continuous innovation and technology transfer is discussed.

An improvement in the productivity of factors intensive in Home's export industry must improve Foreign's welfare as Home's prices fall and the terms of trade move in favour of Foreign.[23] Home citizens need not be so lucky. Consider first the case where Home consumes none of its own export good.[24] Export revenue rises (or falls) as export demand is elastic (or inelastic). Home always gains if demand is elastic, for example, if the terms of trade are fixed. However, inelastic export demand results in *immiserizing technological progress* for Home as the consumption of imports must fall along with the decline in export revenue. If Home consumes some of its own export good, then there are direct consumption gains to set against the terms of trade loss, but the possibility of immiserization remains.[25]

A domestic monopoly would never permit its revenue to fall as a consequence of a cost reduction. Consequently, immiserization can only be a problem if cost reductions are industry wide, the industry is competitive, and the country (or countries) involved is a dominant supplier. This seems more likely in agricultural and mineral markets than in manufacturing industry, though, for instance, technological progress in the watch industry may well have harmed the Swiss (it is hard to think of the Swiss as immiserized!). In such circumstances, *as long as all exporters can reach an agreement*, a joint government policy of an optimal export tax can be applied to emulate the monopolist's expertise at exploiting Foreign consumers, whilst preserving the benefits of lower domestic prices. This is, of course, a straightforward variation on the traditional optimum tariff argument. As a second best policy, though one which may fit in more comfortably with GATT rules, a statutory domestic monopoly might be created, supplemented where necessary by international collusion. Although not related to an immiserizing technological development, OPEC remains an archetype for illustrating the benefits of and problems with such a policy response.[26]

Next consider the related issue of technology transfer. What happens if North initially has a lower cost technology for producing its export good, say computers, and this technology is transferred to South? South must gain as the price of computers falls, but North normally loses. In the absence of comparative advantage, complete transfer (equalizing technologies) erodes North's gains from trade and this must be harmful. The only way North can gain is if South now has a large enough comparative advantage in computers for Northern consumers to benefit from the new pattern of specialization.

With exogenous technical change, there is no obvious way to model the ownership rights to technology. However, suppose the Northern government is able to levy a royalty on technology transfer; then a strictly positive royalty is always desirable for North, and in some circumstances a prohibitive royalty may be optimal. Clearly, now North is able to levy an optimal royalty, it can no longer be harmed by technology transfer. More interestingly, royalty payments reveal another, quite distinct, potential source of immiserization for the innovating country, this time the South. Suppose the North charges maximum royalties such that the transferred technology is only just worthwhile to Southern producers.[27] Product prices are therefore left (almost) unchanged, but the difference from the pre-transfer position is that royalty payments, representing the full resource saving and paid in South's export good, now flow North. This worsens South's trade balance and, on conventional adjustment mechanisms, requires a worsening of South's terms of trade. Such full royalty payments are, therefore, immiserizing unless they are taxed by the South. This argument provides a theoretical justification for the 'oft heard but seldom supported' argument that the import of new technology into developing countries is not always a benefit.

Next consider income distribution and the pressure for lobbying activity in the context of technology transfer. For instance, in a Heckscher–Ohlin world with incomplete specialization, the Stolper–Samuelson theorem can be directly applied to show that North's wage rate rises if computers are capital intensive and falls if they are labour intensive. Trade union pressure against technology transfer is therefore likely to be greatest in labour intensive technologies. This argument can be extended to investigate unemployment in the North due to an inflexible real wage (fixed in terms of a numeraire commodity, not computers). Technology transfer no longer alters the wage rate but, instead, Northern employment and national welfare are raised if computers are capital intensive, and Northern employment and welfare fall if they are labour intensive (always assuming incomplete specialization).

The technical detail of the above analysis is familiar ground for the general equilibrium economic theorist, and it undoubtedly reveals some interesting policy problems. However, the emphasis on the technology of one industry in one country at one point in time fails to neatly capture the stylized fact that some countries are more advanced at producing everything, and particularly good at 'high tech' industries. Krugman (1985) sweeps away all the sectoral details discussed above and focuses on a scalar measure of technological attainment in a single factor (labour) world with a continuum of goods. Countries differ in that they are characterized by a fixed gap (measured in, say, years) behind the world technological frontier in *all* industries. Industries differ in that some are inherently more progressive (measured by the exogenous growth rate of best practice productivity). The combination of a linear gap and exponential growth means that more advanced countries have a comparative advantage in more progressive industries.[28] It is not the level or complexity of technology that matters in this model, but its rate of change. Of course, inasmuch as new techniques are more complex than old ones, the two are not uncorrelated.

Consider the two country case with the North being nearer the technological frontier and so specializing in more progressive products than the South. Krugman chooses a Cobb–Douglas demand structure, which has the effect of ruling out the possibility of immiserizing progress for innovators. He investigates first, the effects of North exogeneously moving nearer the frontier and second, of South narrowing its differential gap with the North. As North moves nearer the frontier, Northern prices fall, North's real wages rise and, though the differential with the South widens, real wages in the South also improve. Things are not so sanguine for the North when the South's technology gap improves. South moves 'up market', producing some of those 'mid tech' goods previously produced in the North, with the consequence that South's real wages rise and so do the prices of 'low tech' goods still produced there. The net effect is that North's real wages may suffer, indeed they must suffer if the North–South gap is closed completely (North's gains from trade are lost). As Krugman puts it 'when the Third World learns to make TV sets, the labour price of TV sets falls, but the labour price of clothing may well rise' (p. 47). These results may also be seen in the context of the more static model discussed above. Technological progress in the North is always in its export industry, while that in the South is in North's import competing industry. Put yet another way, technological progress in the North widens the productivity differential and so the basis for trade, while that in the South narrows it.

It is often thought that a subsidy to 'high tech' industries is a 'good idea'. This need not be true in this model where technological progress is exogenous. South would gain from North's subsidies and North would lose from South's, but the subsidising nation's welfare would not obviously improve in either case. The technology embodied in exports is a symptom, not a cause, of progress. Finally, note that labour in the North should be more worried about the transfer of 'mid tech', which causes the potential harm, but positively support the transfer of 'low tech', which stimulates cheap imports of goods no longer produced in the North.

(ii)   Product innovation

In certain circumstances, product and process innovation can be treated quite analogously. For instance, consider a single characteristic product for which a new technique is developed such that more of the characteristic can be embodied in the product whilst using the same bundle of resources. For divisible products, this is equivalent to product augmenting technological progress. Dixit and Norman (1980) analyze this case, and the results should be familiar from the discussion of process innovation. If technological progress is in Home's import competing industry, Home gains but Foreign loses. Product augmentation in Home's export industry must benefit Foreign, but it is possible that Home is 'immiserized' by an adverse shift in the terms of trade.

A more novel, and probably more fruitful, analysis of the development of completely new products is given by Krugman's (1979) model of monopolistic competition. The dynamic spirit of his analysis is complementary to his 1985 technology gap model just discussed. The world is once more divided into the North, which has the unique ability to innovate and produce new products, and the South, which can copy new products, but only after a lag. Once copied, new products are called old products. Although Northern and Southern workers are equally productive, Northern workers have a scarcity value in that they have a monopoly in the production of new products. Thus, despite production taking place under competitive constant returns, Northern workers earn higher wages than those in the South. This scarcity premium is increasing in the number of new products relative to old, and decreasing in the number of Northern workers relative to the South.[29] An important contrast between this and the models of process innovation can now be noted. A burst of innovation which increases the number of new products increases demand for Northern labour, raises their wages and so the price of new products, and *improves* the North's terms of trade. This is the exact opposite of process innovation and one immediate consequence is that immiserizing progress is not possible with this form of new product innovation. Technology transfer which enables relatively more products to be produced in the South has the opposite effect to new product development and worsens North's terms of trade.

These simple insights are taken into a world of continuous technological progress by making two assumptions which are sufficient to ensure a long-run steady state. New product innovation is a proportion i of the existing stock of products, and technology transfer is such that a proportion t of new products are moved South in each period. Krugman describes the steady state: 'Relative wages are constant, with a fixed differential in favour of the developed country which is an increasing function of the rate of innovation i and a decreasing function of the rate of technology transfer t. The structure of trade remains unchanged in one sense in that North always exports new products and imports old products. But the actual goods involved continually change. Each good is at first produced in and exported by North; then when the technology becomes available to South, the industry moves to the lower wage country. Case studies in such a world would reveal a Vernon-type product cycle' (1979, p. 260).

Total global welfare is improved both by speeding up new product development, i, and by faster technology transfer, t: but each has a very different impact on the distribution of income between North and South. More rapid i has a direct benefit for consumers worldwide by giving them greater variety. The North gains a secondary benefit from improved terms of trade, but this represents a secondary loss to the South. In Krugman's specific example, South enjoys a net gain, but he acknowledges that this need not always be true in a more general model. A slower rate of product development hurts both North and, to a lesser extent, South. Faster technology transfer does not add to variety so the terms of trade effect dominates. South gains and North can lose; indeed, North must be worse off if technology transfer results in the equalization of wages because the gains from trade are eradicated. Once again, the tensions of even a fully employed world in the presence of technological progress are manifest. *The North cannot afford to slow down the pace of innovation without having to cope with both a relative and an absolute decline in real wages.* Adding internationally mobile capital to the model serves to reinforce the advantages of faster i for the North and faster t for the South, as capital flows towards the more rapidly progressing countries. For instance, it becomes more likely that faster i will harm Southern workers as capital flees the South to chase a higher marginal product in the North.

It is interesting to compare these results with Krugman's (1985) own model of process innovation. The South always gains from faster process innovation in the North, but may lose from faster product innovation. The North gains in both cases. With technology transfer, the North always loses if products are more rapidly transferred, but may not with processes. The South always gains. Thus, progress in process technology may lead to less inherent North–South conflict. However, recall the evidence of Mansfield, Romeo and Wagner (1979) that MNEs prefer to transfer product innovations but export the benefits of process development (for security reasons). One implication of Krugman's work is that such a bias towards product transfer may be detrimental to the welfare of Northern labour.

In a recent paper, Dollar (1986) has extended Krugman's product cycle model to endogenize the rate of technology transfer. He assumes that t is an increasing function of the difference between production costs in the North and South (i.e. the terms of trade).[30] He also incorporates capital flows more explicitly. The most interesting result relates to the impact of labour growth in the South. In the short run, before t adjusts and capital is transferred, North's terms of trade improve as Southern wages fall; but in the long term, both capital and technology are attracted South and North's welfare falls.[31] Dollar draws the parallel of Northern boom when the NICs started growing and the stagnant growth experienced in the North more recently. In a world of sticky real wages, downward pressure on equilibrium wages gets translated into unemployment and demands for protection. He concludes: 'The main policy implication of the model would then seem to be that some government control of the process of capital and technology transfer may be desirable in order to prevent further erosion of the world's relatively open trade in goods' (p. 189). This is heady stuff which is not backed up by an explicit analysis of such controls. The model is also very specific and the role of technology transfer, at least, is very sensitive to small changes in specification (see footnote 31). Nevertheless, even if normative policy recommendations from such models need more careful thought, the positive policy pressures that are identified undoubtedly do exist.

(iii) Channels of technology transfer.[32]

Each of the above models is characterized not only by an exogenously determined technological lag (except Dollar, 1986), but also by a 'black box' placed over the means by which transfer takes place. Although there are many ways in which technology may be transferred abroad (e.g. joint ventures, equity swaps) the essential arguments can be illustrated with respect to just two modes – licensing and direct investment (by MNEs). The standard framework for analyzing such choices of markets versus hierarchies is due to Coase (1937) and Williamson (1975). The analysis is shifted away from the industry and focuses on the firm as the decision making unit. A firm in the home country develops some technological advantage (product or process) which is best exploited abroad, at least in order to serve certain foreign markets. This may be because tariffs or transport costs are large, or foreign production costs are potentially lower, or the innovation requires modification to suit the market and there are economies to development taking place locally (e.g. feedback from consumer 'learning by using'). How should the technological advantage be transferred?

Licensing to local firms has several advantages. Local producers understand the traditions, culture and socio-legal environment in which they operate and this gives an advantage when dealing with other local firms, labour and government. Such knowledge can be learnt, but only at a cost that increases with the scale of the environmental differences. The average cost of such knowledge can be reduced if several technologies are expected to be transferred by the same firm. A major problem with licensing is associated with the pricing of licenses. With unpatented products or processes, in explaining the virtues of the new technology and if the innovator is to convince the local producer of the veracity of his claims, the proverbial cat will have leapt out of the bag. The potential licensee has no incentive to pay for the knowledge he has just been given free of charge. Of course, there will be many complex and important details missing, but such details are often difficult to incorporate in a licensing agreement anyway. For many types of patented, trademarked and copyrighted innovations, the problem of maintaining property rights is not much less severe, particularly internationally (e.g. pirating of books, videos, tools etc. is rife in the Far East). Furthermore, even if agreement is reached, there is the problem of policing the licence so that, for instance, the licensee does not start to compete directly with the innovator. Finally, the resource costs of transfer may be much lower within an organization where key personnel can be redeployed, than in the open market where local firms must develop the skills of adopting technology (see Section II). Overall, except for one-off transfers to very different environments (e.g. Eastern Europe), or for products which are simple to produce but for one key and secret ingredient (e.g. Coca Cola), or where legal barriers provide a substantial hurdle (e.g. Japan), or where the innovator faces severe constraints on rapid overseas expansion (e.g. small firms), direct investment is probably the most efficient mode of technology transfer. Finally, Flaherty (1984) provides evidence from the international semi-conductor industry that suggests the advantages of direct investment over licensing are less to do with informational secrecy than the early establishment of long-term contacts with overseas consumers, both for 'learning by using' feedback and to deter entry by local producers.

Findlay (1978) incorporates the informational role of direct investment into a model of technology transfer. The model is very stylized and aggregated, but it does distinguish between transfer due to the technology gap and that due to local diffusion.[33] He argues that MNEs play a crucial role in spreading the 'virus of new technology', and the 'contagion' of local firms provides a limited step towards endogenizing technological progress (innovation remains exogenous). This role of MNEs is incorporated by assuming that foreign owned capital located in the South has beneficial productivity spillovers onto the local economy. The Veblen-Gerschenkron idea of more rapid catch-up the further a country lags behind (provided it is not too poor to take off) is added to the contagion hypothesis in order to study the dynamics of a backward economy. Although this illustrates one way in which to model MNEs and technical progress, there is no welfare analysis and so no policy conclusions can be drawn.

IV Endogenous technological progress

Problems such as potential immiserization do not disappear once technological progress is endogenized. However, since new issues arise, it will often be convenient to abstract from those problems already discussed in order to obtain a clearer focus. The story varies depending on whether trading partners are similar or very different. I begin by looking at countries which are dissimilar in such a way that one dominates in the generation of technological progress. Such North–South models provide a natural development of those described in Section III. Next I look briefly at countries which are basically very similar, but in which the local environment determines the direction of technical change. Finally, I consider a world in which countries are essentially identical, and this brings us into most direct contact with the closed economy view of technology.

(i) Technological leadership

Vernon's (1966) views on why new products should be invented and initially produced in the world's richest countries have already been discussed. Building on the assumption of a leading country having a comparative advantage in innovation, Connolly (1973), Pugel (1982), and Feenstra and Judd (1982) have investigated costly innovation and optimal licensing policy. In these general equilibrium models, labour in the leading country (North) can be freely transferred between production and R&D activity. It turns out that these models yield disappointingly few new insights and only the Feenstra and Judd paper is reviewed here. The remaining three papers discussed in this sub-section are partial equilibrium. Berkowitz and Kotowitz (1982) develop a model of patent policy, Cheng (1984) looks at the benefits of technological leadership, and Dasgupta and Stiglitz (1985) investigate learning by doing. These partial equilibrium models follow the industrial organization tradition and emphasise problems relating to monopoly and competition as opposed to the general equilibrium international trade emphasis on the terms of trade.

Feenstra and Judd (1982) develop a model of product innovation which provides a useful complement to Krugman (1979). Once again the Dixit-Stiglitz CES utility function with many products provides the demand backdrop. On the supply side, a fixed and known investment called R&D is necessary before a good can be produced under otherwise constant costs. Labour is the only factor of production. R&D takes place in the North, but production takes in both North and South. Feenstra and Judd identify technology transfer with R&D carried out in the North for production in the South. Unlike Krugman (1979), they make no distinction between new and old goods (i.e. there is no technology lag) so free trade wages are equalized worldwide. Also, in order to cover the costs of R&D, (constant) wage costs in production are marked up by a fixed, monopolistically competitive margin. They investigate the Northern government's optimal tax policies, though only small taxes around the free trade equilibrium are considered. A positive tax on technology transfer is found to be superior to an import tariff, which beats free trade. Such taxes reduce world variety (and, in their version of the Dixit–Stiglitz model, welfare) but increase the number of products produced locally. The increase in demand for Northern labour, and decrease in demand in the South, moves the terms of trade in favour of the North.[34] Around the free trade equilibrium, this must improve North's welfare as the reduction in world variety has only a second order effect.

Berkowitz and Kotowitz (1982) provide a stimulating analysis of patent policy in an open economy. What does a small country which has little indigenous innovative activity, or which has its R&D dominated by foreign owned MNEs, gain from giving patent protection? For instance, 95% of all Canadian patents are granted to foreigners. Under Article 2 of the Paris Convention, member countries cannot discriminate between local and foreign inventions, though they can set their own patent conditions and duration. Large innovative industrial blocs such as the US and EEC have an incentive to cooperate in setting the global optimum patent life. However, unless a country has a significant degree of monopoly in invention, Berkowitz and Kotowitz show that it is preferable to abandon the patent system (assuming no retaliation). The losses from reduced domestic innovation are outweighed by savings in international royalty payments. The popular demands made for MNEs to locate R&D in developing countries may also be misplaced unless royalty rights reside within the local subsidiary. Failing that, the siting of R&D laboratories locally may actually be a disadvantage if there are tax concessions for R&D, without any compensating advantages in the taxation of royalties.[35]

Cheng (1984b) addresses what he calls the Posner–Hufbauer

hypothesis that the South gains less than the North from trade based on technology. His model incorporates both process and product innovation in that 'technology' is subsumed within a revenue function. There is international duopoly and continuous technological progress over a finite time horizon. Formally, Cheng solves an open-loop differential game with technology as the state and R&D as the control variables. Three possible sources of leadership are identified: a greater initial endowment of technology, lower R&D costs, and preemptive behaviour. It is found that an exogenous increase in the North's leadership will often harm the South (by reducing its flow of profits). However, intriguingly, it is possible that if the initial lead is due only to an initially better endowment, the identity of the technological leader may change. No policy conclusions are drawn, but this last conclusion warrants a mention even in a policy paper.

Finally, Dasgupta and Stiglitz (1985) investigate learning by doing economies. The essential observation to make is that the private incentive to invest in current production (as a means of reducing future costs) is less than the social incentive (unless perfect price discrimination to internalize all potential consumer surplus is possible). Consider an industry which is mature in the North (so learning economies are exhausted), but in which there are potentially substantial learning economies in the South, such that comparative advantage would eventually lie in the South. Assume that Southern firms do not find it privately profitable to enter. Even without recourse to the usual arguments about imperfect capital markets and so forth,[36] if Southern demand is substantial, there may be an infant industry argument for protection to get around the inappropriability problem. Note importantly that North's terms of trade would not worsen as a result of Southern protection because the price of the protected good would not rise. In fact, if North is a substantial consumer, an important subsidy which reduces foreign costs, and so final price, may become optimal!

(ii) National traits

Technological leadership can be thought of as a particular type of national trait – strong comparative advantage in innovation. Other traits are less domineering, but no less important if technological progress is 'localized' due to learning by doing or induced bias along an invention possibility frontier. In such cases, autarky can induce technological divergence which remains entrenched in economies opened up to free trade.

What type of divergence is most likely? Pavitt and Soete (1981) warn against sweeping generalizations such as that technologies develop, on the one hand to compensate for factor scarcities, or on the other to reinforce comparative advantage rooted in factor abundance. Clearly such simplistic views must be in conflict and open to a significant number of counter examples. However, their pessimism in the search for general principles may be unjustified. It is probably possible to state a more careful position based on autarky incentives reinforced by a need for geographical proximity in observing and exploiting opportunities (Linder, 1961). The general principle must be that the return to R&D depends on both the size of the market and the expected price advantage of the technology produced. The idea is best illustrated by a few examples. Consumer products might reflect local tastes forged by climate, politics, history or factor abundance (e.g. socialism in Sweden led to the building of a large stock of smallish apartments which induced an advanced design technology in neat, light furniture). Capital goods (producer products) similarly reflect prevalent local demands (e.g. the British textile and mining machinery industries reflected the profitability of R&D due to substantial local demand by the cotton and coal industries). Thus, the size of domestic demand, perhaps reinforced by export demand, plays a crucial role as an incentive for invention. However, high prices for raw materials (due to local scarcity and international trading costs, including tariffs) also result in a localized search for raw materials saving technology because they raise the return to R&D projects searching for replacements inasmuch as trading costs increase the share of imported inputs in total cost (e.g. German synthetics).

Without more formal modelling,[37] it is difficult to develop such arguments into policy recommendations, though the idea of tariff induced technologies which would become redundant under freer trade is worthy of further investigation. Furthermore, at least one important question remains substantially unanswered. Can a dominant culture lead to technological change which immiserizes a minority culture, perhaps by reducing the availability of products favoured by the minority?[38]

(iii)   Size effects

Thus far, it has been assumed that technological progress is either transcendental or produced in a conventional, competitive industry. In fact, almost no R&D takes place under such stylized circumstances. Economies of scale in the production of knowledge eliminate perfect competition, yet rivalry in entering the R&D industry equally rules out unfettered monopoly. The papers discussed in this section abstract from most international differences, including transport costs, tariffs, and comparative advantage, in order to focus on the essential firm level game theoretic and size effects of opening up the economy. They also assume that competition in the R&D industry eliminates monopoly profits. Each of the models discussed below is in keeping with stylized fact number 4 – that R&D projects have been growing in size at the same time as world trade has been increasing rapidly.

In the introduction to this paper, I suggested that size increases both the aggregate return to invention and the degree of competition, so that, on simple Schumpeterian arguments, the balance of incentives is unclear. Dasgupta and Stiglitz (1980) provide a framework for clarifying matters. In a model in which oligopolists produce a homogeneous product and independently invent the same process innovations (because there is a well defined research path to be followed), and where such innovations are not subject to exclusionary patenting, they find that too much repetitive R&D is carried out but the economy wide rate of cost reduction is too slow. This is because the latter depends on R&D per firm, and not total R&D. Two important parameters in the model are the industry elasticity of demand and the elasticity of cost reduction with respect to R&D. If both of these are constant then the free entry equilibrium number of firms in the industry is independent of market size. Furthermore, both the ratio of socially optimal R&D to actual R&D per firm, and the ratio of socially optimal output to actual output are independent of the size of the economy. However, the levels of each are increasing in size. Thus, an open economy does not tend to eliminate distortions as judged by the current degree of openness, but it does increase the rate of technological progress and it is more socially efficient as judged by autarky standards. Nevertheless, in the short run, a move from autarky to free trade may impede technological progress. Consider the case in which the size of the market and number of producers increase in equal proportion. Current output rises, giving an immediate welfare gain, and if demand is elastic, R&D per firm also rises. However, it is easy to show that inelastic demand may actually reduce R&D per firm as the competitive squeeze outweighs the benefit of market size.

Dasgupta and Stiglitz (1980) go on to investigate the opposite extreme to duplicative research. In a patent race, the winner claims the entire prize. Once again, all firms have identical research plans (this assumption can be relaxed) though the date of invention can be brought forward by heavier investment. Combining these assumptions, it is clear that with free entry into the patent race, and if R&D funds can be committed at the beginning of the race, there will be only one actual entrant who will spend so much on R&D that his potential profits are exhausted. Equally clearly, open economies will experience more rapid innovation. There is, however, no presumption that this is socially desirable. It turns out that this sort of model is very sensitive to the choice of assumptions,[39] but this does not reduce its potential interest in applications to international problems (e.g. should international agreements be made to *slow down* certain types of 'ruinously' competitive R&D?)

The models just discussed relate to homogeneous product industries. Shaked and Sutton (1984) provide an interesting analysis of quality competiton. Fixed investments in R&D are necessary if a higher quality product is to be produced, but marginal costs increase little relative to the marginal willingness to pay. With homothetic tastes everyone would demand the same quality of product and, given the assumption of price competition, only one firm could survive (much as in the patent race just described). However, with an unequal income distribution and willingness to pay for quality increasing with income, several different qualities can survive in the market by selling at different prices. Shaked and Sutton's primary achievement is to show that the number of different qualities is independent of market size, so only inasmuch as trade widens the dispersion of incomes in the market will the equilibrium number of firms increase. In the short run, when an economy is opened up, low quality products are competed out of the market and consumer welfare rises as prices of the remaining qualities fall. In the longer term, marginal returns to R&D are enhanced so more R&D is undertaken and there is a further benefit from the consequently higher quality products that can be enjoyed. The most important policy recommendation to come out of this model is a timely reminder that whatever quibbles concerning free trade have been raised in this survey so far, there are some fairly hefty benefits that should never be ignored.

As they stand, these models have nothing to say about the location of innovative effort and national policies. However, consider what would happen if one country maintained domestic protection while there was free trade in the rest of the world. For simplicity, assume that such protection is prohibitive and there are no transport costs. As long as invention and production must take place in the same country, the incentive to invent is now greater in the protected country (because it has a larger total market). Thus, while reducing global incentives, Home protection can raise Home's share of innovative activity. Home's absolute rate of innovation may either rise or fall. When all profits are competed away (and there is full employment), unless a country values a technological lead for its own sake, or there is a favourable terms of trade effect, then there is no reason to believe that this motive for protection does a country any good. The terms of trade effects have already been

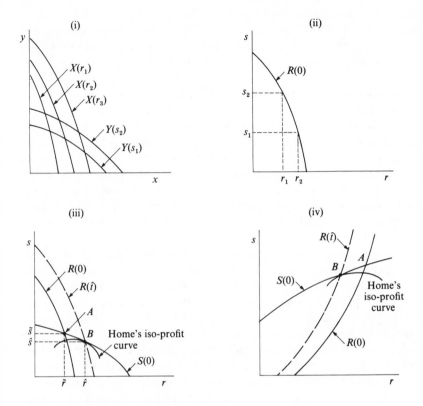

Fig. 7.1 Strategic government policy

discussed. The next section addresses the profit shifting motive for protection, which can arise whenever monopoly profits are not fully competed away.

V   Strategic government policies

The type of government policy so far discussed has been quite conventional. A market imperfection is identified and corrected, or a straightforward opportunity to do down foreigners by manipulating the terms of trade is exploited. In this final review section, a more subtle form of intervention is contemplated. In certain circumstances, governments are able to indirectly place local firms in a better competitive position. The basic idea is to help domestic firms to grab a bigger slice of world profits. The profit shifting policies discussed in this section would be quite irrelevant in a world in which competition either within or for the market meant that firms made zero profits. The analysis is set firmly in an oligopolistic world with positive profits.[40] Because this type of analysis is fairly novel and so may be unfamiliar to those interested in technology policy, it is spelt out in considerably more detail than were the earlier sections.

The simplest way to see the argument is, following Spencer and Brander (1983), to visualize a three-country world. Two firms located in Home and Foreign sell their substitute outputs only in a third country. Each firm has two decisions to make. First it must decide on its R&D, basing its judgement on both expected output and a known function which relates higher R&D to lower marginal production costs. Figure 7.1(i) to (iv) illustrates the basic idea. The following notation is used: x is Home's output (i.e. exports to the third country), y is Foreign's output (i.e. exports to the third country), r is Home's R&D, and s is Foreign's R&D. Suppose Foreign has decided on an R&D expenditure of s_1. This determines marginal cost and, given industry demand, Foreign's best choice of output given any x is $Y(s_1)$. $Y(s_1)$ is known as Foreign's best reply curve or reaction function (see Figure 7.1(i)). Similarly, Home's best reply curves for various levels of r are drawn in as $X(r_1)$, $X(r_2)$, and $X(r_3)$, where $r_1 < r_2 < r_3$. Which r should Home choose? Higher r both reduces variable costs and raises market share, but it also both incurs higher fixed costs and results in lower industry price. With high initial, but diminishing marginal, returns to R&D, there will be some optimum r which maximizes Home profits for any given s. In this case, say r_2 is the best response to s_1. This point is plotted in Figure 7.1(ii) as a point on Home's R&D best reply curve, $R(0)$. Returning to Figure 7.1(i), we can investigate Home's reaction to a higher level of R&D abroad. With s_2 ($> s_1$), Foreign's marginal costs are lower and she tends to produce more. A crucial question now arises: when s is larger, are Home's profits maximized with an R&D budget that is higher or lower than r_2? On the argument that Home's expected market size is lower and that this reduces the marginal return to research, we assume for the moment that r_1 is the best reply to s_2. This is also plotted in Figure 7.1(ii) and justifies the downward slope of $R(0)$; see Fudenberg and Tirole (1984). Figure 7.1(iii) repeats this curve and also draws in Foreign's best reply, $S(0)$.

We are now in a position to discuss various strategic moves. First note that the non-cooperative Nash equilibrium is at A, with R&D budgets of $\bar{r}$ and $\bar{s}$. Exports to the third country are then given by feeding these back into Figure 7.1(i). Next consider what Home can achieve if, by some good fortune, he is able to make a public commitment to his r *before* Foreign is able to make her decision on s. Home will be able to act as a

Stackelberg leader and choose $\hat{r}$, forcing Foreign back to $\hat{s}$. Spencer and Brander's principal insight was to observe that when the Home firm has no clear leadership advantage, the government can subsidise R&D and so confer exactly the same advantage as with Stackelberg leadership. An optimal subsidy of t has the effect of shifting $R(0)$ out to $R(t)$ and generating a Nash equilibrium at B. *Where firms cannot credibly precommit to R&D expenditures, governments sometimes can.* Meanwhile, what if Foreign's government is also in the subsidy game? If Foreign's government tries a similar strategy, then we have a three-stage noncooperative game. First governments choose their subsidies, second firms choose their R&D, and third firms choose their output rates. As compared with no government intervention, each country (except the export market) is made worse off by such competitive subsidies, but neither dares stop, for it would then be made worse off. An international ban on subsidies would be Pareto optimal (except for the export market!).

Several modifications can be made to this type of analysis. Spencer and Brander (1983) show that if export subsidies are possible (which, in practice, they are not because they contravene GATT rules) then these are superior to R&D subsidies because they do not encourage an excessive commitment of scarce R&D resources. In fact, they show that a combination of positive export subsidy and R&D tax is ideal for a single government acting individually.

Another case where an R&D tax is appropriate is if higher Home R&D induces higher Foreign R&D. Such an aggressive response gives an upward sloping $S(0)$ and, as can be seen from Figure 7.1(iv), Home's best interests are served by less r than at the no-intervention Nash equilibrium.[41] The important lesson to learn from this is that this type of government policy works as much by altering the behaviour of Foreign firms as it does by influencing those at Home. In particular, there is no profit shifting role for government policy if Foreign R&D is independent of the level of Home R&D.

Next consider the effect of having a domestic market of significant size. Krugman (1984) demonstrates the important proposition that import protection can then act as export promotion. If Foreign is kept out of the Home market, then her expected market size is reduced and, in the standard case, her R&D falls. Similarly, protection raises Home's expected demand and so his R&D, and these two effects combine to have a double impact in raising Home's market share in export markets. The case of Japan is immediately brought to mind.

Although this section has emphasized R&D, it should be clear that the same basic principles carry over to related issues. For instance, it is straightforward to reinterpret the model as one choosing between an existing menu of production technologies characterized by varying levels of fixed and variable costs. The advantage of commitment to, and subsidy of, apparently excessively large scale technologies is then understood in terms of its value in reducing the scale chosen by rivals, Krugman (1984) discusses a similar case, and also learning by doing. In fact, almost any activity which reduces Home marginal costs or otherwise encourages Foreign to believe that high output levels are unprofitable, can be exploited by, for instance, import protection or export subsidies or R&D (or equivalent fixed cost) subsidies.

Krugman's results on import protection as export promotion contain no welfare analysis and he is careful to make clear that policy conclusions should not be drawn without further analysis. The latter is not straightforward because there is a tradeoff between domestic distortions induced by policy interference and the gains from profit shifting. Once the possibility of retaliation by Foreign governments is acknowledged, the set of possibilities can become infernally complex. For instance, Dixit and Kyle (1985) analyse an apparently simple example. Foreign is already in the market but before Home enters it must incur a fixed R&D entry cost. The Home government has the choice of excluding Foreign from the Home market and/or paying for Home's R&D. The Foreign government can also impose a prohibitive tariff if it wishes. The complexity comes from the differing ordering of, and types of, commitment that governments can make. For instance, Foreign may be able to prevent Home from entering by making a preemptive commitment to protection. However, if this induces a reaction of protection at Home, Foreign may do better by promising free trade conditional on Home doing the same. Home subsidies may be less vulnerable to Foreign retaliation than is Home protection. Explicit treatment of domestic welfare also reintroduces a terms of trade effect. For instance, even if there are no positive profits to be shifted, it may be worthwhile subsidizing Home entry in order to increase competition and so lower the price of imports.

Many more details on strategic trade policy are reviewed with great clarity by Grossman and Richardson (1985). They also make two important points concerning who gains and who loses from profit shifting policies, each based on the fact that the benefits of intervention accrue in terms of profits (unless strong trades unions can appropriate the benefits for their workers). First, many major companies, especially those of a sufficient size to be significant players on the world stage, have shareholders living outside the country of production. The stereotype foreign owned MNE is only one extreme example where all the benefits of profit shifting are gleaned outside the protecting country. The global integration of capital markets severely dilutes the nationalistic benefits of profit shifting. Second, a policy which favours capital owners at the expense of taxpayers or consumers may be unsatisfactory on the grounds of internal equity (let alone international equity). Effective profits taxation can help alleviate such distributional issues, but the usual (if over-stressed) transfer pricing problems remain.

The sheer complexity of the issues involved in strategic trade policy motivates four final comments. First, we always knew that the real world was complex, and we have only just got round to beginning to model it properly (or even half properly). We are still a long way from making confident policy recommendations. Second, even on the basis of what we now know, such complexity does not make for the snappy policy recommendations beloved of politicians. The policies described here are best seen as a recipe for *ad hoc* measures based on a detailed knowledge of an industry's history, structure and competitors. The informational requirements for successful implementation are enormous. Third, *ad hoc* policies are an open invitation for lobbying activities designed to appropriate oligopoly rents, but not necessarily to the social benefit. It may even be that the lobbying costs outweigh the benefits of the genuine occasions on which intervention is desirable. That is a matter for careful empirical investigation and, if untrue, then equally careful policy design is necessary to minimize the costs of policy implementation. Fourth, even if policy applications are abandoned, the theoretical analysis of complex situations will not have been wasted if it gives economists a clearer understanding of, and so credibility with, the business community. Industrialists frequently make protectionist demands that are quite incomprehensible in the context of a competitive world where positive profits are assumed not to exist. Economists must be able to understand such claims whether or not they are to be supported.[42]

VI   Conclusions

This survey has covered a great deal of ground and, in doing so, a number of reasons why technological change may lead to international conflict have been elucidated. A few of the more important conclusions are listed below, but first one important issue needs clarifying.

In this chapter, I have followed Krugman and others in distinguishing between product and process innovation. At long last, I had thought when first drafting this chapter, here is a situation in which the distinction makes a genuine and important difference. In a closed economy, a new product in one industry is a new process to another so from the social viewpoint the one is equivalent to another. The product/process dichotomy is something for students to learn and theorists to ignore. But, if the product is produced in one country and applied in another then, as Krugman has shown (see also conclusions 1, 2 and 6 below), the welfare consequences of each can differ substantially. However, a few moments' reflection should modify the way we interpret these findings. I propose the following alternative dichotomy.

Define vertical technological progress as either: a better way to make the same thing (process innovation); or the same way of making a better thing (product augmentation, e.g. using essentially identical techniques, one is suddenly able to get more memory on the same micro-chip). Define horizontal technological progress as either: the same way of making a different thing (i.e. a new product using a well established technology); or a different way of making the same thing (e.g. a new specialist capital good which complements the existing range of processes available to make established products). In the present context, the crucial difference between vertical and horizontal progress is that while vertical progress, if general to all exporting countries, may lead to a decline in demand for factors intensive in or specialized in the export industry, the same is not true of horizontal progress. With horizontal progress, the increase in available variety always raises demand for the range of exports and so for the factors embodied in them. It is only inasmuch as process innovation is of the nature of vertical progress and product innovation is associated with horizontal progress that the process/product dichotomy can generate interesting results relating to the international distribution of welfare. Clearly, however, the vertical/horizontal distinction (which drives the welfare results) is not always identical to the process/product dichotomy and the latter should be treated with caution.

Finally, I repeat some of the most interesting results relating to international trade and technology policy.

1. If markets are competitive, (vertical) process innovation in an export industry can be immiserizing as the terms of trade move against the innovator. As long as all exporting countries collude, an export tax can help them.

2. (Horizontal) product innovation is much less likely to be immiserizing as demand for resources in the innovating industry increases and puts upward pressure on prices.

3. If royalties are charged on the transfer of process technologies, then South can lose as the terms of trade move adversely.

4. In the absence of the conditions for immiserization, rapid innovation benefits both North and South, but a slowdown in innovation can lead to absolute reductions in equilibrium

Northern wages, and consequently to unemployment. The pressures for a policy response in such circumstances are clear, though the appropriate policy advice is not.

5.   With exogenous technical progress, the gains from trade are increased by living in a world with countries very different to you. With endogenous progress, it may be preferable to live in a world of similar countries if technologies more appropriate to your requirements are then invented.

6.   A tax on the transfer of (horizontal) product innovations is justified on the grounds of improving the terms of trade. For (vertical) process innovation the costs and benefits of a tax depend on the extent of induced competition with import-competing industries.

7.   There appears to be little reason for small countries to adopt a patent system.

8.   Learning by doing economies may provide an infant industry argument for protection; but if learning is taking place abroad, there may equally be an argument for an import subsidy.

9.   Economies of scale are inherent in the production of technology. This both provides an important gain from trade and introduces a significant reason for non-competitive markets. The latter justify policy interventions, such as import protection or R&D subsidies, on the grounds of profit shifting.

10. The complexities of the profit shifting argument make implementation extremely problematic.

11. The global integration of capital markets might mean that profit shifting arguments cannot be made to apply. However, I suspect that they could have a renewed force if there is unemployment. This should be an area for further research.

12. I have paid insufficient attention to the problems of international retaliation.

13. *All but a very few of the policy interventions described in this paper beggar at least one of thy neighbours.*

NOTES

1 Hume was actually underestimating the history of technology transfer. 400 years ago, Bacon observed that three great mechanical inventions, printing, gunpowder and the compass, had changed the face of the world (in literature, warfare and navigation). As Rosenberg (1982) points out, all three originated outside Europe.

2 Hume's main concern was crude mercantilism, and Tucker was troubled by

the logic that if poorer countries advanced only at the expense of the richer, then this might be used as an excuse for war as 'a Kind of Self-defence'. These particular concerns have now given way to such issues as full employment and appropriate technology.

3 The social welfare function may or may not involve conservatism, such that 'any significant absolute reduction in real incomes of any significant sector of the community should be avoided' (Corden, 1974, p. 107).

4 'Nature, by giving a diversity of geniuses, climates, and soils to different nations, has secured their mutual intercourse and commerce, as long as they all remain industrious and civilised' (Hume, 1758, p. 346).

5 See David (1975, ch. 1) for an excellent case study applying such ideas to the controversy over why UK and US technologies diverged in the 19th century.

6 Of course, American firms may have kept away from supersonic airliners because they had better foresight about technological difficulties, oil prices and patterns of demand; but though Concorde has been a commercial failure, the general point should be clear.

7 'Learning by using' is Rosenberg's (1982) phrase.

8 See Soete (1985) for additional references. Deardorff also points out some of the finer distinguishing features within this group of technology and trade models.

9 They also find that 'since the late 1970's, in the OECD as a whole, and in many individual countries, the private sector has replaced the public sector very rapidly as the largest source of R&D financing.'

10 'Reverse engineering' is the practice of buying a new product, then taking it carefully apart in order to learn how it was originally put together. During the post-war years, the Japanese have developed this particular form of technology transfer into a fine art.

11 Except in Japan where legal restrictions have encouraged licensing and sophisticated reverse engineering.

12 A larger sample is studied by Davidson and McFetridge (1984).

13 An early discussion is given by Solo (1966).

14 See, for instance, Behrman and Wallender (1976) who also stress the importance of the MNE in technology transfer, and Davies (1977) on UK transfers to India through licensing agreements and joint ventures.

15 Stewart (1984) argues that there is a tendency for technologies emanating from the developed countries to be increasingly inappropriate for the South (though she stresses that this does not necessarily represent a loss to the South).

16 In a significant minority of cases, they find that technology transfer speeds up foreign technological progress (particularly in processes) either by direct leakage and diffusion or by indirect competitive stimulus. None of the technologies in their sample leaked out before they were transferred within the MNE.

17 Though some small countries which can get by importing technology in an open world would have to increase their R&D effort in an aurtarkic world. Some such R&D, however, would repeat what was being done elsewhere in the world and so cannot be counted as either a national or a global benefit.

18 The first part of this statement is well documented; the second is based on casual empiricism (but see Rosenberg, 1982, ch. 12 for several examples). It may just be that all the easy things have been invented, but reasons to link project and market sizes are discussed in Part IV.

19 Vernon (1979) was one of the first to appreciate this. Deardorff (1984) concludes his survey on a challenging note: 'It will be interesting to see whether the existing technology theories of trade will be refined and convincingly tested before they are left behind by a changing world' (p. 499).

20 The difference between technological progress which results from prior investment and that which comes entirely free (transcendentally) is quite distinct from that between embodied and disembodied innovation. For instance, it is conceivable that the wheel (an embodied technology) was invented almost by accident, and it is certainly true that disembodied organizational advances often require extensive research.

21 Dixit and Norman (1979) provide the simplest, integrated treatment of this subject; McCulloch and Yellen (1982) give a concise statement of the main results relating to technology transfer; and Jones (1979) collects together some of his own thoughts on the subject. See also Dornbusch et al. (1977) for the Ricardian model with a continuum of goods. All results in this section refer either to the standard 2 × 2 × 2 Heckscher-Ohlin model or, where stated, to the one-factor Ricardian model.

22 These cases avoid the (fairly uninteresting) examples involving elasticities of substitution between factors. As Krugman (1985) puts it, 'capital-saving technical change in the labour-intensive sector can actually cause the progressing sector to contract, as Rybczinski dominates Ricardo' (p. 37). This reflects a real possibility, but fails to capture the idea of countries differing in their technological capabilities.

23 Strictly speaking, this only holds for the Heckscher-Ohlin model. In a Ricardian world, if Home's demand for its own export good is very elastic, the demand for imports from Foreign may fall so much that Foreign's ability to import is impaired.

24 And the elasticity of supply is constant so that producers' surplus is a constant proportion of total revenue.

25 Note that this form of immiserization occurs in a Walrasian economy which is free of all distortions. Taxes, tariffs, wage rigidities, etc. provide quite separate possible sources of misery resulting from 'progress' in an open economy.

26 At the global level, it *might* be possible to justify such policy reactions to immiserizing technological progress at the same time as condemning OPEC price rises by invoking a 'conservative social welfare function'. See footnote 3.

27 Of course, it may pay North to charge less than the full royalty if this encourages wider use in the South.

28 Note that despite the fact that Krugman has no R&D in his model, it is fairly consistent with stylized fact number 1, given that R&D is related to nearness to the frontier.

29 If Northern workers are relatively abundant, such that full employment requires some of them to produce old products, then their scarcity rents are lost. Krugman rules out this uninteresting case by assumption. In Dollar's (1986) model, discussed below, this assumption is made redundant as an international wage differential is a necessary condition for endogenous technology transfer to take place.

30 In fact, Dollar expresses transfer as a proportion of old rather than new products, so his *t* is not the same as Krugman's.

31 Once again, Dollar modifies one of Krugman's assumptions. This time he

makes the rate of new product development proportional to the stock of new products as opposed to the stock of new plus old products. Under the latter assumption, Southern labour growth has no effect on the terms of trade and so on technology transfer. His results then rest entirely on capital being attracted South as capital scarcity raises its marginal product. Apart from the fact that the role of technical progress in such transfers becomes superfluous, the exogeneity of the world capital stock then becomes a critical (and unreasonable?) assumption.

32 See also Caves (1982, ch. 7) for a typically eloquent review. For fairly traditional policy analyses, see Rodriguez (1975), Bardhan (1982), Brecher (1982), and Gehrels (1983). Each investigates aspects of national licensing, tariff and tax policies in the presence of exogenous technology transfer. Cheng (1984) gives a summary of their conclusions.

33 Metcalfe and Soete (1984) make a number of interesting observations on gaps and diffusion rates, also incorporating demand diffusion.

34 There may even be a Metzler effect with gross import prices falling in the North.

35 John Black has suggested to me that there may be some other advantages to the small country; in particular, license fees plus the possible usefulness to local firms of having a patents register to consult to see what is available.

36 See Corden (1974) for a full discussion of traditional infant industry arguments.

37 Feenstra (1982) sketches an outline model incorporating environmental factors, but it goes little further than characterizing equilibrium.

38 Venables (1982) makes some progress on this issue.

39 See Reinganum (1984) for a neat survey.

40 Profit shifting should be distinguished from the profit creation that would result from, for example, creation of a domestic monopoly to get round immiserizing technical progress. With profit shifting, total world profits will fall while the share of one country rises (assuming downward sloping reaction curves; see below).

41 The slopes of the best reply curves in the output game are less important since they bear no obvious relation to the determination of the slopes of the R and S curves on which policy is based.

42 Several papers in Krugman (ed.) (1986) provide some empirical examples where deliberate or incidental strategic trade policy has led to competitive advantage.

REFERENCES

Arrow, K. J. (1962), 'Economic welfare and the allocation of resources for invention', in R. Nelson (ed.), *The Rate and Direction of Economic Activity: Economic and Social Factors*, NBER, Princeton University Press.

Atkinson, A. A. and J. E. Stiglitz (1969), 'A new view of technological change', *Economic Journal*, **79**, 573–78.

Bardhan, P. K. (1982), 'Imports, domestic production and transnational vertical integration: a theoretical note', *Journal of Political Economy*, **90**, 1020–34.

Behrman, J. N. and H. W. Wallender (1976), *Transfers of Manufacturing Technology Within Multinational Enterprises*, Ballinger, Cambridge, Mass.

Berkowitz, M. K. and Y. Kotowitz (1982), 'Patent policy in an open economy', *Canadian Journal of Economics*, xv, 1–17.
Brecher, R. A. (1982), 'Optimal policy in the presence of licensed technology from abroad', *Journal of Political Economy*, **90**, 1070–78.
Caves, R. E. (1982), *Multinational Enterprise and Economic Activity*, Cambridge University Press.
Cheng, L. (1984a), 'International trade and technology: a brief survey of the literature', *Weltwirtschaftliches Archiv*, **120**, 165–89.
(1984b), 'International competition in R&D and technological leadership: an examination of the Posner-Hufbauer hypothesis', *Journal of International Economics*, **17**, 15–40.
Coase, R. H. (1937), 'The nature of the firm', *Economica*, **4**, 386–405.
Connolly, M. B. (1973), 'Induced technical change and the transfer mechanism', in M. B. Connolly and A. K. Swoboda (eds), *International Trade and Money*, Allen and Unwin.
Corden, W. M. (1974), *Trade Policy and Economic Welfare*, Oxford University Press.
Dasgupta, P. and J. Stiglitz (1980), 'Industrial structure and the nature of innovative activity', *Economic Journal*, **90**, 266–93.
(1985), 'Learning-by-doing, market structure and industrial and trade policies', *CEPR Discussion Paper No. 80*.
David, P. A. (1975), *Technical Choice, Innovation and Economic Growth*, Cambridge University Press.
Davidson, W. H. and D. G. McFetridge (1984), 'International technology transactions and the theory of the firm', *Journal of Industrial Economics*, **32**, 253–64.
Davies, H. (1977), 'Technology transfer through commercial transactions', *Journal of Industrial Economics*, **26**, 161–75.
Deardorff, A. V. (1984), 'Testing trade theories and predicting trade flows', in R. W. Jones and P. B. Kenen (eds), *Handbook of International Economics*, Vol. 1, North-Holland, Amsterdam.
Dixit, A. K. and A. S. Kyle (1985), 'The use of protection and subsidies for entry promotion and deterrence', *American Economic Review*, **75**, 139–52.
Dixit, A. K. and V. Norman (1980), *Theory of International Trade*, Cambridge University Press.
Dollar, D. (1986), 'Technological innovation, capital mobility and the product cycle in the North–South trade', *American Economic Review*, **76**, 177–90.
Dornbusch, R., S. Fischer and P. A. Samuelson (1977), 'Comparative advantage, trade and payments in a Ricardian model with a continuum of goods', *American Economic Review*, **67**, 823–29.
Feenstra, R. C. (1982), 'Product creation and trade patterns: a theoretical note on the "biological" model of trade in similar products', in J. N. Bhagwati (ed.), *Import Competition and Response*, University of Chicago Press.
Feenstra, R. C. and K. L. Judd (1982), 'Tariffs, technology transfer and welfare', *Journal of Political Economy*, **90**, 1142–65.
Findlay, R. (1978), 'Relative backwardness, direct foreign investment and the transfer of technology: a simple dynamic model', *Quarterly Journal of Economics*, **92**, 1–16.
Flaherty, M. T. (1984), 'Field research on the link between technological innovation and growth: evidence from the semiconductor industry', *American Economic Review, Papers and Proceedings*, **74**, 67–72.

Fudenberg, D. and J. Tirole (1984), 'The fat-cat effect, the puppy-dog ploy, and the lean and hungry look', *American Economic Review, Papers and Proceedings*, **74**, 361–66.

Gehrels, F. (1983), 'Foreign investment and technology transfer: optimal policies', *Weltwirtschaftliches Archiv*, **119**, 662–85.

Grossman, G. M. and J. D. Richardson (1985), 'Strategic trade policy: a survey of issues and early analysis', *Princeton Special Papers in International Economics*, No. 15, International Finance Section.

Horst, T. (1972), 'The industrial composition of US exports and subsidiary sales to the Canadian market', *American Economic Review*, **62**, 36–45.

Hufbauer, G. C. (1966), *Synthetic Materials and the Theory of International Trade*, Duckworth, London.

(1970), 'The impact of national characteristics and technology on the commodity composition of trade in manufactured goods', in R. Vernon (ed.), *The Technology Factor in International Trade*, NBER, New York.

Hughes, K. S. (1986), 'Exports and innovation: a simultaneous model', *European Economic Review*, **30**, 383–99.

Hume, D. (1758), 'Of the jealousy of trade', Essay VI in T. H. Green and T. H. Grose (eds) (1964), *The Philosophical Works*, Vol. 3, Scientia Verlag Aalen.

Jones, R. W. (1979), *International Trade: Essays in Theory*, North-Holland, Amsterdam.

Kierzkowski, H. (ed.) (1984), *Monopolistic Competition and International Trade*, Oxford University Press.

Krugman, P. A. (1979), 'A model of innovation, technology transfer and the world distribution of income', *Journal of Political Economy*, **87**, 253–66.

(1984), 'Import protection as export promotion', in H. Kierzkowski (ed.).

(1985), 'A "technology gap" model of international trade' in K. Jungfelt and D. Hague (eds), *Structural Adjustment in Developed Open Economies*, International Economic Association.

(ed.) (1986), *Strategic Trade Policy and the New International Economics*, M.I.T. Press.

Linder, S. B. (1961), *An Essay on Trade and Transformation*, Wiley, New York.

Mansfield, E. and A. Romeo (1980), 'Technology transfer to overseas subsidiaries by US based firms', *Quarterly Journal of Economics*, **95**, 737–50.

Mansfield, E., A. Romeo and D. Teece (1979), 'Overseas research and development by US based firms', *Economica*, **46**, 187–96.

Mansfield, E., A. Romeo and S. Wagner (1979), 'Foreign trade and US research and development', *Review of Economics and Statistics*, **61**, 49–57.

McCulloch, R. and J. L. Yellen (1982), 'Technology transfer and the national interest', *International Economic Review*, **23**, 421–28.

Metcalfe, J. S. and L. Soete (1984), 'Notes on the evolution of technology and international competition', in M. Gibbons *et al.* (eds), *Science and Technology Policy in the 1980's and Beyond*, Longman.

OECD (1986), *Science and Technology Indicators 2: R&D, Invention and Competitiveness*, OECD, Paris.

Pavitt, K. and L. Soete (1980), 'Innovative activities and export shares: some comparisons between industries and countries', in K. Pavitt (ed.), *Technical Innovation and British Economic Performance*, Macmillan, London.

(1981), 'International differences in economic growth and the international location of innovation', in H. Giersch (ed.), *Emerging Technologies:*

Consequences for Economic Growth, Structural Change and Employment, J. C. B. Mohr, Tubingen.

Posner, M. V. (1961), 'International trade and technical change', Oxford Economic Papers, 13, 323–41.

Pugel, T. A. (1982), 'Endogenous technological change and international technology transfer in a Ricardian trade model', Journal of International Economics, 13, 321–35.

Reinganum, J. F. (1984), 'Practical implications of game theoretic models of R&D', American Economic Review Papers and Proceedings, 74, 61–66.

Rodriguez, C. A. (1975), 'Trade in technological knowledge and the national advantage', Journal of Political Economy, 83, 121–35.

Roman, D. D. and J. F. Puett (1982), International Business and Technological Innovation, Elsevier, New York.

Rosenberg, N. (1982), Inside the Black Box: Technology and Economics, Cambridge University Press.

Shaked, A. and J. Sutton (1984), 'Natural oligopolies and international trade', in H. Kierzkowski (ed.).

Soete, L. G. (1981), 'A general test of technological gap trade theory', Weltwirtschaftliches Archiv, 117, 638–60.

Soete, L. (1985), 'Innovation and international trade', in B. R. Williams and J. A. Bryan-Brown (eds), Knowns and Unknowns in Technical Change, Technical Change Centre, London.

Solo, R. (1966), 'The capacity to assimilate an advanced technology', American Economic Review Papers and Proceedings, 56, 91–97.

Spencer, B. J. and J. A. Brander (1983), 'International R&D rivalry and industrial strategy', Review of Economic Studies, 50, 707–22.

Stern, R. M. (1975), 'Testing trade theories', in P. B. Kenen (ed.), International Trade and Finance: Frontiers for Research, Cambridge, Mass.

Stewart, F. (1984), 'Recent theories of international trade: some implications for the South', in H. Kierzkowski (ed).

Sveikauskas, L. (1983), 'Science and technology in US foreign trade', Economic Journal, 93, 242–61.

Teece, D. (1977), 'Technology transfer by multinational firms: the resource cost of transferring technological know-how', Economic Journal, 87, 242–61.

Venables, A. J. (1982), 'Optimal tariffs for trade in monopolistically competitive commodities', Journal of International Economics, 12, 225–41.

Vernon, R. (1966), 'International investment and international trade in the product cycle', Quarterly Journal of Economics, 80, 190–207.

(1979), 'The product cycle hypothesis in a new international environment', Oxford Bulletin of Economics and Statistics, 41, 255–67.

Walker, W. B. (1979), Industrial Innovation and International Trading Performance, JAI Press Inc., Greenwich, Connecticut.

Williamson, O. E. (1975), Markets and Hierarchies, The Free Press.

Wolff, B. M. (1977), 'Industrial diversification and internationalisation: some empirical evidence', Journal of Industrial Economics, 26, 177–91.

8 Some new standards for the economics of standardization in the information age*

PAUL A. DAVID

I Technological standards, business strategies and public policy

Technological standards and product standardization today are subjects of active policy concern in business and government. Standards have a significant bearing upon both the development and the diffusion of new technologies and products, and the process of technological innovation obviously exerts a powerful force upon the structure of markets and the performance of industries. So it is not surprising that issues concerning 'standards', although once quite neglected, have emerged since the mid-1970s as a focus of analytical and empirical attention among economists, especially among those preoccupied with the economics of industrial organization and international competition (see Hemenway 1975, Kindleberger 1983, LeCraw 1984, and Farrell and Saloner 1985b for recent surveys).

The direction of inventive activity itself has to be assigned some of the responsibility for this intellectual re-awakening. Modern advances in microelectronics and microwave, laser and fibre optics technology have given heightened prominence to economic and political issues posed by network externalities and system scale economies in the encoding, processing, and transmission of information. Compatibility and standard-setting have arisen lately as central questions in the development and marketing of computer operating systems and software,

* While the opinions and mistakes contained in these pages are my responsibility exclusively, I wish to thank Brian Arthur, Timothy Bresnahan, and Edward Steinmueller for responding with many corrective criticism and suggestions on a previous draft of Sections I, IV–VII, and to Shane Greenstein, who helped especially with the development of the taxonomy in Section III. Extended conversations with Karl F. Habermeier have helped to clarify my views, in Section V, on the conditions for the occurrence of a 'lock-in' of inferior technology. Julie Bunn supplied very capable research assistance on many more points in the history of systems competition than are reflected in this paper. Financial support received under a grant to the High Technology Impact Program of the Center for Economic Policy Research at Stanford University is gratefully acknowledged.

commercial data or 'value added' networks (e.g., TELENET and TYMNET), local area networks (LANs), cellular radio-telephones, and 'smart cards' for electronic funds transfer. While these are a source of new economic opportunities, they have also created new and difficult problems of strategy for corporate managers and public policy-makers alike.

When should a company strive for standardization of product features and technologies, and when should it seek to thwart standardization? Can dominant firms choose technological standards so as to further extend their own market power? How, if at all, will standards evolve from the interplay of competitive market forces, and how is the course of their evolution likely to be influenced by governmental intervention? Can national governments adopt policies towards standards that will promote both the economic welfare of domestic consumers and the international competitiveness of their own firms?

Addressing questions such as these raises still more questions, uniform answers to which remain largely non-existent. What effects does the establishment of a technical standard have upon the rate and direction of innovative activity in the field itself, and in related technologies? Are there important differences in this regard among different categories of standards? Is there some general taxonomic principle which economists might use in distinguishing among the many varieties of 'standards'? When are public policies best directed toward fostering standardization, or, alternatively, when should government actions be interposed in an effort to slow an adoption 'bandwagon' that appears to be leading an industry into premature standardization? Are there some principles that may guide policy-making under conditions in which, most typically, the technical optimality of proposed standards, and the magnitudes of potential economic benefits and costs from their adoption, remain clouded by engineering and market uncertainty?

Rather than risk engendering false hopes that answers to all these questions will be forthcoming shortly, I should announce my purpose here to be a far more modest one. I want to address some special problems of formulating economically sensible standardization policies suitable for the era of the 'information revolution' which we have entered. These concern the use of various modes of direct and indirect governmental intervention to promote network compatibility, achieve interchangeability among functionally equivalent components, and foster systems integration – by specifying standards for physical product characteristics, procedures, and linguistic (code-writing) conventions. At best, I can hope to succeed in suggesting the usefulness of adopting a fresh approach, a non-standard way of thinking about how such policies may affect the development of new technological systems.

II   Network technologies, present and past

Telecommunications and information processing 'network technologies' of the variety just mentioned provide paradigms of the particular class of systems which are especially interesting in this connection. Two distinct features of such technologies will be seen both to occasion a need for public policy interventions and to pose awkward problems for the intervenors: *technical interrelatedness* and *economies of system scale* (or *network integration benefits*) each give rise to differing forms of 'externalities'. These were typical of the classic network industries, but today production processes and consumer products having such properties seem to be pouring forth, at an accelerated rate, from the microelectronics cornucopia. Consequently, it is now quite widely appreciated that users of such technologies are at the mercy of the social mechanisms available for maintaining efficient system performance by providing compatibility among all the constituent elements (see, e.g., Kindleberger 1983, Hartwick 1985). It is also believed that in such situations decentralized resource allocation through markets leads, in general, to an insufficiently high degree of standardization to avoid efficiency losses in systems operations (see Carlton and Klamer 1983).

Of course, we did not have to wait until being stuck with an IBM PC in the office and an Apple Macintosh computer at home to understand this point. Residents of Baltimore, Maryland, must have grasped it (and perhaps also the underlying economic logic) in February of 1904, when a fire broke out of control in the city's downtown area and soon threatened to overwhelm the capacity of local fire-fighting equipment. Fire engines were summoned from the surrounding communities; units from Washington, D.C., reached the scene within three hours, and others arrived eventually from as far afield as Philadelphia and New York City. Although there was no shortage of water, many of them proved utterly incapable of helping throughout the thirty hours in which the fire laid waste an area of seventy city blocks; the screw couplings on their hoses would not fit the fire hydrants in Baltimore (see Hemenway 1975). That's what we call a static efficiency loss.

I have now fulfilled at least your minimal expectations of me as a practicing economic historian, by indicating that the special opportunities and problems posed by the emergence of today's information-technology systems are not without instructive historical precedents. Older technologies in the fields of transportation and communications, such as those which laid the foundations for the canal, railway, telegraph, wire-based telephone, and radio industries, also were characterized by significant 'network externalities' which rendered the achievement of compatibility an issue of recognized importance (see, e.g., Aitken 1976, Chandler 1977, Jennings 1984, Puffert 1985, Sturmey 1958). The experience of the electrical manufacturing industry and electrical utilities in the development of generation, transmission and applications systems, too, may hold many highly pertinent lessons about the nature of things yet to come (see, e.g., Bowers 1982, Byatt 1979, Hannah 1979, Hennessey 1971, Hughes 1983, Passer 1972, and David with Bunn 1986).

Far more is involved here than technological and business history narrowly construed. Efforts to adapt to technological needs and opportunities in the area of communications – notably telegraphy, railway rolling-stock exchanges, and radio transmission use of the electromagnetic spectrum – led to national conflicts and coalitions; the outcome in some cases was the creation of entirely new international organizations, many of which remain largely unstudied. Moreover, a reorientation of one's thinking along these lines quickly reveals a wealth of only casually examined historical experience, involving non-esoteric consumer products for which the question of compatibility with other, complementary elements of a technological system has long been of practical economic importance for consumers' welfare and business success: coin-operated vending machines, phonograph records, photographic films and lenses, automobile spare parts, and so forth, recently joined by colour TV and VCR's.

Indeed, there seems to be considerable heuristic value even in so simple a story as that of the system of typewriters and touch-typists based upon the notoriously inefficient standard keyboard known as QWERTY – the prosaic and serendipitous technological foundations of that design notwithstanding (David 1985, 1986b, Hartwick 1985). A sense of the historical experience in this particular case, as in others, has the salutary effect of encouraging one to adopt an explicitly dynamic approach. Specifically, it instructs us to look beyond the more familiar dilemmas facing policy-makers who seek to avoid static efficiency losses by promoting cooperative standard-setting among network industry firms, or by mandating compliance with governmentally designated 'interface standards'.

Before proceeding to that task, however, some brief attention to the nature and functions of 'standards' may prove helpful. Section III offers a taxonomy which has the virtue of bringing technological 'interface standards' into sharper focus by distinguishing them from others, while also indicating the breadth of relevant experience that might be brought to bear on future policy analyses in this area. Static economic welfare considerations pertaining to standardization policy are then reviewed very briefly in Section IV, before I turn to the argument for taking a less standard approach, emphasizing the dynamics of competition among alternative systems designs that are each characterized by network integration benefits. To help fix ideas concretely, Section V presents an elementary model of sequential technological systems choices on the part of competitive users under conditions of symmetrical network externalities. This explicitly synthesizes the simplest class of 'probit' models of equilibrium diffusion (following David 1969 and Davies 1979) with the analysis of technological competition under increasing returns as a path-dependent stochastic process, along the lines provided by Arthur (1985). A slight extension permits formal treatment of the effects upon diffusion dynamics of the expectations that are formed concerning the eventual outcome of the rivalry between contending systems.

Section VI takes up three generic technology policy problems that are highlighted by the preceeding heuristic modelling exercise. Elsewhere (David 1986a), I have affixed to these some colorful labels – referring to them as the problems of 'narrow policy windows', 'blind giants', and 'angry orphans' – in order to compensate for the fact that they previously have been allowed to pass without much notice in discussions of the economics of standardization. The first one derives from the likelihood that, where strong positive network externalities exist, the momentum of market-driven adoption processes operates to 'lock in' some system configurations, and to 'lock out' others. Consequently, there may be only comparatively brief and uncertain 'windows in time', during which effective public policy interventions can be made at moderate resource costs. The second is a dilemma posed by the realization that governmental agencies are likely to have greatest power to influence the future trajectories of network technologies, just when a suitable informational basis on which to make socially optimal choices among alternatives is most lacking. The actors in question, then, resemble 'blind giants' – whose vision we would wish to improve before their power dissipates. A third problem arises from the virtual inevitability that rivalries among alternative technological systems, whether driven purely by market forces or publicly managed, will leave some groups of users 'orphaned'; they will have sunk investments in a system whose maintenance and further elaboration are going to be discontinued. Encouraging the development of gateway devices (converters, adaptors, translators) linking otherwise incompatible systems can help to minimize the static economic losses incurred by orphans. But 'premature' reductions of gateway costs may exact unforeseen economic penalties, by discouraging investment in R&D programmes aimed at establishing the technological dominance of one system over its rivals.

In place of proper conclusions in Section VII, I am obliged to close by giving notice to the main respects in which my treatment of technology policy dilemmas pertaining to network standardization represents a drastic oversimplification of reality; of the need in future applied research to attend more closely to the nature of the specific constraints imposed by particular network technologies, standards-writing organizations, and regulatory procedures and institutions. Above everything else, however, I would urge that the dynamic stochastic approach to modelling technology choices under increasing returns which is essayed so simplistically in these pages, be elaborated upon by others for the purpose of analysing public policy issues. It is to be hoped that they will be better able than I to take account of the essentially political nature of the process of setting domestic and international technology standards, and to analyse the additional theoretical complexities created by the scope for strategic behaviour on the part of private firms and the various interested agencies of government.

III   Interface and other standards: a proposed taxonomy

The term 'standards' has been used here in more than one way. It is employed substantively in the ordinary, dictionary sense, when referring to the means used in determining 'the way things should be'. This is broad enough to include something established by authority, customary usage, or general consent as a model, exemplar, or criterion; as well as something which has been set up and established by authority as a rule for the measure of quantity, weight, extent, value, or quality. In modern parlance the noun 'standard' also has acquired a special meaning, which is the one invoked when the International Standards Organization, or the US Federal Trade Commission (1978) uses it to refer to *a technical document* intended to describe design, material, processing, safety or performance characteristics of a product.

The economics of standards, interpreted in either the commonplace or this special sense of the word, forms a subject the dimensions of which extend well beyond the purview of the present essay. Seen from the most general theoretical perspective, it properly belongs to the domain of information economics; the establishment of standards has greatest significance when economic agents cannot assimilate without substantial costs all the relevant information about the commodities that may be exchanged with other agents, and the processes by means of which those goods and services can be produced. Many features that have been noticed as problematic about the demand for 'standards', and the supply thereof, are not peculiar to standards as such. They are, instead, generic attributes of information as a commodity. Lack of super-additivity is one example: just as having the same bit of information twice does not convey more information than having it once, so having two standards for the same thing does not mean one has more 'standardization' – indeed, quite the opposite may be true.

Broadly construed as information, standards may be held to have the function of reducing transactions costs. 'Voluntary standards' is a term used in reference to technical documents formulated with this ostensible purpose; they have been described as 'agreements intended to facilitate communication within an industry' (see Link 1983, p. 393). Having a standard can lower transactions costs by making it simpler for all the parties to a deal to recognize what is being dealt in, and also by limiting the scope for the exploitation of informational asymmetries through practices such as giving short weight, short measure, adulteration, debasement of payment media, and so forth. Private agents' costs of information acquisition obviously can be reduced by the elimination of variety, so, 'standardization' – the action of bringing things to a uniform standard – has the effect of facilitating economic transactions. Elimination of variety also may yield savings in unit costs of physical production, as is the case when achievement of greater uniformity permits economies of repetition, more intensive (larger scale) utilization of fixed facilities, and reductions in the relative importance of setup vs. operating time.

A great diversity of standards is subsumed under the foregoing general rubric, and some distinctions of potential economic interest among them are bound to be obscured by concentrating theoretical attention upon their shared properties. Kindleberger (1983) suggests that the distinction between the two economic effects just noticed – reducing transactions costs and realizing physical economies of scale in production – provides a basis for categorizing standards. Some practical problems arise with this particular proposal, because a given 'standard' evidently can perform both functions: the dimensional standards for lumber would appear to fall into one category at the sawmill and the construction site, but into the other when considered at the retail lumber yard. There is a more serious objection, however, against starting out to classify standards according to their ultimate economic effects. The latter should not be prejudged for the purpose of locating a standard within a taxonomic framework; rather, the question of the effects upon market structure and industrial performance is a proper subject of applied economic analysis, and so must be permitted to remain unresolved in particular instances.

Virtually the same objections can be lodged against selecting as a taxonomic principle the manner in which a standard comes to be set up – that is, whether it has been formalized *de jure* (through legislative mandate, administrative decree, legal ruling), or established without force of law by explicit voluntary agreement, or arisen *de facto* through customary usage or the congruence of many individuals' independent actions. This, too, is an important matter which is better left for the conclusions of a systematic politico-economic inquiry. Moreover, the origins of particular standards are likely to turn out to be as much a product of the institutional and market contexts as of any intrinsic qualities of the standards themselves.

Standards have been classified according to the nature of the information conveyed. The American Society for Testing and Materials, an important standard-writing organization (see Hemenway 1975, p. 87) recognizes five categories: definitions, classifications, practices, test methods, or specifications. While this taxonomy obviously can be implemented, even if there are occasional overlaps, it does not give the economic analyst much to work with. How then might the various forms of standards be better represented for purposes of formal economic modelling? If one focused upon the aspect of standards as measures of one sort or another, a standard's relevant features could be described mathematically as involving the establishment of one of the following:

(1) an ordinal scale or measure against which the relative extent of some quality dimension is compared, of which gradation measures of the quality of many consumer products are typical;

(2) a cardinal scale for a quality against which some minimum or maximum bound is defined, as exemplified by the typical environmental standard;

(3) dichotomous sets, one being compatible with a standard and the other not, which typically holds for standards intended to assure compatibility among components or products. Standardization of technical interfaces characteristically falls into this category.

Yet, this formalism does not overcome the problem of lack of mutual exclusivity. A given 'technical standard' could be placed in more than one of the three foregoing categories. For example, being greater or less than some bound establishes two dichotomous sets, and the notion or 'partial compatibility' further blurs the distinction between class (3) and classes (1) and (2). This is somewhat disappointing because drawing distinctions along these lines might prove useful in applied studies where enforceability of standards is a matter of interest: it may be that it is easier to insure conformity with a cardinal scale, because monitoring is cheaper to effect when it has some foundation in a scientific procedure, even though only an ordinal property of the standard (not giving short-weight) has major interests for the customers. Conformity to the standard of accuracy for the weighing-machine at the butcher-shop is of

Table 8.1. *Taxonomy of standards*

	Standards of Technical Design	Standards of Behavioural Performance

Standards for Reference, Definition	currencies
	weights, measures
	chemical properties
	grades, dimensions of
	  materials & products
		professional licensing
		accreditation of insti-
		  tutions
		precedents in law

Standards for Minimal Admissible Attributes	safety levels (system)
	safety features (com-
	  ponent product)
	product quality
		legal codes
		job qualifications
		certification of com-
		  petence

Standards for Interface Compatibility	physical design of
	  interfaces
	codes
	screw threads
	signal frequencies
		contractual forms
		diplomatic protocols
		vernacular languages
		standards of commercial
		  conduct ('honesty')

less relevance to shoppers than the standard's ordinal property: that the machine should not overstate true weight. A second difficulty with trying to construct a taxonomy based on this formalization of the quantitative characteristics of standards is that it does not so readily accommodate the broader notion of standards defined over aspects of human behaviour, as well as over characteristics of inanimate objects. The relevance of much social experience could be obscured by giving such prominence to distinctions based upon measurement modes.

The foregoing suggests that generating a satisfactory categorization of standards from a single classification principle is not easy, but that a taxonomy helpful for economic analysis might be constructed using the two orthogonal principles of classification: one that refers to the nature of the things with which the standard is concerned, and another that refers to the informational function performed by the standard in reducing transactions costs. I would begin, therefore by dividing standards between instances in which the standard deals with features of an inanimate object (principally its material and design properties), and those in which the standard describes human behaviour, procedures, and performance. This distinction creates a major separation between the entire class of *technical standards*, which are easier to specify *ex ante* in a fully quantitative manner, and standards for human behaviour, which are typically codified *ex post* and generally retain greater elements of ambiguity. The indicated separation may have some heuristic value, in calling attention to the fact that several distinctions that appear within the family of technical standards can be extended with little difficulty into corresponding distinctions among *behaviour standards*. Social experience with the latter may then clarify our thinking about the former.

Restricting attention to the left side of the 2-way tableau shown as Table 8.1, one can distinguish three general categories or types of technical standards. First comes the category of reference standards, within which we may place definitions, terminologies, and classification and labelling schemes. A key feature of *a technical reference standard* is that it functions as a reference point in only one dimension; the informational categorizations or definitions alone serve to divide objects into sets. These sets can have either mathematical representation in a cardinal scheme such as weights and measures, and conventional dimensions (as in the case of 2 × 4 lumber, which has been standardized to be $1\frac{1}{2}'' \times 3\frac{1}{2}''$, sawn and dried); they can simply be a categorization scheme, such as chemical properties, and grades of meat. Thus, this class is more general than measurement type (1) above. The right-most column of the tableau suggests that the behavioural counterparts of technical reference standards include such things as specific precedents in the law, and standards for the identification of agents performing specialized complex services, as in the case of professional liscensing and accreditation standards.

The next class of standards can be viewed as providing information in the form of sharply drawn dichotomies. Technical standards belonging in this category generally involve the combination of a numerical and a categorical reference standard, in order to categorize objects on the basis of a *minimum admissible attribute*. It is a combination of measurement modes (2) and (3), because the designation of a dividing line turns a numerical standard in one dimension into a dichotomous classification scheme in the same dimension. (While it resembles the categorical reference class of standards because of the existence of a rule for inclusion and exclusion, the rule employed in the numerical case is an inequality.) The satisfaction of a safety level for the operation of a technological system, and the existence of technical safety features in an individual product or device, are exemplars of technical standards of this sort. Standards assuring some minimal level of quality in products belong here, too – such labelling standards fix a maximum for the proportion of chicken allowable in a 'beef frankfurter', or the amount of gum arabic that can be present in a product sold as 'mayonnaise'. Among the behavioural analogues of this category of standards one would want to place legal codes that separate licit from illicit conduct, and job qualifications such as minimum educational attainment levels.

The third functional class of standards provides information required to facilitate physical interactions and behavioural 'transactions' at interfaces between objects, or between agents, and also between objects and agents (as in the layout of airplane cockpits, and the oft-cited case of typewriter keyboard layouts and touch-typists). Technical standards here may possess all the measurement features found in the first two functional classes, but they are more complex and present in more than one dimension. One feature of this class of standard is the multiplicity of judgements and labels that typically go into the exclusion and inclusion rule, but it is possible to think of special instances in which a single-dimensional minimal admissible attribute standard functions as a standard assuring the compatibility of components – e.g., in receipts for food preparation.

Rather than risk over-simplification, however, it seems better to consider the following illustratively complex example from the field of microelectronic circuit design, which W. Edward Steinmueller has brought to my attention. There is a standard referred to as 'TTL', to which a large class of integrated circuits conform. Features of TTL ICs include the universal use of 5v. supply voltages, designation of 3v. or greater as a binary state of unity, and of 2v. or less as a binary state of zero. Although the standard itself is named after the original circuit design (Transistor–Transistor Logic) employed in fabricating a type of IC device, an IC can be classified as TTL if it conforms to the interface specifications that assign those voltage ranges to the binary codes – regardless of whether or not its actual circuitry uses transistor–transistor logic to perform logical functions. Notice that although here the 'physical design of interfaces' standard stops at the boundary of the IC with its external environment or interface, functional compatibility depends upon the standard of signal levels which is defined in terms of minimal admissible attributes ($\leqslant$2v. = '0', and $\geqslant$3v. = '1'), and the 5v. supply reference standard. Moreover, the performance and operating cost of an electronic *system* built with TTL-standard ICs is by no means determined when the interface issues are resolved by specification of that standard; because the operating speed of a system is often limited by the component device whose 'switching speed' is the slowest, system performance may be determined by specification of a reference standard switching speed. Thus, in realistically complex technological systems, although the attributes of constituent design standards may be labelled according to the taxonomic scheme of Table 8.1, the type of standard controlling the construction of systems appears to be distributed arbitarily across the main categories that have been distinguished.

Technical design interfaces, such as those between spark-plugs and automotive engine cylinders and electrical circuits, or the thread-sizes of nuts and bolts, and formal codes (like computer languages), are perhaps more familiar members of this category, and many of the most difficult economic policy questions surrounding interface standards concern the way that compatibility among components affects the benefits and costs of forming and operating complex technological systems. These will occupy the discussion in the two following sections, but, as the taxonomic tableau points out, there are significant parallels that may be drawn in this regard between technological systems on the one hand, and the organization of commercial, social, and political networks, on the other hand.

IV   Network externalities and interface standardization: statics

The *technical interrelatedness* of the components that form, say, a communications network, requires strict compatibility at each interface, node, or linkage point, in order for the system as a whole to perform efficiently in an engineering sense. Hence the functioning of any component of an integrated technological system cannot be evaluated in isolation, and its within-system performance can be affected by the attributes or behaviour of other components. A second point to notice is that the existence of *system scale economies*, or benefits of more extensive *network integration*, means that the economic value of any technically defined variant of system design can in some degree be enhanced for those using it by enlarging the size of the user-community. When technically interrelated components of a system are supplied by independent economic agents, both features give rise to 'network externalities'.

The first form of externality impacts immediately upon the technical performance of the particular system as a whole, and feeds back to affect the costs and profits of other component suppliers, through the influence of the system's performance characteristics upon users' demand for it in comparison with alternative technologies. The second form operates directly upon the demand side of the market, where the benefits derived by users increase with the number of others whose decision to use compatible products enlarges the coverage of the network. In both sets of circumstances, it is commonly understood, markets are likely to work poorly as mechanisms for quickly achieving the degree of compatibility or standardization required to maximize the benefits obtainable with an already existing network technology. (See Brock 1975, Kindleberger 1983, Carlton and Klamer 1983, Katz and Shapiro 1985a, and the recent survey by Farrell and Saloner 1985b.)

This is not to say that *uncoordinated networks* do not arise via the decentralized profit-seeking actions of agents who will not or cannot be bound by enforceable contracts to maintain stipulated interface standards. What is most likely to happen early in the development of a network technology is that there will be a multiplicity of configurations, each of which is not fully compatible with the others. The fire departments in Baltimore, Washington, and Philadelphia did have engines equipped with hoses fitting the (standard) hydrant in each of their respective cities. In the early days of the computer boom, although peripheral equipment such as tape drives had to be designed to interface with central processing units (CPUs), little was done to allow data recorded on one type of machine to be read by another: by 1960 there existed fifty models of tape drives, with physical tape widths ranging from one-half inch to two inches and the number of parallel data tracks ranging from seven to forty-eight (see Brock 1975, p. 77). More prosaically, the owners of Nikon and Pentax SLR cameras on an outing today can lend 35mm film to each other if one of them has an extra roll and the other has run out; yet they cannot share lenses unless they have equipped themselves with special adaptors.

Societal advantages which could justify government action to induce interface standardization are therefore seen both in the greater benefits afforded to those users who would adopt the new technological system in any event, and the marginal benefits derived through the extension of its use to others who otherwise would have had to bear the costs of installing adapters, or 'gateways' to achieve *ex post* network integration. Further, standardization of component interfaces sometimes can allow customization which better suits the varied needs and tastes of users, as has proved to be the case with hi-fidelity audio systems. Beyond these, there may also be generic standardization gains for complex system users: design information and engineering costs may be reduced, along with search costs and uncertainty regarding system performance. Greater price, and/or quality competition among suppliers of standardized components is more likely to ensue, supposing that the latter can enter the market more readily than can firms who must undertake to provide an entire system. Market structure and conduct may well be improved by the standards for interchangeability which restrict the scope for 'tying' arrangements (see Leland 1979, LeCraw 1984).

On the other hand, in a pure market environment, *coordinated network technologies* may be developed through the private sponsorship of a set of interface standards which are embodied in a proprietary system: all the necessarily interrelated components of a consumer product or a production facility can, in many instances, be readily packaged together by a single provider. Such a supply-agent may be referred to as an *integrated system sponsor*; and the particular product or service supplied as a *system variant*. A difficulty, however, may be that the entailed capital costs are so large that they pose effective barriers to the entry of rival system variants, and so give rise to natural monopoly systems such as exist in the paradigmatic network industries: railways, telephones, electric utilities. Hence the problems of achieving standardization can be replaced by those which arise when firms acquire great market power.

The literature on the economies of standardization recognizes an alternative route to network coordination, which may look attractive in eschewing the creation of natural monopolies requiring regulation: public authorities may hope to foster network integration, and so to promote competition among suppliers of network components, by promulgating uniform interface standards for systems purchased by government agencies, or by mandatory imposition of standards in regulated industries. That losses of potential efficiency may result from the legislative or administrative setting of technology standards, and also from governmental efforts to induce cooperation among firms in the voluntary setting of standards, is generally regarded as the central dilemma facing public policy-makers in this arena.

The problem of *voluntary* standard-setting is that it may be impossible to achieve without arranging for elaborate 'side-payments': in the telecommunications field the standards arrived at in this way often are the ones that allow participants to earn some quasi-rents on the respective 'components' of the network in which they had developed a special competence. Such compensation will be needed, generally, to induce the cooperation of firms who believe they would surrender a valuable competitive advantage by relinquishing their freedom to switch to the use of some new proprietary standard; or that rents which they enjoy as integrated system sponsors would be competed away once standardization permitted easy entry into the market by suppliers of separate components. Feasible arrangements for side-payments among 'stake-holders' could be facilitated by changes in anti-trust policy, favouring formation of joint ventures among rival system suppliers for the purpose of developing industry standards. These, however, soon begin to assume the features of a cartel which, in turn, would call for some measure of continuing governmental oversight.

However difficult it may be to achieve confined cooperation in a timely fashion, voluntary standard-setting is nevertheless viewed by many as the appropriate public policy course because it represents the lesser of two evils. The greater evil, in this case, is regarded to be the potential efficiency losses arising from governmental imposition of 'wrong' standards. It is pointed out frequently that public authorities do not generally possess the technical expertise required to write technical standards, and so must in any event rely upon information obtained from sources closest to the technology in the private sector.

A property common to the foregoing observations is that they are dominated by an essentially static conceptualization, in which the core problem is seen to be the fact that market competition does not lead to enough standardization to optimize the efficiency of existing network technologies. Yet the world takes on a very different appearance when one turns to consider the dynamics of market rivalries among alternative variants of a network technology – whether these are sponsored or unsponsored. Under competitive conditions, and in the absence of governmental intervention, the existence of significant increasing returns in system scale can give the result that one variant will drive out all the others and so emerge as the *de facto* standard for the industry. Moreover, the winner need not be the most efficient among the available alternatives, nor the one which adopters would have chosen – if a different historical sequence of choices on the part of others had preceded their own. The inefficient layout of the QWERTY keyboard bears witness to the practical relevance of such theoretical considerations (see Arthur 1985, David 1985, 1986b).

V   Some elementary dynamics of technological systems rivalry

To fix the latter ideas more concretely here, it may be helpful to consider a formal representation of the dynamics of a 'systems rivalry'. We may start from the most elementary micro-decision model of technology choice: a diffusion model of the 'probit' type (see David 1969, Davies 1979, and Stoneman 1983: pp. 97–102 for further discussion). Assume there are just two interesting variant formulations of a particular network technology: D and A, which might stand for electricity networks based upon direct current and alternating current, respectively; or, for that matter, the Dvorak typewriter keyboard layout and any other Alternative to QWERTY. Let there be potential users, indexed by $i = (1, \ldots, N)$ where N is large, and suppose that at a particular point in time, t, the i-th agent will have to make an irreversible choice between D and A. Denote the probability of the ith agent choosing system variant A by $p^i(A) = 1 - p^i(D)$.

Assume that the ith agent would derive an inherent benefit from selecting system D rather than A, and let the measure of that be z^i. The latter could arise from objective circumstances intrinsic to i's economic activities, or could be a pure 'taste' variable. Further, assume that all users would derive a benefit (net of installation costs) from using system variant A instead of variant D, measured by B_A^i. Let absolute (gross) system-use benefits be b_A^i, and b_D^i, and inherent absolute benefits be Z_D^i and Z_A^i, respectively; define the differential benefits: $z^i = Z_D^i - Z_A^i$, and $B_A^i = b_A^i - b_D^i$. Then $B_A^i \geqq z^i$ is equivalent to $(b_A^i + Z_A^i) \geqq (b_D^i + Z_D^i)$. The more compact notation will be employed below.

For simplicity of exposition, the choice behaviour of the i-th agent can be taken to be purely deterministic:

$$p^i(A) = \begin{cases} 1 \text{ if } B_A^i \geqq z^i \\ 0 \text{ if } B_A^i < z^i \end{cases} \tag{1}$$

This simplistic choice-model follows very much along the lines of the earliest 'equilibrium theories' of innovation diffusion, and also resembles Arthur's (1983, 1985) elegant exposition model, save for the fact that the z^i-variate is assumed here to have a continuous distribution in the population of potential adopters, whereas Arthur specialized the model to the case in which the agents were of only two types.

Now I shall introduce a crucial specification intended to represent the influence of network externalities upon individual agents' choice-behaviour: denoting the proportion of existing users of the technology who already are committed to system variant A as $F(A)$, I say that the differential system-use benefit derived from A by i depends upon this measure of the extent of the system's 'coverage', as of the date t when i must make a choice:

$$B_A^i = B^i\{F_t(A) \mid t=i\}, \quad i = 1 \ldots N, \tag{2}$$

where, without loss of generality, the index of individual agents has been ordered so that $i=t$. As there is no strong reason to suppose that the users would not be symmetrically effected by network externalities – whether those took a positive form (integration) or a negative form (congestion)– matters should be kept as simple as possible. I will therefore impose the further restriction:

$$B_A^i = B\{F_t(A)\}, \quad i = 1 \ldots N. \tag{3}$$

Two remarks are in order. First, there is no requirement thus far for $B^i\{.\}$ to have any particular shape, so it could be a monotonic or a non-monotonic function in $F(A) = 1 - F(D)$. Second, the resemblance of the formal structure of the model to that of the models of Stoneman and Ireland (1983) and David and Olsen (1984) becomes strong, once one imposes the 'increasing returns' condition: $B_{F(A)}\{.\} > 0$. In those models, however, it is the 'learning effects' on the technology supply side

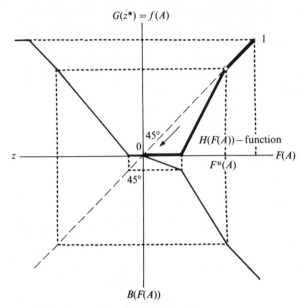

Fig. 8.1   Generation of the *H*-function

that drive the diffusion process forward in time; whereas here the interpretation is that increasing network externalities are operating on the demand side.

Now a stochastic element can be introduced into the picture, by following Arthur (1985) in supposing that agents arrive at the market (to select a system variant) in random order. Assume there is a time-stationary distribution of the characteristic z over the population of such agents, with p.d.f. $g(z)$, and c.d.f. $G(z)$, so that at each moment in time: $\Pr[z \leqq z^*] = G(z^*)$.

What is the unconditional probability that variant A will be chosen by an agent who arrives at the market at time t? Given equation (1), it is simply the probability that at that time an agent will appear whose inherent benefits from choosing the other variant (D) will be matched or exceeded by the current level of the net system-use benefits that can be obtained by joining network A. Using $f_t(A)$ to denote this unconditional probability at time t, equations (1)–(3) allow us to write

$$f_t(A) = G(z_t^*), \text{ where } z_t^* = B\{F_t(A)\}, \text{ for all } t. \tag{4}$$

This leads immediately to a convenient reduced-form expression:

$$f_t(A) = H\{F_t(A)\}, \text{ for all } t. \tag{5}$$

Figure 8.1 shows how the H-function will be generated by specification of a cumulative distribution function, $G(z)$, and a benefits curve for system variant A. The resulting H-function is mapped into the $f(A)$–$F(A)$ plane *in its limiting position*, i.e., the one that is approached as the absolute numbers of users becomes sufficiently large that their distribution between the alternatives is the determinant of the level of net system-use benefits from either.

What can be said about the dynamics of the sequential process of technology choice? From the viewpoint of the formal theory of stochastic processes the model before us is equivalent to a generalized 'Polya urn scheme'. In one simple set-up of that kind, beloved by probabilists, an urn containing a large number of balls of various colours is sampled with replacement, and every drawing of a ball of a specified colour results in a second ball of the same colour being returned to the urn; the probabilities that balls of specified colours will be added are therefore increasing (linear) functions of the proportions in which the respective colours are represented within the urn. (While the model under examination here corresponds to the diagramatically easier two-colour case, the mapping from the distribution of colours in the urn to the probable colour of the next ball added is more general than the classic linear example.)

A basic tool for investigating limiting properties in path-dependent dynamic processes of this sort recently has been made available, in the form of an important theorem of Arthur, Ermoliev, and Kaniovski (1983, 1985). Leaving aside technicalities, the A–E–K theorem says, in essence, that if the process is extended indefinitely, the respective shares of the user population held by the variant systems (colours in the urn) must converge *with probability one* to a fixed point; but it can converge only to points of 'stable' equilibrium, namely those which *expected* motions lead towards; and it cannot converge with positive probability to 'unstable' fixed points, namely those from which the *expected* motions lead away. (This rendering is based on the exposition in Arthur 1984.)

Returning to look at Figure 8.1, we can see that wherever the H-function crosses the 45-degree line in the $f(A)$–$F(A)$ plane there will exist a fixed point; so in this case many equilibria will be 'in contention' as potential outcomes of the process. The point corresponding to $F^u(A)$, marked with the open dot, is unstable in the downwards direction. Since to the left of $F^u(A)$ the probability of system A being adopted by the latest arrivals in the market lies below the proportion of users already committed to that variant, the expected motion of the latter share will be downwards, until it converges to $F(A) = 0$. But as the H-function happens to coincide with the 45-degree line to the right of $F^u(A)$, every

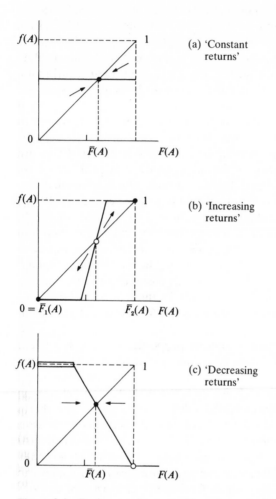

Figure 8.2   Basic cases in stochastic systems rivalries

one of the infinity of equilibria up to and including $F(A) = 1$ is a stable, 'attractor' point. This is a rather special situation, which can serve to alert one to the possibilities of bizarre outcomes in the world of path-dependent stochastic processes.

A more conventional array of economic cases is represented by the three diagrams of Figure 8.2: (a) corresponds to the case of constant returns to system scale, i.e., no network externalities of either kind; (c) to a case of decreasing returns (system congestion?). Whereas the dynamics of system rivalry under these conditions leads to a unique outcome, $\bar{F}(A)$,

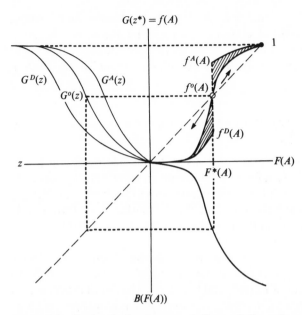

Figure 8.3   Rational adaptive expectations reinforce the normal dynamic effects of positive network externalities

in which the market will be shared indefinitely among the contending variants, the unbounded (symmetrical) positive network externalities case which is depicted by Figure 8.2(b) points to a strikingly different conclusion. The alternative systems cannot coexist indefinitely, and a *de facto* universal standard will emerge 'naturally,' with probability one!

The foregoing elementary framework can be modified in a correspondingly simple way, in order to give at least token notice to the potent role that expectations on the part of users may play in dynamic processes of adoption when network externalities are significant (see Hanson 1984, and Katz and Shapiro 1985a, b and, more generally, Ireland and Stoneman 1986 and David and Olsen 1986 on effects of technological expectations).

Suppose one replaced the assumption regarding the time-stationarity of the $G(z)$ distribution with a different supposition, based on the notion of 'adaptive expectations'. Let there then be some critical market share, $F^*(A)$, defined as a point, or a range, above which there would occur a reduction in the inherent z-benefits from adopting system variant D. The latter, it will be recalled, are what new entrants to the market treat as their opportunity costs of opting to join network A; the posited reduction could be interpreted as reflecting a bigger write-down of the anticipated future worth of an investment in linking oneself to a network whose relative coverage of the user population will be shrinking secularly. When the market share of A fell *below* $F^*(A)$, on the other hand, just the opposite direction shift of the z-distribution should occur. This is expressed formally by

$$G(z) = \begin{cases} G^D(z) & \text{if } F(A) < F^*(A) \\ G^o(z) & \text{if } F(A) = F^*(A), \\ G^A(z) & \text{if } F(A) > F^*(A) \end{cases} \tag{6}$$

where the following first order stochastic dominance condition holds: $G^A(z) > G^o(z) > G^D(z)$, for all t. Notice that if potential adopters were here held to possess complete information about the process underlying the rivalry, they would have to put the critical market share level $F^*(A)$ at the unstable equilibrium point – where Figure 8.3 shows it to lie.

It is only a trivial matter now to show that if the unconditional probability of an adoption of A at time t in the absence of adaptive expectation effects is $f_t^o(A)$, corresponding to $G^o(z)$, then $f_t^A(A)$ must lie above it to the right of $F^*(A)$, and below it to the left of that point, or range. Figure 8.3 gives an illustration, from which it is apparent that the existence of adaptive expectations of the sort imagined would *reinforce* the effects of positive network externalities, thereby accelerating the emergence of one of the two variants as the *de facto* standard for the industry.

Which standard will triumph in this fashion, however, cannot be predicted with corresponding certitude from an *ex ante* vantage point. For, from Figure 8.2(b), it will be seen that the particular details of the initial conditions can make all the difference in determining the identity of the eventual victor. Under unbounded increasing returns, the dynamic process of systems rivalry takes on a truly historical nature in the sense of being *non-ergodic*; it can never shake loose from the grip of past events and is in that sense *path-dependent*. Moreover, there is nothing to guarantee that efficiency will prevail along the path followed by such a process (see Arthur 1985). Nor need the ultimate outcome be the one which is globally optimal. In the simple model just presented, the victory of system variant A, which is no less likely *ex ante* than that of variant D, could deprive the entire population of users of some greater level of benefits that would have been enjoyed had the ultimate outcome have been reversed.

A superior network technology that arrived on the scene unanticipated, could successfully challenge the incumbent if the latter's installed base was comparatively small in relation to the flow of gross additions to the facilities accessed by users of the network. The foregoing model simply abstracted from the question of the durability of additions made to the network, but, evidently a high rate of physical depreciation of the installed base would tend to undermine the position of a technologically inferior incumbent. Substantial durability of capital equipment embodying a technological standard – or even an overlapping positioning of successive generations of moderate durability – will reinforce it against more efficient challengers.

The analysis just presented dealt with alternative systems that were unsponsored, whereas Katz and Shapiro (1985b) have observed that technological sponsorship may prevent the installation of an inferior technology as the unintended consequence of mere accidents of history. If there are sponsors who hold property rights in a technical standard, say, in the form of patent protection, they may be able to internalize the externalities resulting from network expansion. A firm which is convinced that the system whose benefits it can internalize will be superior in the future to the existing incumbent system, may find it worthwhile to subsidize the initial adoption of its system by 'penetration pricing' (below cost). This is a strategy not without substantial risks, however, and finance constraints may easily prevent superior technologies from finding sponsors with sufficient resources to unseat inferior incumbents.

Farrell and Saloner (1985a) have pointed out that if a new system would be economically superior to the incumbent system when everyone had switched to it, complete information in the possession of all users would be sufficient to induce everyone to decide independently to make the necessary switch-over. But this route of escape from sub-optimal lock-in depends upon a rigorous backward induction process, which leads the last user to switch given that all others have switched; and the next-to-last to correctly anticipate the decision of the last user, and so to switch himself, given that all before him have already switched; and so on, back to first user, who will switch in the expectation that all following him will do likewise. Incomplete information will readily break this chain, and therefore prevent it from even starting to form.

While it does, therefore, require some rather exacting circumstances for an inefficient technological system, or a technically inferior standard to become historically 'locked in', this analytical conclusion cannot warrant taking comfort in a belief that those conditions obtain only rarely in the experience of real industries. Here, then, we need to confront a potential source of standardization policy dilemmas, quite different in character from those that have been most readily perceived by economists trained to think in terms of convex production technologies. In activities conducted under conditions of incomplete information, and dominated by unappropriable increasing returns due to learning

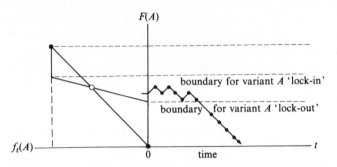

Fig. 8.4   The 'Arthur-gram' for the (linear) increasing returns case of systems rivalry

phenomena, habituation, and network externalities, public agencies may have to intervene *to mitigate the tendency of market competition relentlessly to lock the system into 'wrong' standards.* Quite a number of other unconventional implications for the formulation of 'standard policies' would follow quite naturally when one re-examines the subject from the non-standard analytical vantage point thus gained. Three of these offer focal points for the brief reconsideration of public policy issues in the next section.

VI   Three non-standard dilemmas of standardization policy – managing windows, giants and orphans

Three problem-areas for policy makers are highlighted by the foregoing heuristic exercise. To compensate for the fact that these have passed without much notice in previous discussions of the static welfare economics of standards and standardization, I have affixed colourful labels to them. First is the problem which I refer to as the Narrow Policy Window Paradox. Increasing returns in system scale makes available 'windows' for effective public policy intervention at modest resource costs – involving the manipulation, with high-leverage effects, of private sector technology adoption. by means of taxes and/or subsidies, or informational programmes and announcements designed to shape expectations about the future adoption decisions of other agents. Publicity about government procurement decisions may be a potent and relatively inexpensive instrument to use in this connection. But, for public agents to take advantage of these 'windows' while they remain open is not easy; the point at which such interventions can have maximum leverage over the course of diffusion and development of network technologies tends, under natural conditions, to be confined towards the very beginnings of the dynamic process, and to have an uncertain but generally brief temporal duration.

The brevity of the phase which leaves widest latitude for policy interventions aimed at altering decentralized technology adoption decisions is, of course, a relative matter – the comparison indicated here being that with the course of the market competition which may ensue as one system or another progresses towards *de facto* emergence as the industry's universal standard. Actual temporal durations would depend upon the real time rate at which system users were becoming sequentially committed to one network formulation or another, in the fashion depicted by the foregoing model.

What is it, exactly, that defines these policy action 'windows' and causes them to narrow? Essentially, it is the growing weight attached to considerations of network externalities – as determined by *the size and distribution of installed base* – among the range of factors influencing the system-choices of new users. The diagram in Figure 8.4 (inspired by simulation results reported by Arthur 1985) shows how the increasing returns version of the formal model considered here generates stochastic time-paths for the proportions of users who become connected to each of the alternative technological systems. The dashed horizontal lines indicate levels of $F(A)$ above (below) which variant A (variant D) becomes 'locked in' – in the sense of approaching complete market dominance with probability one. In the left-hand quadrant the H-function is shown in its limiting position, approached as the number of users becomes sufficiently large that changes in the relative size of the system-use benefits depends upon changes in the distribution of users between the two networks, rather than upon the absolute enlargement of the entire user community. But, from Figure 8.1 it is easily seen that at the outset of the diffusion process, when there are few members of either network, the use-benefits function, $B\{F(A)\}$, would be less steeply sloped; closer to the beginning of the process, therefore, there will be a wider range separating the $F(A)$-levels corresponding to 'lock-in' ($f(A) = 1$) and 'lock-out' ($f(A) = 0$) for variant A.

If the rate of flow of new customers into the market is variable and not known precisely, it can be hard to predict the rate at which the 'window' defined by these boundaries will be closing. But it is no less true that new windows may pop open quite suddenly, as a result of the unanticipated appearance of a technologically superior or economically more attractive formulation of the system. An obvious implication for those charged with making technology policy is that instead of being pre-occupied with trying to figure out how to mop up after the previous 'battle between systems', or manage competitive struggles which currently are well-advanced, it would be better to spend more time studying nascent network technologies in order to plan ahead for the dynamic systems rivalries that are most likely to emerge.

This brings me directly to what I have called the Blind Giant's Quandary. The phrase is meant to give capsule expression to the dilemma posed by the fact that public agencies are likely to be at their most powerful in exercising influence upon the future trajectory of a network technology just when they know least about what should be done. The important information they need to acquire concerns which characteristics of the particular technology are the ones that users will eventually come to value most highly; and what possible differences exist between the potentialities which the available variants have of undergoing future technical enhancement as a result of cumulative, incremental innovation. Prescribing action guidelines for Blind Giants is a dubious business at best.

One strategy worth considering, however, is that of 'counter-action'. A suitable objective for an inadequately informed public agent might be to prevent the 'policy window' from slamming shut before the policy-makers are better able to perceive the shape of their relevant future options. This requires positive actions to maintain leverage over the systems rivalry, preventing any of the presently available variants from becoming too deeply entrenched as a standard, and so gathering more information about technological opportunities even at the cost of immediate losses in operations efficiency. A passive, 'wait and see' attitude on the part of public agencies is not necessarily what is called for by the prevailing state of uncertainty, profound though those uncertainties may be. Private sector commitments to specific technologies surely will be made in the face of ignorance; in circumstances where positive network externalities are strong and, consequently, markets beg for technical standards, governmental passivity leaves a vacuum into which will be drawn profit-seeking sponsors of contending standards, and private standard-writing organizations that are dominated (typically) by industry constituencies.

Regarded from this vantage point, the prevailing US public policy stance which seeks to avoid mandatory standards, but which encourages the formation of widely representative committees to write voluntary technical standards, would be misguided were it to lead more often to the early promulgation of technical interface standards. Voluntary standards-writing exercises do not converge quickly, however, especially not in areas of technology where scientific and engineering fundamentals are perceived to be changing rapidly. This is not necessarily a failing that should be laid entirely at the door of committee politics and strategic behaviour by self-interested sponsors of contending standards; as an engineering task the writing of technical standards involves a continual interplay between efforts to be currently cost-effective and ambitions to 'push the state of the art', in which it is quite natural for new designs to be proposed even when they are not meant to serve as placeholders for nascent competitors. Thus, inventive and innovative responses to the opportunities perceived in such circumstances have a side effect, in contributing to delaying the work of voluntary standards-writing organizations.

The present perspective suggests, however, that something more may be needed than so unreliable a device for postponing the establishment of a standard until more information has been gathered. Quite possibly, government agencies should be urged to pursue purchasing and other policies that, in effect, handicap the leader and favour variant systems that remain behind in 'the race for installed base'. A particular form for such counter-active policies would involve *subsidizing only the second-place system*: it addresses some part of the moral hazard problem created when leaders are saddled with handicaps, since one has to make an effort to avoid being left in third-place, or even further behind.

What would be the effect upon the rate of adoption of the system that was in first place, were such a policy to be announced? It is not self-evident that the adoption of the leader-technology would be delayed. Instead, one can imagine conditions under which knowledge that government intervention would eventually be directed towards building momentum for a second-system bandwagon might lead to strategies that sought to accelerate the speed of the bandwagon carrying the first-place system. The matter is complicated and deserves more detailed examination than it can be given here.

In addition to whatever effects a public program of second-system subsidization might be found to have upon the dynamic competition among existing system variants, attempting to keep the policy window from closing would be likely to encourage continuation of private R&D devoted to creating new variants, or fundamentally enhancing the older ones. The very fact that the identity of the victor in an ongoing rivalry remains more uncertain, rather than less, may be seen to reflect the persistence of conditions that hold out stronger, not weaker incentives for profit-seeking firms to invest in more basic explorations of the technological opportunity space.

This may seem a rather paradoxical assertion, since it is nowadays so commonplace to be told that private investment in basic R&D is much inhibited by the great margins of uncertainty surrounding its economic payoffs. But the paradox is resolved when it is recognized that the market situation envisaged must be evaluated from the viewpoint not only of the existing rivals, but from that of potential entrants; a would-be entrant – say, the sponsor of a newly developed network technology which enjoyed a specified margin of superiority (in cost or performance dimensions) – will have a greater expectation of being able eventually to capture the market when there is no incumbent holding so large a share of the installed base that the 'lock in' of an inferior technology must be considered a high probability outcome. In markets characterized by increasing returns *that remain substantially unrealized*, system sponsors and would-be sponsors confront a situation having a pay-off structure resembling *a tournament*. The certainty of market dominance by one system or another implies that a firm having exclusive property rights – in at least one, strictly complementary component of the winning system – could count on collecting some monopoly rents as a tournament prize.

It is socially costly, however, to continue trying to offset the advantages conferred by installed base in order to induce a high rate of learning about the potential trajectories along which a network technology might be developed. There are, *ex hypothesi*, some positive network externalities that remain unexhausted, and which might be gained through a movement towards standardization and complete system integration. We therefore cannot ignore the realistic prospect that even if no one system variant eventually managed to gain a clear technological superiority, any rationally conducted public policy course would call for an end to handicapping the leader in the competition for market dominance. But, when suppliers and sponsors of vanquished rival systems are left to fend for themselves and possibly to perish in what Schumpeter referred to as the 'competitive gale', their withdrawal or demise is likely to make orphans of the users of the now-unsupported network technologies.

Angry technological orphans, who can complain publicly that their technological expectations were falsely nourished by governmental programmes, pose a political problem and an economic problem. The economic difficulty is that the existence of the proposed technology management policy tends to induce the allocation of resources to non-market activities, by firms seeking to protect the value of sunk investments. The political trouble is that they may find it comparatively easier to form lobbies and pressure groups to protect themselves from injury by perpetuating the governmental programmes which originally were designed only to prevent 'premature' standardization (*de facto* and *de jure*).

Bygones are just bygones when one is concerned with economic efficiency (as I am at this point), rather than with considerations of equity. Unless, of course, memory draws the past into the present and makes it a basis for actions affecting efficiency in the future. So, a third policy dilemma cannot be evaded: how to cope with the problems of those Angry Orphans of the passing competitive storm, so as to maintain the credibility of the government's announced technology policies for the future? One must do so, moreover, without encouraging behaviour on the part of future network sponsors that would tend to add moral hazard to the already appreciable risks that adopters face in choosing among alternative technologies.

Since this is likely to be a difficult task, one reasonable approach is for public agencies to anticipate the orphans' problem and render it less serious, by reducing at least the costs to society that result when otherwise functional hardware or software is discarded because it has become incompatible with the emergent standard for the industry. Governmental support for R&D can be focused upon the development of 'gateway technologies', such as physical adapters, power transformers, code translators, and electronic gateway devices, which will permit the *ex post facto integration* of distinct system variants into larger networks.

Profit-seeking firms may find their own incentives, without any public interventions, to develop gateway innovations. In recalling the constructive resolution of the late-nineteenth century 'battle of the systems' between AC and DC, one may point to the role played by the 'rotary converter', an invention of 1888 attributed in the US to Charles S. Bradley, a former Edison Co. employee, who soon after set up his own company to manufacture the device. Rotary converters allowed existing DC electric motors to be supplied with current from AC generation plants and transmission lines, and so was soon recognized by General Electric and Westinghouse as an important area for further technological innovation, as well as a profitable line of manufacturing activity (see Passer 1972, pp. 300–05, Hughes 1983, pp. 121–25). The recent introduction of 'PC to MAC and Back' may not be on quite the same level of engineering and economic significance, but it stands as testimony to the fact that markets still do work. The question, however, is whether they can be trusted to work sufficiently well to generate the right amount of gateway innovations.

There is still room for doubts on this score, and consequent grounds for considering suggested modes of public intervention. Private systems-sponsors may be justifiably wary about supplying customers with cheap 'gateways' to other systems. Public management of the preceding phase of open dynamic rivalry in accordance with the principle of second-system subsidization, as previously proposed, therefore may carry side-benefits in this regard. It may provide additional market incentives for new entrants to supply missing gateways, *ex post facto*; by concentrating the population of users in a relatively small number of variant systems, the costs of engineering gateways among them can be reduced, and the potential number of customers for any specific type of gateway device may be enlarged.

But, equally, public policy-makers seeking to mitigate the costs of inherited incompatibilities must recognize that even in this regard there can be such a thing as 'too much, too soon'. The achievement of *ex post* compatibility in respect to some part of an interrelated system may render it vulnerable to 'take-overs' that will allow the tastes of a minority of users to impose losses upon the majority who do not share those tastes but may nonetheless be obliged to share the costs. Moreover, providing easy connections between existing variant systems that cater to somewhat different user-needs is likely to promote the technological specialization of those variants, rather than the further development of a broader range of capabilities within each. It is arguable that the advent of the rotary converter resolved the battle between AC and DC in North America in a way that suspended fundamental research on the possibilities of an integrated electricity system utilizing direct current, delaying the development of high voltage DC transmission (see David with Bunn, 1986). The trade-off between immediate cost savings and 'pushing the state of the art', thus, remains an ineluctable one for the makers of technology policy in this connection as in others: premature reductions of gateway costs may exact unforeseen economic penalties by discouraging investment in R&D programmes aimed at establishing the technological dominance of one system over its rivals.

VII   Towards a political economy of technological interface standards

The special set of technology standards policies within the focus of the foregoing discussion have not been concerned with the reliability of 'labels' or the assurance of minimum quality. They belong, instead, to the class concerned with the ways in which levels of economic welfare in the present and future may be raised through the manipulation of products' 'interface' characteristics, those affecting the compatibility of sub-components of existing and potential 'network technologies'. Public policy interventions of this kind indirectly can channel market-guided microeconomic resource allocation processes that otherwise would determine the development and diffusion trajectories of emerging technologies.

This initial delimitation of the discussion simply set aside probably the

greater portion of the range of policy interests that occasion governmental actions having intended or unintended consequences for the
generation and diffusion of technological innovations. Into the excluded
category went ethical and political considerations raised by the potential
redistributive effects of technical 'progress'; also, the hardy perennial
question of new technology's impact on job creation and job displacement, and such bearing as it may have upon short-run dimensions of
macroeconomic performance, such as unemployment and price stability.
Issues of military defence, national power and the maintenance of
sovereignty, have been ignored, even though they may be affected
crucially by interface standards in the telecommunications field (see
Blatherwick 1986).

Yet even with these blinkers held firmly in place, the subject matter
immediately in view remains so complex – especially in proportion to my
analytical powers – that the foregoing treatment has fallen far short of
being comprehensive, much less conclusive. Most of it remains on a
frankly speculative plane. For this, however, I will make no apologies
and, instead, would claim justification for the effort – by reference to the
obvious importance of the issues at stake and the consequent value of
directing to the subject the attention of others more capable of pursuing
it successfully. One cannot fail to recognize that the public policy choice
problems surrounding technological standards have been presented here
in a drastically oversimplified and, possibly, a misleading form. In place
of a conclusion, therefore, it seems more appropriate for me to leave
some notice of these deficiencies, as they indicate the tasks that remain
ahead if economists and political scientists hope eventually to contribute
intelligently to improving the actual policy-process.

A first and most obvious limitation of the foregoing discussion derives
from the highly stylized, general representation of system-technologies
themselves. Further headway towards usefully concrete results
undoubtedly will require investigation of the implications of particular
technology structures that give rise to different forms of network
externalities. Second, nothing has been said concerning the possibility of
strategic interactions among participants in the sequential process of
choice between alternative network designs, a crucial subject that
recently has begun to receive welcome attention from economic theorists
employing the tools of game theory (Hanson 1984, Farrell and Saloner
1985a, c).

A third and perhaps most serious qualification is that I have essentially
suppressed all consideration of what might be called 'the political
economy of standards', by not attending to the institutional contexts in
which public policy decisions are taken and implemented, and by simply

positing that a coherent social policy actually could be formulated and implemented by a modern representative government. Guidelines for framing such policies in respect to specific network technologies have therefore been approached here from the perspective of some imagined monolithic and benign political authority, external to the dynamic rivalry among contending potential technologically-based systems, and concerned only with promoting the growth of society's economic welfare. One may doubt that such a vantage point exists. In reality it is likely that more than one of the many departments of government will be in a position to exert leverage over the outcome with respect to the specific form assumed by a new technological network.

The various governmental agencies that are able to influence how, when, and which network standards will be set do not automatically act in unison. Rather, they are likely to encounter some of the very same dilemmas of achieving policy 'coordination' in this sphere – the problem of setting a standard policy on technological standards! They have diverse and sometimes opposing goals, as well as common interests; whatever their respective special missions may be, they may find themselves also in the role of prospective major users of the technology in question – as was the case, for example, with the early development of mainframe computers in the US. In international negotiations concerning the adoption of systems standards or the transfer of specific (military and civilian) technologies, they may be obliged to represent the proprietary interests of firms who happen to be based in their own national constituency. By virtue of the leverage they are recognized to possess within the domestic arena, and the potential influence they may exert over the terms of international competition through advocacy of particular standards, it is thus to be expected that individual governmental agencies will become entangled thoroughly in dynamic market rivalries between sponsored system-standards. They become interested actors in the drama, both as customers of suppliers in the private sector, and as regulators (and sometimes captive agents) of evolving network industries in which natural monopolies are expected to arise.

Just as domestic standard-setting may take on the flavour of political coalition formation resembling a legislative process, so attempts at transnational standard-setting pose many of the dilemmas peculiar to international politics (Crane 1979; Blatherwick 1986). There are externalities here too, so that long-term national purposes – including the improvement of domestic economic well-being and maintenance of national security – may be served by forgoing exploitation of existing short-term competitive advantages, and relinquishing the 'protection' afforded by autarky, in order to negotiate agreements on standards that would promote closer economic interdependence and the strengthening of cooperative alliances.

Indeed, we would do well to reflect upon the power of recent accelerating advances in the whole complex of telecommunications and information technologies to further diminish the economic meaning of historically defined national boundaries, but for the arbitrary constraints which the exercise of political sovereignty continues to impose. The piecemeal emergence of a comprehensive standard for digital transmission of voice and other forms of data, the Integrated Services Digital Network (ISDN), provides a striking example of the prospective creation of world-wide markets that can be serviced at virtually zero marginal cost. In the light of such developments we must start to think seriously about the larger drama which is in progress on the global stage, involving incipient competition between alternative international political systems grounded in old and new technologies. To come to grips eventually with this prospect, it would seem essential to approach the 'political economy of standards' in a way that emphasizes the aspects of path dependence in the dynamic evolution of network technologies, and the institutional structures with which they become intertwined.

REFERENCES

Aitken, H. G. (1976), *Syntony and Spark: The Origins of Radio*, New York: Wiley & Sons.
Arthur, W. Brian (1983), 'On Competing Technologies and Historical Small Events: The Dynamics of Choice Under Increasing Returns', IIASA (Laxenburg, Austria). Paper presented at the Technological Innovation Program Workshop, Stanford University, Department of Economics, November 1983. Revised version available as Arthur (1985).
   (1984), 'Why a Silicon Valley: The Pure Theory of Locational Concentration in High-Tech Industry', paper presented at the Technological Innovation Program Workshop, Department of Economics, Stanford University, November 1984.
   (1985), 'Competing Technologies and Lock-in by Historical Small Events: The Dynamics of Allocation Under Increasing Returns', Technological Innovation Project Working Paper, Center for Economic Policy Research Publication, No. 43, Stanford University (January).
Arthur, W. Brian, Yuri M. Ermoliev, and Yuri M. Kaniovski (1983). 'On Generalized Urn Schemes of the Polya Kind', *Cybernetics*, **19**, 61–71.
   (1985), 'Strong Laws for a Class of Path-dependent Urn Processes', in *Proceedings of the International Conference on Stochastic Optimization, Kiev, 1984*, Munich, Springer-Verlag.
Blatherwick, David E. S. (1986), 'The International Politics of Telecommunications' (unpublished manuscript: Department of Political Science, Stanford University).

238 Paul A. David

Bowers, Brian (1982), *A History of Electric Light and Power*, New York, Peter Peregrinus Ltd.

Brock, Gerald (1975), 'Competition, Standards and Self-Regulation in the Computer Industry', in R. Caves and M. Roberts (eds), *Regulating the Product: Quality and Variety*, Cambridge, MA, Ballinger Publishing Company.

Byatt, I. C. R. (1979), *The British Electrical Industry, 1875–1914: The Economic Returns to a New Technology*, Oxford, Clarendon Press.

Carlton, Dennis W. and J. Mark Klamer (1983), 'The Need for Coordination Among Firms, with Special Reference to Network Industries', in *The University of Chicago Law Review*, **50**, pp. 446–65.

Chandler, Alfred E., Jr (1977), *The Visible Hand: The Managerial Revolution in American Business*, Cambridge, MA, Harvard University – Belknap.

Crane, R. (1979), *The Politics of International Standards: France and the Color TV War*, Norwood, NJ, Ablex Publishing Co.

David, Paul A. (1969), 'A Contribution to the Theory of Diffusion', Center for Research in Economic Growth Research Memorandum, No. 71, Stanford University.

(1985), 'Clio and the Economics of QWERTY', *American Economic Review*, **75**, 2 (May), pp. 332–37.

(1986a), 'Narrow Windows, Blind Giants and Angry Orphans: The Dynamics of Systems Rivalries and Dilemmas of Technology Policy', Technological Innovation Project Working Paper, No. 10, Center for Economic Policy Research, Stanford University. Paper presented to the Conference on Innovation Diffusion, held in Venice, Italy, March 17–22, 1986.

(1986b), 'Understanding the Economics of QWERTY: The Necessity of History', in *Economic History and the Modern Economist*, W. N. Parker (ed.), Oxford: Basil Blackwell.

David, Paul A. and Julie Bunn (1986), '"The Battle of the Systems" and the Evolutionary Dynamics of Network Technologies', paper prepared for presentation to the Economic History Association Meetings in Hartford, Conn., September 26–28, 1986.

David, Paul A. and Trond E. Olsen (1984), 'Anticipated Automation: A Rational Expectations Model of Technological Diffusion', Technological Innovation Project Working Paper No. 2, Center for Economic Policy Research, Stanford University.

(1986), 'Equilibrium Dynamics of Diffusion when Incremental Technological Innovations are Foreseen', Technological Innovation Project Working Paper No. 9, Center for Economic Policy Research, Stanford University. Paper presented to the Conference on Innovation Diffusion, held in Venice, Italy, March 17–22, 1986.

Davies, Stephen (1979), *The Diffusion of Process Innovations*, London: Cambridge University Press.

Farrell, Joseph and Garth Saloner (1985a), 'Standardization, Compatibility and Innovation', *Rand Journal*, **16** (Spring), pp. 70–83.

(1985b), 'Economic Issues in Standardization, Working Paper No. 393, Department of Economics, Massachusetts Institute of Technology, October.

(1985c), 'Installed Base and Compatibility, with Implications for Product Preannouncements', Working Paper No. 385, Department of Economics, M.I.T. Press, August.

Hannah, Leslie (1979), *Electricity Before Nationalisation: A Study of the Development of the Electricity Supply Industry in Britain to 1948*, Baltimore, MD, Johns Hopkins University Press.

Hanson, Ward A. (1984), 'Bandwagons and Orphans: Dynamic Pricing of Competing Technological Systems Subject to Decreasing Costs', paper presented at the Technological Innovation Program Workshop, Department of Economics, Stanford University, January 1984.

Hartwick, John M. (1985), 'The Persistence of QWERTY and Analogous Suboptimal Standards', unpublished paper, Department of Economics, Queens University.

Hemenway, D. (1975), *Industrywide Voluntary Product Standards*, Cambridge, MA, Ballinger.

Hennessey, R. A. S. (1971), *The Electric Revolution*, Newcastle upon Tyne, England, Oriel Press Ltd.

Hughes, Thomas P. (1983), *Networks of Power: Electrification in Western Society, 1880–1930*, Baltimore, MD: The Johns Hopkins University Press.

Ireland, Norman and Paul Stoneman (1986), 'Technological Diffusion, Expectations, and Welfare', *Oxford Economic Papers*, **38**, 283–304.

Jennings, Frederick B. (1984), *Interdependence, Incentives, and Institutional Bias: An Organization Perspective on the British Canals*, unpublished Ph.D. Dissertation in Economics, Stanford University.

Katz, Michael L. and Carl Shapiro (1985a), 'Network Externalities, Competition and Compatibility', *American Economic Review*, **75** (May), pp. 424–40.

(1985b), 'Technology Adoption in the Presence of Network Externalities', Discussion Paper in Economics, No. 96, Woodrow Wilson School, Princeton University.

Kindleberger, Charles P. (1983), 'Standards as Public, Collective and Private Goods', *Kyklos*, 36 (Fasc. 3), pp. 377–96.

LeCraw, Donald J. (1984), 'Some Economic Effects of Standards', *Applied Economics*, **16**, pp. 507–20.

Leland, Hayne (1979), 'Quacks, Lemons and Licensing: A Theory of Minimum Quality Standards', *Journal of Political Economy*, **87**, pp. 1328–47.

Link, Albert N. (1983), 'Market Structure and Voluntary Product Standards', *Applied Economics*, **15**, pp. 373–401.

Passer, Harold C. (1972), *Electrical Manufacturers, 1875–1900: A Study in Competition, Entrepreneurship, Technical Change, and Economic Growth*, New York, Acno Press.

Puffert, Douglas J. (1985), 'Standardization of Gauge and the Integration of Railway Networks in Britain and America: A Conceptual Framework', paper presented at the Technological Innovation Program Workshop, Department of Economics, Stanford University, May 1985.

Stoneman, Paul (1983), *The Economic Analysis of Technological Change*, Oxford, Oxford University Press.

Stoneman, Paul and Norman Ireland (1983), 'The Role of Supply Factors in the Diffusion of New Process Technology', *Economic Journal*, Supplement **93** (March), pp. 65–77.

Sturmey, S. G. (1958), *The Economic Development of Radio*, London, Gerald Duckworth.

U.S. Federal Trade Commission (1978), *Standards and Certification* (Proposed Rule and Staff Report, Bureau of Consumer Protection), Washington, D.C., G.P.O.

Index